Foreword

Welcome to the second edition of UCAS' guide to getting into university and college. If you have already made the decision to apply for higher education, the advice in this book will support you at every sta

This updated publication is desigi choice for you, and to give you a

Accepting a place on a full-time u The aim of the UCAS guide is to with confidence.

In this new edition are fresh case application process. There is alsc everyone should know before arri

Inside the guide you will learn hov to write a persuasive personal sta

Included are sample interview qu days), checklists and even some

In writing this second edition we h gone before you. They wanted a university and college and this gu and I wish you every success wit

MARY CURNOCK COOK
CHIEF EXECUTIVE, UCAS

Introduction

Introduction

This book offers a wonderfully comprehensive guide to the process of applying and preparing to go to university and college. It's important to think about the environment you are preparing to enter, the one you will hopefully get a glimpse of when you go to some open days.

Universities and colleges are environments where groups of people work to satisfy their intense curiosity about their world. In whatever subject they work in, lecturers, and other members of staff, are there to study and learn more about their chosen subject. By going to university, you will join that world, and will learn the skills required to help you fulfil your own curiosity about your chosen subject.

Lecturers at university and college aren't there to teach you in the way you are probably used to, where a teacher passes on information, which you then learn and then use that information to pass an exam. A lecturer's role is to guide your learning and to assess how well you are developing an understanding of your subject.

Universities and colleges are very exciting places to be. Research going on around you will be pushing forward the frontiers of knowledge. It's a world where debate and discussion are relished. You will be shown how to question and research in the subject you most enjoy studying, surrounded by like-minded people. You will hopefully find it a very intellectually fulfilling experience; and this guide will help to get you to the start of the experience.

DR HARRIET JONES
SCHOOL OF BIOLOGICAL SCIENCES
UNIVERSITY OF EAST ANGLIA

Key to symbols

Key to symbols

You'll find these symbols throughout this book to make it easy to locate the information relevant to you.

Case studies. The experience of others.

Did you know? A great idea.

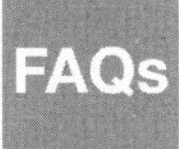

Frequently asked questions and the answers.

International students. Worldly advice.

Mature students. Older and wiser!

Myth buster. Blow those myths from your mind.

Tips. Advice from universities, advisers and students.

Students with disabilities. Unlock your potential!

Top tip. Pinpointing key tips from UCAS.

Contents

Contents

Foreword 1

Introduction 3

Key to symbols 5

Where to start

What is higher education? 13

UCAS - Our role in your journey 25

Mature students 29

Students with disabilities 35

Non-UK students 43

Money: how much will uni cost? 49

Chapter summary 57

Step 1 **Choosing courses**

Do your research 61

Look at league tables 85

Money: scholarships 95

Summer schools and taster courses 97

Admissions tests 101

UCAS Card 115

Chapter checklist 118

Contents

Step 2 **Applying**

When to apply ... 121
How to apply ... 125
How to complete your UCAS application ... 129
Personal statement ... 147
Applying for medicine, dentistry, veterinary science or veterinary medicine ... 177
Applying for Oxbridge ... 187
Chapter checklist ... 194

Step 3 **Offers**

After you apply ... 197
Track ... 201
Money: apply for student finance ... 209
Making changes ... 213
Interviews, portfolios and auditions ... 219
Unis' decisions ... 237
Replying to your offers ... 247
If you've no offers, Extra could be for you ... 255
Chapter checklist ... 261

Step 4 **Results**

Preparing for exam results ... 265
Exam results ... 269
What happens after the unis have your exam results ... 275
Chapter checklist ... 288

Step 5 **Next steps**
What next? ... 291
Adjustment ... 295
Clearing ... 299
Studying in another country ... 305
Taking a gap year ... 311
More options... ... 319
Chapter checklist ... 323

Step 6 **Starting university and college**
Preparing to study and getting support ... 327
Making friends ... 335
Starting university – leaving home ... 341
Accommodation ... 343
If you have a disability ... 351
If things go wrong and you want to make a complaint ... 353
Money: making it go further ... 355
Domestic life ... 361
Practical matters ... 367
Employment ... 373
Parents, grandparents, guardians, and other family members ... 375
Chapter checklist ... 377

Resources
UCAS Tariff ... 381
Jargon buster ... 397
Useful contacts ... 401
Map of major UK cities and airports ... 411

Acknowledgements ... 413

www.ucas.com

Where to start?

So you're thinking about doing a higher education course. In this chapter we explore what higher education is, why you might want to do it (in case you're yet to be convinced!), what's available and what help there might be financially.

Higher education is an excellent way to pursue a subject you're interested in at the same time as meeting new people and gaining independence. Student life can also provide opportunities to develop skills through societies and group work – skills that will prove beneficial when applying for jobs in the future.

Where to start?

www.ucas.com

What is higher education?

Student tip:

'If you're unsure about going to university it's handy to look at prospectuses to see what might catch your eye. I also recommend open days and university applicant groups on Facebook and Twitter. Research is key – you can't do too much!'

Higher education offers a diverse range of courses and qualifications, such as degrees, Higher National Diplomas (HND) and foundation degrees. Many higher education courses take place in universities, but plenty are also taught at colleges, specialist art institutions and agricultural colleges.

Why choose higher education?

It's a must for some careers. A higher education qualification is essential for pursuing some vocational careers, like dentistry, chartered engineering and architecture. Some courses offer vocational programmes directly related to particular work areas, like accountancy, sports science and teaching.

To improve your earning power. A higher education course can help you gain a fulfilling job and reach higher earnings.

It can strengthen your understanding of different cultures and beliefs. Unis and colleges bring together students from a variety of backgrounds.

Student tip:

'I feel this is the start of my life – I feel like anything can happen, that things people tell me are just dreams can actually become real. It sounds cheesy but I think if you believe in something you can make it happen – nothing is impossible.'

Higher education develops important transferable skills. Skills like communication, timekeeping, management, research and creative thinking – these can give you an edge in the fast-changing world of employment.

To show other people what you can do. Your qualification will show employers that you can learn and give them an idea of how well you might do in the future.

For academic debate. If the course includes seminars, you can use this time to challenge each other's views in a neutral and stimulating environment.

To show yourself what you can do. Gaining a higher education qualification boosts your self-confidence and self-awareness. You may even be at a time of life when you can study a subject just because you like it.

Types of qualifications available

Higher education isn't just about getting a degree. There are other qualifications you can get at uni or college too – in both academic and work-related courses.

The main courses offered are:

Bachelor's degree

A three- or four-year course where graduates gain a bachelor's degree. A degree helps you develop in-depth understanding of a subject and helps you move into a relevant job, profession or postgraduate course. Sometimes known as a 'first' degree, it can lead to an 'ordinary' bachelor's degree or a bachelor's degree with honours. Generally, gaining honours requires a higher academic standard, possibly based on a successful dissertation. Most first degrees are honours degrees, although ordinary degrees are offered by some institutions. Honours degrees in England, Wales and Northern Ireland tend to take three years to complete, or four years with a work placement or year abroad.

Honours degrees in Scotland normally take four years to complete, although you can jump straight into the second year if you have appropriate qualifications. An 'ordinary' degree in Scotland is usually a three-year full-time course, whereas an 'honours' degree is usually a four-year full-time course.

Part-time degree courses are taken over a longer period – usually five years or more – and institutions can often offer flexible arrangements to suit your needs.

Case study

Name: Melissa Gloria Larsson
Applying for: Creative courses

I found choosing to go to university a difficult thing because I wasn't 100% sure what I wanted to do. If you don't know what to do, maybe take a gap year and think about it. However, if you have a slight idea, read about every course, research every industry you're interested in and try to imagine what you see yourself doing in the future.

I decided I wanted to go into the kind of area including the art/technology side of things, like media or games design. Make sure the course would be something you'd be good at and would definitely enjoy. What's the point of torturing yourself for three years doing something lame - let alone working as something similar for the rest of your life?

Even if you're worried about being a shy type, you'd still be able to show the universities that you're good and willing to learn. You won't be perfect and 100% knowledgeable yet, but that's why you'd be applying for a university course - to further your education. And don't try to fake your personality - just be yourself.

I ended up applying to completely different courses at completely different universities, (though luckily I still found it possible to write a personal statement that applied to them all), and I ended up with an offer from each of them. My advice is show the universities what your good at and don't panic!

You're generally assessed by a mix of exams, coursework and a written dissertation. Honours degrees are marked so that you're awarded a first-class (top mark), upper-second (2:1), lower-second (2:2), or third-class degree.

Higher National Certificate (HNC) and Higher National Diploma (HND)
The HNC is a one-year work-related course and the HND a two-year work-related course. If completed with high grades these can lead to the second or third year of a bachelor's degree.

HNCs and HNDs are highly valued by employers because they're designed to give you the skills to put the knowledge you learn to effective use in a particular job. They're mainly assessed through assignments, projects and practical tasks.

Certificate of Higher Education (CertHE) and Diploma of Higher Education (DipHE)
These are the first year (the certificate) and second year (the diploma) of a degree course. They're academic rather than vocational qualifications, and can be used for entry to the second or third year of a related degree course.

Foundation degree
A foundation degree is a flexible vocational qualification combining academic study with workplace learning. A full-time course usually takes two years to complete – a part-time course may take longer. Often linked to a degree, you might be able to progress directly to the third year of a bachelor's degree. You're likely to work on real projects which enable you to pick up the technical and practical skills needed for your chosen line of work. As well as building up skills for a particular area of work, it also gives you general skills useful in any job. You'll be assessed in various ways – from project work to exams and presentations – and there are courses available you can study through distance learning, online, or at college.

Adviser tip:

'Foundation degrees may be offered by partner institutions despite appearing to be offered by a specific university when you apply. Find out exactly where the course will be delivered.'

Postgraduate

Higher education qualifications that require you to already have a bachelor's degree are known as postgraduate qualifications. They're often taken to build on the knowledge and skills gained during a bachelor's degree, but you can also study a subject that's new to you. There are postgraduate diplomas and certificates – which can be academic or vocational – and there are master's degrees which are academic and can be research-based or a taught course, or a mixture of both. They can take around 12 months of full-time study to complete.

A doctorate qualification is longer term – taking at least three years of full-time study to complete. For doctorates you'd be expected to work independently, with guidance from a supervisor, on an original piece of research.

What level are these qualifications?

Each qualification has a different volume of learning. The Government has indicated the level of each qualification in a framework for higher education – see the table over the page. It shows how different higher education qualifications compare in terms of how hard they are – the higher the level, the harder the qualification. For example the bachelor's degree is a higher level than the HNC. The levels also indicate the differences in the range of intended learning outcomes.

Levels 1-3 (for England, Wales and Northern Ireland) and levels 1-6 (for Scotland) precede higher education and include A levels and Scottish Highers.

If you complete A levels, Scottish Highers or similar you can go straight into a bachelor's degree – and for a doctorate you wouldn't need to have studied all the levels beforehand. You might even have taken a route through employment rather than school or college that demonstrates your suitability for higher education.

Framework for higher education qualifications level in England, Wales and Northern Ireland	Scottish credit qualifications framework level	Examples of higher education qualifications within each level
4	7	- certificates of higher education (CertHE) - Higher National Certificates (HNC)
5	8	- diplomas of higher education (DipHE) - foundation degrees (eg FdA, FdSc) - Higher National Diplomas (HND)
6	9 10	- bachelor's degrees - bachelor's degrees with honours (eg BA, BSc, BEng, BEd, BMus)
7	11	- master's degrees (eg MA, MSc, MPhil, MRes) - postgraduate certificates - postgraduate diplomas
8	12	- doctoral degrees (eg PhD/DPhil)

Myth buster

Uni isn't just for people who are good at academic courses

Universities offer many different types of courses. While some courses are mainly academic, others can be practical, physical or creative – leaving the lecture hall behind to gain work experience, learning through scenario-based assessments or developing a practical skill.

Look at the different course structures to see which suits you – there are courses which offer time away from the university, like a year in industry and work placements in the UK or abroad.

Course Finder on **www.ucas.com** will tell you a lot about how academic a course is, and its method of teaching. So get to know what's available and choose those that you'll enjoy most.

The Choosing courses chapter has more information on Course Finder

Single and combined courses

Single honours degrees are courses where one subject is studied. It allows you to focus on that one subject throughout the course.

Combined courses are ideal for anyone wanting flexibility and the variety of knowledge and skills offered by a combination of subjects – eg history and French. There are three types of combined courses:

- Joint honours degrees allow you to divide your time equally between two subjects – 50/50.
- Major/minor courses allow you to study two subjects, one as a major part of your course, the other as the minor. The time spent is usually 75/25.
- Combined honours programmes are flexible courses that allow you to do two, three or four subjects – maybe specialising in just two subject combinations once you're in the second or third year.

The use of 'and', 'with' and the ampersand ('&') in course titles

The course title should indicate whether a course is a single subject or joint subject course. Generally, the words 'and', 'with' and the ampersand ('&') have a specific meaning within a course title:

- Where there are two elements to a single subject, an ampersand ('&') is used to link the two elements – eg art & design.
- Where two subjects are studied (for a joint honours degree) in a balanced combination, the subjects are joined with 'and' – eg French and German.
- Where there are two elements to a main subject (within a joint honours course), the elements are joined with an ampersand ('&') and the main subject with 'and' – eg physics & applied physics and French.
- For major and minor subjects, 'with' is used as the link word and the major subject is listed first – eg 'French with German' is French major with German minor.

Modular courses

The majority of higher education institutions use a modular structure for courses. This means you can build a personalised course by choosing modules or units of study from different subject areas. Unis have lists of modules that can be taken for each course – some compulsory and some you can choose between. Uni websites

often list which modules are available to you – but watch out for timetable clashes.

Unis often have links with employers who might be able to arrange a placement for you, but you could also search for your own placement, as long as the uni agrees it's suitable.

Sandwich courses

Some vocational courses include a year of working in the industry as part of the course. This will usually be for the third year of a degree course or the second year of an HND and, depending on the employer, may be full-time paid employment. The purpose of this is to introduce you to the world of work, while gaining valuable experience in a profession you might consider after completing your higher education course.

Foundation year – year 0 of a degree course

Some unis include a foundation year in the degree. You can see if they do with Course Finder on the UCAS website by searching on the subject 'foundation'. They're designed to prepare students who have qualifications which are acceptable for entry in general but aren't appropriate for a specific course of study. Alternatively they can be used as year 0 of a degree course to enable students with non-traditional qualifications to enter higher education – using year 0 as preparation for a full degree. For more info about foundation years get in touch with universities.

Foundation courses for international students

It's easy to get muddled with the different 'foundation' courses available. Foundation courses for international students are usually nine-months long and cover English skills and academic courses. They can help you prepare for university entry but they're not accepted in every UK university. You can find information about them on university websites.

Don't confuse them with the foundation year (year 0 of a degree course – explained above), the foundation degree (a vocational qualification – see page 16) and the art and design foundation course, a one-year further education course designed to broaden and deepen the student's art skills before specialising and applying to an art-related degree.

Higher education – a different way of learning

Give yourself time to get used to the new teaching and learning environment.

Learning at a university or college is different from learning at school. At school you're dependent on teachers, the routine and timetable set by them and the structure of the school. You might be used to being directed to a resource and rewriting (or cutting and pasting) information. Achieving academic success at A level doesn't necessarily mean you can cope easily with the more independent and self-directed style of learning expected of universities. Many students have to quickly learn these skills at the start of their course.

Adviser tip:

'Contact hours vary depending on the type of course you are studying. Make sure you ask how many contact hours your course typically has.'

At uni you're expected to take on a more independent way of learning – taking responsibility for planning and organising your own work (as well as balancing work with pleasure). You'll still get deadlines to hand in work but you might not have to hand it in for weeks and weeks. No one will tell you how many hours of study you should be doing – you'll have to work all this out for yourself. You might only get eight hours of contact time a week (lectures, tutorials etc) so you'll be expected to study on your own the rest of the time.

This requires a lot of self-motivation and dedication. You'll need to discover your own learning style – when to work alone, when to work with others and when to seek advice. Independent learning involves in-depth questions, learning from resource materials, (either in libraries or at home), analysing and evaluating content, doing practicals and listening to feedback.

FAQs

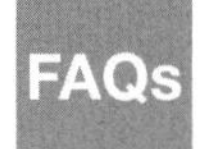

Is there an age limit for going to university or college?
No. People of all different ages apply for courses, and those who are more mature are equally welcome as they contribute not only their academic ability but also life experience.

Where can I study? Is higher education limited to universities?
Traditionally higher education has been associated with universities alone; however there's now also a large number of colleges – meaning with over 300 institutions

there's currently more choice than ever. You can find out about each of the institutions by visiting **www.ucas.com**.

I have been educated overseas, so which courses are right for me?
The UK welcomes many international students each year so it's likely you'll be able to find a course that's right for you. The institutions themselves can answer any questions you might have about their entry requirements and the support that's available. Don't be afraid to get in touch with them.

How does higher education in the UK differ from other countries?
Applications to higher education in the UK are usually made through UCAS, which means you only have to submit one application form. In other countries you often have to make applications to each institution separately, making the process time consuming and potentially expensive.

What qualifications do I need to reach higher education?
Institutions often set minimum entry requirements for their courses in terms of qualifications. You can find this information for the courses you're interested in by using Course Finder at **www.ucas.com**, or by looking on uni and college websites.

Institutions often accept a wide variety of qualifications, from both the UK and overseas. If you have any questions about their entry requirements then it's a good idea to contact them direct.

Is higher education just for school leavers?
Higher education is available to people from all stages of life, whether you've recently left school or you left some time ago. It's no longer the case that students all start courses at the same age – nowadays the choice to do further study can come about for different people at different times, for many different reasons.

Do many employers look for graduates?
Many employers recruit individuals with degree level qualifications, as the relevant knowledge and experience these provide might be essential for the role.

For jobs where there's fierce competition, this kind of knowledge could offer an advantage over competitors. It's worthwhile visiting the websites of a few employers to find out what type of experience and qualifications they look out for.

What experience will I gain from higher education?
Higher education will expand your knowledge on a given subject – sometimes including hands-on experience in more practical-based courses. You'll learn to manage your time in order to meet deadlines and you'll build on your analytical skills.

Aside from the educational gains, there are many other ways you can benefit from higher education. For starters, living away from home can help you develop independence, and mixing with students from around the world can broaden your cultural awareness.

How can I contact UCAS?
Our website **www.ucas.com/about_us/contact_us** has details of how to contact us.

You can also email us at enquiries@ucas.ac.uk for an automated response with general information and guidance.

Do I have to apply through UCAS or can I apply to institutions directly?
For all courses listed on **www.ucas.com** you'd have to submit an application through UCAS as we are the central admissions system. Your application will allow you to apply for up to five choices at the same time.

www.ucas.com

UCAS – our role in your journey

We're responsible for managing applications to higher education courses in the UK. We aim to help you make informed choices about higher education, guiding you, your parents and advisers through the application process. That's what this book is all about! But it's not your only source of help.

After looking at this book, you'll need help finding a course. We list all full-time higher education courses in the UCAS scheme (that's around 43,000 courses) on our website **www.ucas.com**. You can use Course Finder to read information that includes entry requirements, course descriptions and student services.

When you decide to make your application to university, you'll need to use Apply, our online application system. After you send us your application, we pass it on to your chosen universities and colleges so they can view it online. They won't see where else you have applied – they'll simply consider your application and send their decision to us.

Student tip:

'UCAS helped me discover so many unis that I would never have heard of before.'

Yougo conversation:

User 1: Have an unconditional for Brighton to do Humanities: War and Conflict. Good luck with everyone and their offers.

User 2: That sounds like one complicated subject!

User 1: Maybe, but it all depends on what you're interested in :P To me Television Production sounds complicated.

User 2: Aha fair point :) Yeah Television Production comes natural to me lol.

You'll be able to see those decisions in Track, our online system where you can follow the progress of your application. In Track, you can see what's happening with your application – like whether you've received any offers – and you can then make replies to any offers you get, accepting or declining them.

During summer we receive many exam results direct from the exam boards and pass them on to the unis and colleges that are holding a place for you (see page 269). When you get your results, you then check Track to see if you've got a place on your chosen course. Depending on what happens you might want to use Adjustment or Clearing (see pages 295 and 299) which allow you to search for further courses with vacancies remaining.

Of course you can consult this book and our website at any stage to check what to do next. You can also watch video guides on UCAStv at **www.ucas.tv**, follow us on Twitter at **twitter.com/ucas_online**, ask us a question on Facebook at **www.facebook.com/ucasonline** or see your questions answered on YouTube at **www.youtube.com/ucasonline**. You can also check out our blogs on **www.ucasconnect.com/blogs**, and we have a Twitter feed for advisers in schools and colleges – **twitter.com/ucas_centres**. If you'd like to speak to us, you can find our contact details on **www.ucas.com/about_us/contact_us**.

Another way to find useful information is to ask other students – you can do this on yougo, the UCAS student network on Facebook. Register to use the yougo app on the UCAS Facebook page – then you'll be able to talk to other students on your course or at your university.

We've summarised our role in your journey in six easy steps…

Six steps to applying – the applicant journey

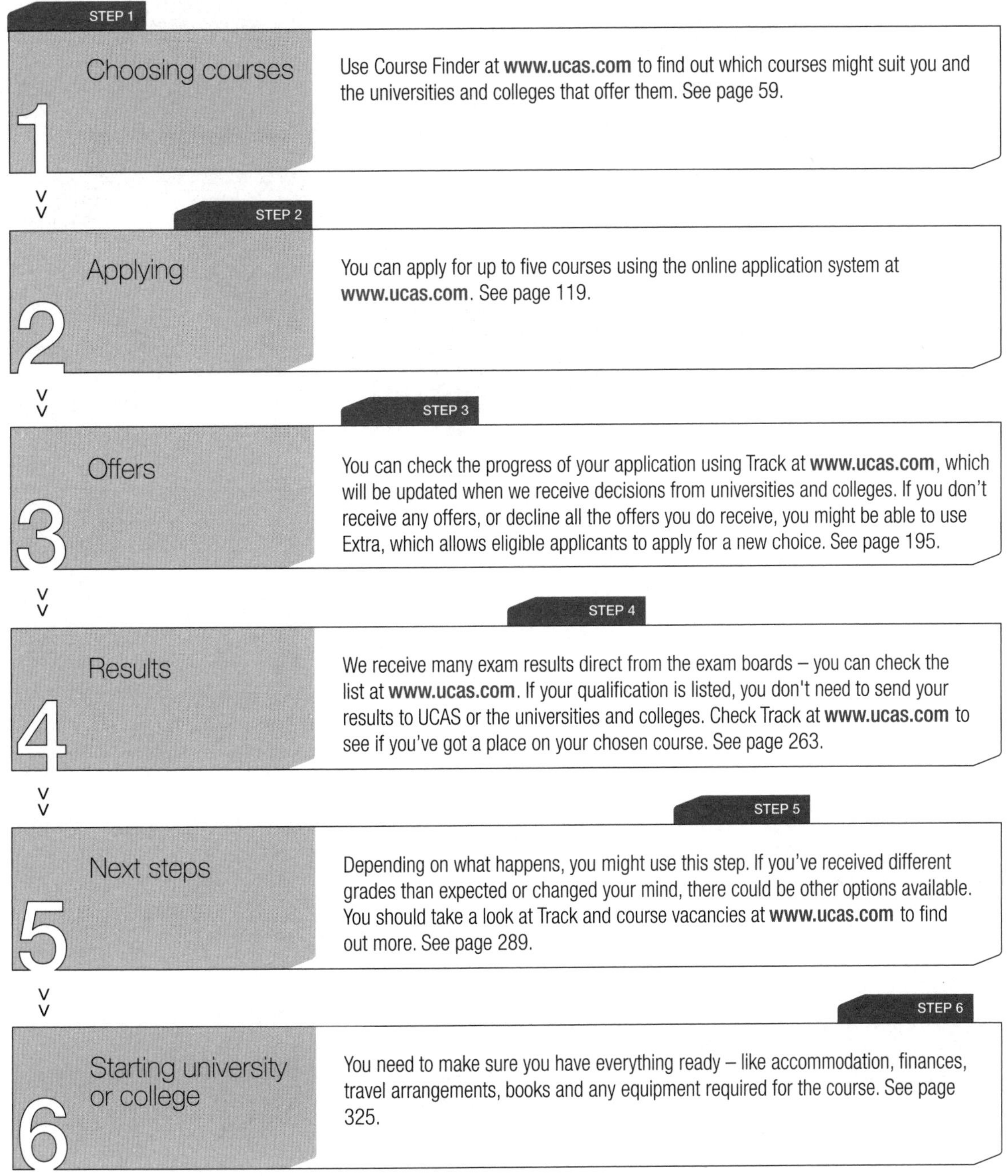

STEP 1
Choosing courses
1
Use Course Finder at **www.ucas.com** to find out which courses might suit you and the universities and colleges that offer them. See page 59.
STEP 2
Applying
2
You can apply for up to five courses using the online application system at **www.ucas.com**. See page 119.
STEP 3
Offers
3
You can check the progress of your application using Track at **www.ucas.com**, which will be updated when we receive decisions from universities and colleges. If you don't receive any offers, or decline all the offers you do receive, you might be able to use Extra, which allows eligible applicants to apply for a new choice. See page 195.
STEP 4
Results
4
We receive many exam results direct from the exam boards – you can check the list at **www.ucas.com**. If your qualification is listed, you don't need to send your results to UCAS or the universities and colleges. Check Track at **www.ucas.com** to see if you've got a place on your chosen course. See page 263.
STEP 5
Next steps
5
Depending on what happens, you might use this step. If you've received different grades than expected or changed your mind, there could be other options available. You should take a look at Track and course vacancies at **www.ucas.com** to find out more. See page 289.
STEP 6
Starting university or college
6
You need to make sure you have everything ready – like accommodation, finances, travel arrangements, books and any equipment required for the course. See page 325.

Mature students

People are increasingly taking courses at any stage of their lives, so don't be put off higher education by thinking it's too late or you might not fit in. Mature students are welcomed by universities and colleges for their experience, skills and enthusiasm.

Getting to know yourself and mixing with school leavers can be interesting and educational in itself! Mature students can play important roles as figures younger students can relate to. Your life and work experience will bring an extra dimension to seminars and lectures, and will be valued.

When applying for university or college you'll need to provide evidence of your ability to study at the appropriate level, or evidence of relevant experience (or both). Course admission requirements are flexible for mature applicants and exact requirements will vary, depending on the course and university. If you left school with few or no qualifications or you haven't been in formal education for some years, you could take an Access course at a local college to brush up your study skills.

Adviser tip:

'Some students don't perform at their best while studying in their teenage years – for widely varying reasons. They may then find themselves in roles they don't find fulfilling – but remember there is still the opportunity to study for a new career at any age.'

A lack of qualifications shouldn't stop you going for undergraduate study – unis and colleges will consider your experience and other qualities too.

Access to higher education programmes

Access courses are known as Access to Higher Education courses in England, Wales and Northern Ireland and SWAP (Scottish Wider Access Programme) in Scotland. They're designed to provide a good grounding in the knowledge and study skills needed for entry to higher education.

Some programmes are linked to particular degree subjects and on completion might offer a guaranteed place at a university or college. Others aren't tied to a subject area and concentrate on offering general progression to higher education by developing key transferable skills, English or communications, numeracy and information technology – all with tutorial support.

Most courses are modular in structure so you can build up credit at a pace that suits you and your circumstances. Find out more at **www.accesstohe.ac.uk** or **www.scottishwideraccess.org**.

Case study

Name: Nicky West
Studying: Events Management
At: University of West London

At college I was interested in languages but then went on to work in customer services and management. I then reached a point in my previous career where I realised I couldn't progress any further in the role, and as I was always organising social events at work a friend suggested that I try events management. I started looking for jobs in the industry and my partner encouraged me to study for a degree.

I did an evening course at the Events School of London - I didn't want to give up my job just yet - and it was there that someone recommended that I attend a networking evening. Contacts at the networking evening recommended that I study for a degree. I then completed a diploma at another university - for which I achieved a distinction - and finally enrolled at the University of West London.

I was nervous about giving up a full time job but quickly found out about the role of Student Ambassadors - student staff who help out at university events - which fitted around my studies and allowed me to gain experience. Having the skills to write essays was also a worry, but I think being a mature student makes you very determined and focused. Also, the university lecturers have always been very friendly and helpful, especially in the beginning when I needed it most.

I'd say go and do an evening class first and see if you like the subject. There are also lots of ways you can volunteer, with charities perhaps or the Olympics, which will also help you to gain experience. You are never too old for anything!

FAQs

Mature students' FAQs

Am I a mature student?

A mature student normally refers to anyone who is aged 21 and over (or 20 if in Scotland).

Do I have to complete a different application?

No, it's the same application for all applicants.

Who should I ask to provide my reference?

If you're a mature student and can't get an academic reference, you should ask a responsible person who knows you to provide your reference – but not a friend or relative. Maybe an employer, training officer, careers adviser, a teacher on a recent further education course, or a senior colleague in employment or voluntary work.

Can I get funding?

Yes, you'll still be able to apply for funding – the exact amount will depend on your personal circumstances. For further information visit **www.gov.uk/student-finance**.

Is there a maximum age for higher education?

No, there's not an age requirement for applying to higher education. Some courses do have specific requirements, so we advise you to contact the institution if you're unsure.

Will institutions consider experience if I don't quite meet the qualifications they have listed as requirements?

For a mature applicant many unis and colleges will look at your life experience relevant to the subject you're applying to, so you might not need to meet the specific entry requirements. You should contact the institutions you're interested in for further advice on this.

Can the courses be more flexible to meet my needs?

The majority of higher education institutions offer either modular programmes – which enable students to build a personalised degree – or part-time study options. There could also be the option of distance learning, depending on the subject you'd like to study.

I'm no longer at school so where can I get careers guidance?
There are many websites offering advice aimed at mature students – for example **www.careers.ed.ac.uk**.

Do institutions provide childcare?
Some unis and colleges do offer this facility – check with the student services office of your chosen institution before applying to see what's available. The charity The Daycare Trust promotes childcare in higher education and is a good contact point for advice on provisions and benefits.

Where can I live while I'm studying?
As a mature student you might have commitments that mean you'd need to attend a local university to stay living at home. However if you do decide to move away there are many accommodation options. Many institutions have halls of residence which could be an option for some mature students. However for students with spouses, children or both, some institutions are able to make specific housing provisions.

What are the basic study skills I will require?
Unis and colleges often look at a mature student's life experience rather than purely their formal qualifications. They'll also consider whether you're able to understand how to learn, organise time, read effectively, take notes, research, draw conclusions and write essays and reports.

www.ucas.com

The information for disabled students in this chapter and the rest of the guide has been contributed by Disability Rights UK.

Disability Rights UK

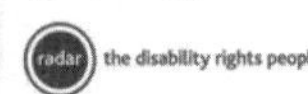

Disability Rights UK – **www.disabilityrightsuk.org** – is a pan-disability organisation led by disabled people and formed in 2012 from the union of three major disability charities. Its work includes promoting equality in education, training and employment and it runs some of the policy and information services formerly provided by Skill.

Disability Rights UK provides a free information and advice service for individual disabled people and the professionals who work with them, with a freephone helpline, email and website **www.disabilityrightsuk.org/contact.htm**.

Students with disabilities

Definition of disability

A person has a disability if they have a physical or mental impairment which has a substantial and long-term effect on their ability to carry out normal day-to-day activities (Equality Act 2010).

Disability support

Under the Equality Act (2010), universities and colleges have a duty to make reasonable adjustments to their services, so disabled students are not placed at a substantial disadvantage. The Special Educational Needs and Disability Order (SENDO) 2005 is similar in Northern Ireland. However, it's still important to contact the disability support person at the institution to discuss how your individual needs will be met. They'll usually be called the Disability Coordinator or something similar. You might find some institutions have more experience in supporting people with a certain type of disability or impairment. You can find a link to the contact details of all the disability coordinators across the UK at **www.disabilityrightsuk.org/disabledstudents.htm**.

You can research individual uni and college websites and other materials to gain a better understanding of their support for disabled people. For example you could look at its Student Charter and whether it covers equality and diversity, health and welfare support and complaints procedures. You might also want to look through the university's access agreement published on the Office for Fair Access website. You could even ask or information in relation to its Public Sector Equality duty on the effect of its policies on disabled students.

Disability Rights UK

Disability Rights UK's vision is of a society where everyone with lived experience of disability or health conditions can participate equally as full citizens. As part of this it promotes opportunities to empower young people and adults with any kind of disability to realise their potential in further and higher education, training and employment.

As well as extensive policy work, Disability Rights UK runs a free helpline for disabled students, parents, carers and key advisers.

Telephone 0800 328 5050 (telephone) or email **skill4disabledstudents@disabilityrightsuk.org**.

Disability Rights UK publishes Into Higher Education, a guide for disabled people planning to study at university. It contains detailed answers to the common questions disabled students have about choosing where to study, disability support services in higher education, disclosing your disability and applying for Disabled Students' Allowances (DSAs).

Case study

Name: Fred Suter
Studying: BA (Hons) Modern Languages
at: University of Southampton

Being deaf might seem a huge hurdle and studying languages an even bigger one.

On the academic side of things, such as finding different pathways for listening exercises, it may be a bit of a challenge sometimes. However it is definitely far from impossible as many might think. With the support of my tutors and especially the disability team here, everything is done to ensure that my university experience matches the one of a hearing student.

From my Disabled Students' Allowances (DSAs) any extra equipment which I require at university, such as a printer or specific books, are paid for by Student Finance. This is important as I rely more on sources which I can read than the average student.

The greatest piece of support is Remote Captioning. Thanks to this system, I manage the biggest hurdle, which is communication. I even wish I had this service 24 hours a day! I can read from my laptop screen every word being said in the classroom, just like subtitles, milliseconds after it is said. I feel totally equal to the other students.

Of course this support doesn't just fall into my lap, what I do is work actively together, help sort out things where I can. And this also counts for other kind of support that I get.

I am open to discussing needs with tutors and the disability team, searching for the best equipment available and handing in signatures quickly when required. I think that way I benefit from it in the best way possible, because what goes around, comes around.

Of course university isn't all positive. It hurt to see students from my corridor in halls making friends in the first week but hardly ever knocking on my door. I kept telling myself at the beginning to stay calm and that it takes time, and I think I was right.

While others may make their friendships really quickly, I need to find the people who are worth it and who I want to go into deeper relationships with and I am surprised how quickly that actually happened. I already have my social circle built and I can't wait for my second year!

I think if you are deaf, you are much more in charge of yourself. You have to take the first steps and that can be pretty challenging because deafness no doubt causes a lack of confidence. But if you build the larger part of the bridge towards other students, work closely together with the people who want to help you, then it is worth it and I can absolutely recommend having the courage and taking the step towards university.

Case study

Name: Catherine Alexander
Studying: BA (Hons) English
at: Lancaster University

I have congenital muscular dystrophy, which means I use a powered wheelchair to get around. I also need help with most day-to-day tasks, including washing, dressing, preparing meals and getting to lectures and seminars. I also need help overcoming the physical barriers of my course, so I get assistance with things like note-taking and collecting books from the library.

I decided to go to university as it was the obvious next step for me. I achieved good grades in my A levels and the kinds of jobs I am interested in require a degree.

After a lot of thought and research, I decided to move away from home as the universities near where I live did not really provide the course I wanted. I also felt that if I stayed at home, I would miss out a lot on the social part of university life. However, I was very nervous about this decision. At home I had a reliable care package and people who knew my needs well and I felt comfortable with. I was also worried about getting full-time care. At home I only had carers come in for my personal care and my dad did all the other things like meals.

I heard about Community Service Volunteers (CSV) from the disability officer at Lancaster. The volunteers would live with me on campus and provide my care for up to a year. Social

Services were quite keen on this idea from a financial point of view, as it was relatively inexpensive for a 24-hour care package – they would only have to pay for the volunteers' accommodation, food and living costs. However, it still had to be approved at 'panel', which was an anxious wait!

On the whole, I feel that CSV is a great way of providing care. It allows me the flexibility to be able to decide what I do, rather than being tied to a schedule of carers coming in and out at certain times. I also feel I have made friends for life with several of my volunteers. However, it can be difficult if you don't gel with a volunteer – you do spend a lot of time together so it's important you get on with them! I would also say it is hard to get used to having different volunteers every year.

It is a huge change and takes a lot of getting used to, but I now love living away from home and my new-found independence.

FAQs

Disabled students FAQs

Am I eligible for extra financial help?
Disabled Students' Allowances (DSAs) can help you with the extra costs of attending your course. DSAs are available for both full-time and part-time students.

Should I disclose my disability to the institutions I apply to?
Generally we advise students to disclose their impairment as this allows institutions to ensure they can offer the correct support.

How much information do I need to provide about my disability?
We advise providing as much info as possible about your support needs as this helps to ensure that all necessary reasonable adjustments are in place when you start your course.

Will I be less likely to secure a place?
No – all applications gain equal consideration as long as they've met the required deadlines. Information about your disability is protected by the Equality Act and Data Protection Act, and if you have any questions you can contact your chosen unis and colleges for further information.

Is there an organisation that provides advice to me as a disabled student?
Disability Rights UK provides a free information and advice service for individual disabled students and the professionals who work with them, with a freephone helpline, email and website **www.disabilityrightsuk.org/contact.htm**.

How can I find out if my preferred institutions can meet my needs?
The best option would be to contact them direct as they'll be able to discuss their facilities and they might have a disability coordinator they can put you in touch with. An open day is also a good idea so you can see whether the institution meets your needs.

Non-UK students

The UK has a long history of welcoming international students to study in its universities and colleges. The most recently available figures for 2010/11 for those studying full-time at publicly funded higher education institutions are:

European Union (EU) students	130,120
Non-EU students	298,110
Total	428,230

Source: HESA

When looking to study in the UK, there are many places and people that can help. There are people at each university and college ready to answer your questions, help you through the application process and support you while you're in the UK. Many universities and colleges organise a programme of events before you start your course to welcome you, and to help you make new friends and get used to your new surroundings.

Student tip:

'If you want to know which university has the best research program in a specific area of study, looking up the most recent Research Assessment Exercise is the way to do it.'

Student tip:

'British universities are recognised by their academic excellence and international reputation – but never forget, as well as enjoying your studies it's about loving the experience! Be sure to check Student Union websites to see the events, societies and groups you can join.'

Social and cultural activities are often run for international students throughout the year. Universities and colleges also provide a variety of clubs and societies that you might want to join.

UCAS is also here to help you in your journey into UK higher education. We understand what a life-changing decision this can be and we're here to help you every step of the way. You can also meet some of our staff in your own country, as UCAS attends a number of international events to guide you, your parents and advisers through the application process. You can check where we will be visiting next by going to: **www.ucas.com/students/wheretostart/nonukstudents/internationalevents**. Many universities and colleges also visit a number of countries. You should check with their websites for further information. Finally, you might also want to check with your local British Council office to see if they can assist you.

Immigration requirements for study in the UK

You need to give yourself plenty of time to deal with your visa application to come to study in the UK. The evidence you need to provide can sometimes take several months to collect and has to be in the required format – otherwise your application for entry clearance (visa) will be refused.

The UK Border Agency (UKBA) is responsible for considering applications to enter or stay in the UK, including student visas. For more information on the requirements to obtain a student visa you should visit: **www.ukba.homeoffice.gov.uk/visas-immigration/studying**.

Similarly, UKCISA (the UK Council for International Student Affairs) produces information on immigration requirements at **www.ukcisa.org.uk/student/immigration.php** and **www.ukcisa.org.uk/student/info_sheets/applying_home_country.php**.

These pages also contain links to the UK Government's relevant application forms and guidance.

Furthermore there will be staff at the universities and colleges where you plan to study who can answer questions you have about this process.

Case study

Name: Alina Ludviga
Applying for: Interior Architecture and Design

English is not my first language so I knew I would have to pass IELTS.

Lesson one - don't wait until the last minute when applying to IELTS. When I finally got the courage to apply it turned out all test dates in 2011 were fully booked. Oh, where was I earlier!? I knew I could take it after the deadline of 15 January, but I wanted to make sure I had fully completed my application, so that I wouldn't have pressure of getting place on the course IF I passed IELTS. (And imagine if I got really unlucky and had to resit it, then it might have been really tight with time.)

My first offer was not from my first choice, but it still felt good. Condition was the one I already knew - the required IELTS score. By then I had finally managed to get a place on one of the test dates, giving me a month to live in growing fear and to improve my English.

Luckily my friend and I had to take the test on the same day, so we arrived early and when we ran out of things to do while waiting we decided to listen to each others' voice recordings we made while preparing for IELTS. Turns out it's an excellent method how to have a laugh and relax, as well as a great way how to practise speaking; when you get over that 'I hate my voice on recordings' feeling you can really notice mistakes you're making, which ones repeatedly and where your pronunciation sounds weird or unclear.

After taking the test, I knew I didn't get all the answers right on the first part which was listening. When I realised I had already missed a section I got quite nervous and had to force myself to let it go and focus on what was left. But all in all my biggest fears of hearing strange accents or low quality recordings didn't come true. That's for sure, on your IELTS you don't have to worry about technical things.

About my reading part I felt much more confident - I seemed to understand all the questions and found the answers quite quickly. I strongly advise to make yourself familiar with the type of questions and tasks you will see on IELTS. When you do a couple of practice reading tests it gets easier and easier on the next ones.

The writing part was the one where I had problems with the time limit. I finished both tasks, but I didn't have much time to check errors.

Well, and about speaking part, I don't know - I believe I was too nervous and because of that I was mumbling too much and speaking even more chaotically than usual... Maybe, just try to think about it as of a casual conversation with a friend. And breathe.

When I received the magic envelope from IELTS examination centre it turned out I did very well. I was right about reading part, that's the one where I got the highest score and I should probably spend more time writing essays as that's where I did the worst. Anyway, all in all, I got an overall band which was even a couple of points higher than necessary for my chosen course. And receiving a piece of paper which gave me rights to ring my mum and proudly announce that I'm very clever, made me feel so good and got me through the weekend flying a few centimetres above the ground.

Non-UK students' FAQs

Can I apply from outside the UK?

Applications are made online so you can apply from anywhere in the world with an internet connection.

Will I need to pass an English test first?

If English is not your native language, or if a university or college has a concern that your English language ability may be insufficient for the course you are applying for, they may ask you to take a recognised English language test – such as IELTS, TOEFL, CAE or CPE. The university or college may set a condition on an offer that you obtain particular grades in the test. Check with the universities or colleges directly to see which tests and what scores you would require.

How can I find out how much the fees are and whether I can get student funding or scholarships?

The profile of the course on the Course Finder section on **www.ucas.com** usually includes the fees for both home and international students. Your chosen institutions will check whether you are a home or international student when they decide whether to offer a place. Funding information can be found at **www.ucas.com/students/studentfinance**. UKCISA also provides a detailed outline of fee status requirements: **www.ukcisa.org.uk/student/fees_student_support.php**.

How can I tell if my qualifications will meet the entry requirements of my chosen institution if the qualification I've taken isn't in the UCAS Tariff or the course description?

Contact the institution to discuss your qualifications. They will decide whether your qualifications will meet their entry requirements. Many universities and colleges will also have specific information listed by country on their own websites, which you should make sure to check.

Is there a different application for students from outside the UK?

Everyone applying through UCAS uses the same electronic Apply form available on **www.ucas.com**.

Adviser tip:

'Different from other English speaking university systems, UK unis consider 'EU nationals' as distinct from 'international students'. When researching tuition fees and funding opportunities, make sure you read all the details regarding citizenship and domicile to determine the correct category for your circumstances.'

Adviser tip:

'If in doubt over your fee status, firstly check UKCISA and refer to the individual institution.'

Will I need a visa to study in the UK?
If you are not normally resident in the UK you may need to apply for a student visa. Information on student visas can be found at **www.ukba.homeoffice.gov.uk/visas-immigration/studying**.

Will I be required to attend an interview and when will it be?
Each institution will decide whether they need to interview for their course and when interviews will take place. If you will have any problems attending an interview at the institution during the year you should contact the institution to discuss when an interview can be scheduled. Sometimes universities and colleges will come to your own country to conduct an interview.

Do I need to send academic transcripts and where should I send them to?
You must fill in details of ALL qualifications you have, or will receive, on your UCAS application. Although you cannot attach transcripts to your UCAS application, the institutions you have applied to might want to receive copies. They will tell you when they would like to receive a copy, but you won't need to send any copies to UCAS.

Does my reference need to be in English?
Your reference must be written in English, although it can be a translation. Institutions may also wish to contact the referee directly for additional information, so the referee should be contactable and able to respond in English if possible.

Can the institution help me find somewhere to live while I'm studying?
Contact your chosen universities and colleges for information. Many have halls of residence which you can apply to stay in, and they might also be able to help you find private accommodation.

Can I work while studying in the UK?
Currently, most students on a Tier 4 Adult student visa are able to work up to 20 hours a week during term time, and full-time outside of term time. However this may change, so for more information on working in the UK go to **www.ukcisa.org.uk**.

The information about student finance in this chapter and the rest of the guide has been contributed by NASMA.

The National Association of Student Money Advisers (NASMA) strives to relieve the poverty of students through the provision of advice, information and training. We aim to provide for the public benefit, the profession of student money advice.

Visit **www.nasma.org.uk**

Money: how much will uni cost?

Now you've decided to study, you need to think about how you'll survive financially. The 'money' sections in this book advise you on funding that might be available, and how to get your hands on it so that you can relax and enjoy your time at university.

Sort this out before you start!

If you've already been bored by budgeting sessions at school, and talk of student grants and loans makes you yawn, you might be thinking about skipping these sections and moving on to something more interesting. STOP!

These sections might change your life!

The cost of studying in the UK

As a student, you'll usually pay for two things – tuition fees for the course, and living costs like rent, food, books, transport and entertainment. Fees charged vary between courses, as well as between universities and colleges, so it's best to check these before you apply.

Tuition fees are set by the uni or college – check how much before you apply.

You can find out the tuition fee by looking at the university or college websites or on Course Finder at **www.ucas.com** which has specific details on fees and financial support for each course. The maximum tuition fee for 'home' students is usually £9,000. If you're classed as 'overseas' for fee purposes, you're liable to pay the full cost fees which are set at a higher rate. See page 131 to see how your fee status is assessed.

If you live in Scotland and you want to study there, you aren't normally required to pay tuition fees. Check the Student Awards Agency for Scotland (SAAS) website **www.saas.gov.uk** for further information.

Eligibility for student funding

Eligibility is based on where you've lived before starting your course (this is referred to as your residency) and also if you've studied in higher education before. If you have studied before (even if only for a short time) it's strongly recommended you seek advice before starting another course, as there are restrictions on how many years you can get funding.

The rules are quite lengthy, but it's worth taking time to find out all the information at **www.gov.uk/student-finance**, or you can ask at your school, college or prospective university.

Each country in the UK has its own rules and procedures. You should check the website for the country where you're hoping to study as well as for the country where your family is living. See page 54 for a list of the websites to visit.

Cash support

Financial support for students in England, Scotland, Wales and Northern Ireland covers the following main areas. It's a good idea to get used to the different terminology so that you know what people are talking about and you don't look daft!

Tuition fee loans – repayable

As long as you've not been to university before, and you meet the residency rules, you'll not have to pay your tuition fees up-front to cover the cost of being taught on your course. Instead you can take out a loan to cover the cost. If you take out this loan the money will be paid directly to your university on your behalf.

If you want to pay your tuition fees yourself instead you can make arrangements to do this with your university.

However, eligible Scottish domiciled students and EU students studying at a uni or college in Scotland are currently entitled to free tuition.

Maintenance Loans – repayable
You can have a Maintenance Loan to cover your living costs, like rent, food and travel. For England, Wales and Northern Ireland Maintenance Loans are paid into your bank account in three instalments, at the start of each term.

Many part-time students are eligible for loans, as long as they study at least 25% of their time. However, they won't be eligible for maintenance support.

Be aware that there could be differences in loan rates for students living at home, those living away from home and studying in London, and loans for longer courses.

In Scotland you can receive a student loan. The amount of loan you can get depends on the level of your family's income, and payments are made on a monthly basis into your bank account.

Maintenance Grants – non-repayable
Maintenance Grants are intended to help students from lower income households with their living costs. You don't have to get a loan to be eligible for this grant.

Maintenance Grants are paid at the same time as Maintenance Loans.

However, Maintenance Grants aren't available everywhere in the UK – instead bursaries are provided in Scotland and Assembly Learning Grants in Wales.

Special Support Grants – non-repayable
This grant is for students eligible for (but not necessarily receiving) means-tested benefits. As a general rule this is students who are parents or disabled students.

Special Support Grants are paid into your bank account in three instalments – at the start of each term.

Note: you can only apply for either the Special Support Grant or the Maintenance Grant in any academic year – not both.

University bursaries – non-repayable
Bursaries might be available at the uni or college you choose. This varies greatly between different institutions and courses – you can find out more on Course Finder at **www.ucas.com** or on uni and college websites.

National Scholarship Programme

New students starting university in England from September 2012 may be eligible to receive an award through the National Scholarship Programme, depending on the criteria set by the university.

You should check the criteria for your chosen institution, and also look at whether or not you need to apply for the support or if the university is using an automated checking process.

Scholarships – non-repayable

Scholarships are usually given to students because of achievement and excellence. This is one area of additional financial support where you might have to do some of your own research. (See more information on this in Step 1 Choosing courses on page 95.)

Interest and repayments

Despite what you might have heard, Student Loans aren't interest free, but rather than a commercial rate, the interest is linked to inflation plus up to an additional 3%. So basically you're not likely to get a better deal on the high street, but be aware that you'll be charged interest from the day you take out your loan.

The main difference between Student Loans and commercial loans is that the repayments on Student Loans are linked to how much you earn rather than how much you borrowed.

The loan is only repayable when you finish your course and your income goes over the set threshold. These thresholds increase annually by the rate of inflation. In England and Wales the earnings threshold will be £21,000. In Northern Ireland the rate will be £15,795. Repayments are deducted from your salary (like tax and national insurance) at 9% of your income over the threshold amount.

This table gives examples of how much your monthly repayments would be if you're from England or Wales:

Salary £22,000	9% of £1,000	£90 per year	£7.50 per month
Salary £24,000	9% of £5,000	£450 per year	£37 per month
Salary £36,000	9% of £15,000	£1,350 per year	£112 per month

Bournemouth University has produced a short animated film to explain the new fees system and repayment scheme – take a look at **www.bournemouth.ac.uk/fees2012**.

Additional money or support you may be eligible for

Please note, the information here is what's available at the time of writing and it may change.

If you're unsure whether you'll have enough money to go to uni or college, the additional money or support listed here might make all the difference. However it's also worth thinking ahead about how you can make the most of the money you do have – take a look at the 'Money: making it go further' section on page 355 to find out more.

Care leaver's grant

If you've been in local authority care before going to university you'll find both your leaving care team and your uni have loads of additional support for you. Obviously you need to tell the university that you've been in care, but don't worry about other people knowing; it's all kept confidential. It's not like being at school where everyone knows all about you. At uni you're an adult so nobody will know anything about you if you don't want them to.

Extra help for students who are parents

Childcare – if you have children you'll have different worries and priorities when you're thinking about starting university. Unis employ specialist staff to advise you about childcare, funding and benefits. The website **www.gov.uk/childcare-grant** has information about the Childcare Grant.

When you apply for student funding you can also apply for help with childcare costs. This is a means tested grant which can cover up to 85% of your childcare costs.

You can also apply for a Parent's Learning Allowance.

These grants will be disregarded when Jobcentre Plus calculates your entitlement for benefits, and they're both non-repayable.

Child Tax Credit – if you have children financially dependent on you and you receive Child Benefit for them, you can also claim Child Tax Credit from HM Revenue and Customs. You don't have to be working to claim them (and students are classed as unemployed). But if you'll be working alongside your studies you can still claim Working Tax Credit as well as Child Tax Credit –

depending on your age and the amount of hours you work. Check **www.hmrc.gov.uk/taxcredits** to find out more.

Disabled Students' Allowances

If you have a disability, ongoing health condition or specific learning difficulty you could be eligible for additional support via the Disabled Students' Allowances. When you apply for your funding you'll need to send some evidence – maybe an educational psychologist's report or a letter from your specialist or doctor. Once this is accepted you'll be sent on an assessment of your needs – this provides a list of recommendations for the support you'll need to attend your chosen course. Then this will be paid for on your behalf.

In addition your uni will be able to put support in place for you – like extra time in exams. Most unis have teams of staff that deal with this – look on their website and contact them well before you start – as the more notice you give, the more time staff will have to make arrangements for you.

Once again, a lot of this support can be done discreetly, so don't feel embarrassed about seeking help or advice.

Emergency and hardship funding

All universities have emergency money they can use to assist students in hardship – this could help you if your loan hasn't turned up or something unexpected has happened. If your circumstances mean you'll find it hard to work alongside your studies, perhaps due to the intensity of your course, your children or your disability, you might also qualify for additional financial support from your university.

Find out more about student finance from the relevant sites

England: Student Finance England – www.gov.uk/student-finance

Northern Ireland: Student Finance Northern Ireland – www.studentfinanceni.co.uk

Scotland: Student Awards Agency for Scotland (SAAS) – www.saas.gov.uk

Wales: Student Finance Wales – www.studentfinancewales.co.uk

Funding in summary

Funding	How is it paid?	Where does it come from?	Additional information	Means tested or non-means tested	Repayable or non-repayable
Tuition fee loan	Direct to university	Student Loans Company		Non-means tested	Repayable – once completed and earning £15,000
Maintenance Loan	Directly to students in three instalments	Student Loans Company	Used by students to live off, pay rent, buy food etc	72% non-means tested 28% means tested	Repayable – once completed and earning £15,000
Maintenance Grant*	Direct to students in three instalments	Student Loans Company	Used by students to live off, pay rent, buy food etc	Means tested	Non-repayable
Special Support Grant*	Direct to students in three instalments	Student Loans Company	Used by students to live off, pay rent, buy food etc	Means tested	Non-repayable
Childcare Grant	Direct to students in three instalments	Student Loans Company	For students that have to pay for childcare	Means tested	Non-repayable
Adult Dependants Grant	Direct to students in three instalments	Student Loans Company	For students that have an adult that is dependent	Means tested	Non-repayable
Parents Learning Allowance	Direct to students in three instalments	Student Loans Company	For students that have dependent children	Means tested	Non-repayable
University scholarships	Will depend on university – check their website	University	Students that excel at certain things – may be sport, academic, arts etc	Not normally means tested	Non-repayable

* Students can only be eligible for one of these grants in any academic year.

FAQs on money

How does UCAS help with student finance?

UCAS isn't directly involved in providing or organising student finance, but we do have lots of advice on our website to help you out – **www.ucas.com/students/studentfinance**.

What if my loan doesn't give me enough money to live on?

Many students work in part-time jobs during their studies – which as well as earning you extra money also increases your work experience and develops new skills. Maybe you could work part-time during term time, or maybe just over Christmas and summer – it could make all the difference.

It's worth checking if there's any additional support on offer at your chosen university or college – you might be entitled to a bursary or a scholarship.

Then it's a case of making your money go as far as possible – think about getting an NUS discount card at **www.nus.org.uk/nusextra**, and have a look at **www.studentcalculator.org.uk** to see an online budgeting tool.

Whatever you do, make sure you apply for your student loan on time or your money might be delayed.

When do I have to pay back my loan?

You can make repayments of your loan plus the interest whenever you like, and there's no deadline – but after your earnings increase above a certain rate, a small percentage of your earnings will automatically be deducted each month.

View **www.gov.uk/student-finance** to find out more about the rates, methods of repayment and how much you could be repaying each month.

Chapter summary

These are the things you should now know:

- ☐ Why you want to go to higher education.
- ☐ The differences between the types of qualifications available:
  - bachelor's degree
  - Higher National Certificate (HNC) and Higher National Diploma (HND)
  - Certificate of Higher Education (CertHE) and Diploma of Higher Education (DipHE)
  - foundation degree
  - postgraduate.
- ☐ What are single subject and combined subject courses.
- ☐ What's meant by modular courses.
- ☐ What's meant by a sandwich course.
- ☐ How learning at university is different to learning at school.
- ☐ UCAS – our role in your journey.
- ☐ Six steps to applying – the applicant journey.
- ☐ Extra information for:
  - mature students
  - students with disabilities
  - non-UK students.
- ☐ Money: eligibility of student funding and cash support.

www.ucas.com

Step 1
Choosing courses

Once you know you want to do a higher education course, you need to start thinking about what you want to study and where you want to go. There are lots of resources available to help you but at the end of the day you'll have to make up your own mind. Spend time exploring what you want to do and what best fits your interests and abilities.

This chapter will guide you through your research – starting with where to find course details and where to find info on universities and colleges.

Step 1 **Choosing courses**

Thinking of going to university or college?

No → Employment, Apprenticeship, Part-time course, Gap year, Re-sits, Other ...

Yes →

Do your research!

Which subject?

Ask your school, family, etc

Visit **www.ucas.com** for Course Finder links to uni websites

Library

Summer school

Which career?

Careers service

Connexions

Work experience

Dreams, inspirations, heroes & heroines

Which course?

Which university or college? (see websites and prospectuses)

Check whether you need to sit an admissions test or are likely to be called to interview or audition (see **www.ucas.com**)

Joint degree – can restrict or open choices of career

Check out teaching and assessment methods

Attend an open day to look around and meet current students

Step 1

Do your research

Choosing the right course can be crucial to your career path, so it's important to look at what you want to do early. Then when it comes to applying you'll be more certain you're aiming for the right courses for you.

Many potential applicants don't know what they want to study at uni or which subjects suit them best, so if you're not sure yet, don't worry – you're not alone. It's essential that you spend time exploring and researching what to study. Every year a significant number of students drop out of their course because they failed to do enough research before they applied.

You can choose up to five courses to put down on your UCAS application. You don't have to use all your choices though – you can apply for just one if you know exactly where you want to go. Remember to check out course entry requirements too – you'll want to be realistic about which universities are likely to make you an offer.

Student tip:

'Pros and cons lists are always welcome, as well as making a list of your abilities, qualities and what you think would suit you most on a longer period of time, rather than stating something you only wish you could do or something you perceive as a hobby.'

Here's a list of the things you should be doing to research the right course for you – each is then explained in more detail over the following pages.

Page	
62	Think ahead and explore your career path
65	Be aware of the different types of qualifications available
67	Look at Course Finder at **www.ucas.com** and check the entry requirements
71	Look at university and college websites and prospectuses
71	Attend a higher education convention
75	Think about the type of university that would suit you
80	Go to open days
84	Watch **www.ucas.tv**
85	Look at league tables
95	Check available scholarships

Think ahead – going to university should be one of the most enriching and enjoyable experiences of your life. A big decision deserves a lot of thought. You can apply for five course choices and you want to decide on the very best ones for you.

Think about your career path

Some careers require you to take a particular subject at a particular level while others will be happy with any subject. If you have an idea of what kind of a job you'd like after education, check what qualifications employers look for. On the other hand, if you're starting with an idea of what subject you'd like to study, see what career opportunities come with it.

There are many places to check the career paths that different courses lead to.

- University and college prospectuses and websites often mention which careers their graduates go into.

- *What Do Graduates Do?* (published every year and available online from the Higher Education Careers Services Unit website (**www.hecsu.ac.uk/what_do_graduates_do_archive.htm**) provides stats and articles indicating the variety of careers graduates get involved in.
- Ask your school or college tutors and advisers, as well as your local Connexions, Careers Wales, Careers Scotland or Northern Ireland Careers Service offices.
- If you have a career in mind, talk to someone already doing the job and see if it has a professional representative body. Check job ads too – they might give an idea of what a career is like and how it could develop.

There's a wealth of information on the internet. Spend a few hours each week surfing and collecting information.

Students with disabilities

If you know what career you want to follow, talk to a careers adviser about what degrees would suit your needs. You could also talk to a professional organisation connected to the career you're interested in. By talking to someone already doing the job you can get practical advice about the best courses. You might want to do a foundation degree if you're already working and want to develop your skills, or if you have a specific career in mind.

In some cases you may need to think about how your impairment might affect your future career path. There are some courses and professions which have their own 'fitness to practise' regulations. These relate to the physical demands of the job and health and safety requirements. This might involve completing a health questionnaire and having an occupational health assessment.

No one should assume that a disabled person cannot enter a specific career. The Equality Act (2010) means that employers have to remove barriers in the workplace for disabled people, and financial support is available to help them do this. Always start exploring your options based on what you want to do, then afterwards you can think about any advice and support you might need.

Remember, you may get a better degree – which employers will like – if you study something you enjoy.

No idea what to study?

If you know that a higher education course is for you but you find the choice of subjects too much, a good place to start is by asking yourself the following questions:

- Which subjects interest me?
- What are my talents?
- What job would I like to do after university or college?
- Which academic skills would I like to improve?

International students

The most important part of higher education in the UK is choosing a course. Unlike other countries, what you want to study determines where you might study it.

FAQs on choosing a course

How do I choose a course?

Find a course that matches your interests, career aspirations and talents. It's important to choose a qualification that suits you. Unis and colleges offer a whole range of higher education courses including undergraduate degrees, foundation degrees, HNDs and HNCs – look into what these involve so you can then decide what to apply for.

Once you've decided which subject to study, you can decide which universities to apply for. You can look at league tables, which compare universities by subject, or even better you can go to an open day or arrange a tour.

Often the best way to decide if a university is right for you is to just visit it!

How do I know if I'm eligible for a course?

Universities list the entry requirements for their courses on their websites and on UCAS Course Finder. Often these listings include how many UCAS Tariff points you'd need to get on the course. If you're not sure you have enough points, or your qualification isn't included in the Tariff system, contact the university directly and ask them if you meet their requirements.

Can I defer my place for a year?

Check with the university or college you're interested in to see if they're happy to consider an application for deferred entry. When you add the choice you'll need to state that you'd like to defer your application when you select the start date you want.

Adviser tip:

'Consider this – if you were given a textbook this very second and told it was the only thing you could read for the next 3 or 4 years (no magazines, newspapers, Facebook or Twitter), what would the book be about? If you can answer that then maybe that's the subject you should study at university.'

Choose a qualification that suits you

Most people think higher education means studying for a degree, but there are many more qualifications you can take at university or college. See the different types of qualifications there are on page 14.

Consider combination courses if you would like to study more than one subject

If you're interested in more than one subject you can choose a combination of subjects – eg English literature and psychology. Use Course Finder at **www.ucas.com** to find out which combinations you could go for.

You can often decide for yourself how much time you'd like to spend on each subject. See the section 'Single and combined courses' on page 18 for more information.

Did you know?

You can study waste management and dance…

It's amazing what combinations you can do. Over 1,000 different subjects are available in well over 43,000 different courses. So before jumping in with a favourite subject you're studying now, it could be worth seeing what else is available. For example, if you're studying biology, maybe you'd be interested in a course in zoology, marine biology or forensic science. Or if you prefer English, what about journalism, creative writing or primary school teaching?

International students

If you plan to work back in your home country, be sure to check the course is recognised there.

Vocational or non-vocational course?

A vocational course is job-specific – so it could be the more secure route into employment. A non-vocational subject on the other hand might not lead directly to a specific job but could prepare you for a career you'd enjoy more.

You could also think about taking a sandwich course – these involve working for a year in the industry you're aiming for, giving you really valuable experience. You can search for sandwich courses on Course Finder.

Student tip:

'Erasmus is brilliant – I recommend looking into it when you're first applying to uni. See if the course you want has an Erasmus option, and check what connections the uni has with international institutions – then research them to see if they're right for you.'

Studying abroad

Erasmus is the European exchange programme for higher education students. You get to study or do a work placement for a few months (anything from three to 12) in other European countries as part of your degree course. Students from all subjects can take part – it's not just for language students, (although studying in another country will involve foreign languages in some way).

If you're interested, you need to choose a uni or college that offers the Erasmus programme for the course you want to study. You can find more info on the British Council website **www.britishcouncil.org/erasmus**.

It's a great opportunity to improve your academic experience and job opportunities, as well as developing your personal confidence and maturity.

Alternatively you could apply to study a full degree abroad. There would be a lot of additional factors to think about – such as funding and different application processes (not managed by UCAS) – but it could be an ideal option for you.

For more information on studying abroad, either for a year or a whole course, take a look at the Studying in another country section on page 305.

Look at Course Finder at www.ucas.com

Course Finder on the UCAS website lists around 43,000 full-time higher education courses, so narrowing down your search might seem daunting.

You'll recognise the core subjects available to study, like maths, English and chemistry. But you might not recognise the more creative and varied courses which branch out from these core subjects. For example, if you enjoy chemistry, there's also chemical engineering, environmental chemistry or forensic science. Or if you prefer English, you could study English literature, journalism, creative writing or primary school teaching.

Course Finder provides info including:

- course title, duration, type of qualification and application deadline
- university contact details and website links
- links to the relevant employability profile
- the content of the course
- entry requirements
- skills, qualities and experiences admissions staff are looking for
- fees, bursaries and financial support
- details about the institution.

You can search by subject on Course Finder to see courses in that subject area. When you click on the course title you'll find all the info the uni or college has provided about that particular course. Here you can check you'll have the right qualifications, experiences and personal qualities to gain entry onto the course.

Many courses with the same title are actually very different in terms of content and study methods, so check the course details to help you see what suits you best.

Adviser tip:

'Even if you are certain of what it is you want to study, be careful to look at the course descriptions – courses with the same course title or code can vary widely.'

Student tip:

'Thanks to Course Finder on www.ucas.com I could easily find a university for me, with information including the grades required, locations, uni website links and feedback.'

Often certain subjects will be required and you must be already studying these in order to have your application fully considered.

Be realistic. A popular degree at a prestigious university will set challenging entry requirements.

Be sure of the entry requirements

When you check the entry requirements see if there are any admissions tests or interviews you have to attend. Also check if there are specific GCSE or Standard Grade subjects and grades you need to have – many courses require English and maths at grade C or above. Any A level or Higher grades you need will be listed too, as well as any specific subjects and grades you'll need for that particular course.

Often entry requirements also include Tariff points – these are from the UCAS Tariff system which allocates points to the qualifications students use to enter higher education. Most qualifications are included in the Tariff – but if yours isn't all you have to do is contact the unis you're interested in to check if they'd accept it. Take a look at page 272 or **www.ucas.com** to check if yours is on the list.

International students

If you've been asked for GCSE equivalents, find out what that means for your country's educational system. And if entry requirements for your country's national exams are not specified, resist the temptation to guess your entry requirements based on numbers for other exams, such as the International Baccalaureate. Entry requirements for one country's system will probably not directly correspond to another academic system. Take the time to contact universities to make sure.

If your first contact at the admissions office is unfamiliar with your qualification, ask to be put through to international admissions. Furthermore mention the region of your qualification, (eg USA for AP exams), rather than the country in which you are studying.

Myth buster

If one course has lower entry requirements than another, it doesn't mean that it's not as good.

Try not to decide which courses to apply for based on just the grades or points they require – although you'll need to check that you can realistically meet these, you also need to think about the course itself. It's more important that you choose a course based on what it offers you, rather than whether it has high entry requirements or not.

Read through a course's content to see if it's what you want, or check the university's website.

Ask friends, family and advisers about courses and universities, but whatever anyone says about a course, make sure it's right for you.

FAQs on Course Finder

How do I find out which universities or colleges run the course I want to apply for?
The Course Finder facility on the UCAS website allows you to see what's available. You can just search by subject or you can narrow down your search by geographical region, a specific institution or course type as well. You can also look for courses leading to Qualified Teacher Status (QTS) or professional accreditation.

What qualifications do I need?
The majority of courses on Course Finder have information on course content and entry requirements. These differ between courses and universities so it's important to check carefully before applying.

Can I search for just universities or colleges that will accept my qualification(s)?
Unfortunately not – you'll need to find a course you're interested in and then check the specific entry requirements.

How do I search for part-time courses?
UCAS processes applications for full-time courses only. However, we do have a part-time course search from July-September where you can search for part-time courses at the unis and colleges that also recruit for their full-time courses through us. Plus, you can contact individual universities and colleges to find out if they have part-time options, or you can check on their websites.

What information is included in the course details?
As well as entry requirements you'll also find more info about the course, selection criteria, admissions policy, fees, bursaries and financial support, specific information about the institution, and details regarding any admissions tests required.

Can I search for courses in other countries?

No – UCAS only processes applications for courses in England, Wales, Scotland and Northern Ireland, but you can find more information about studying abroad by contacting the Embassy for that country (see page 309).

International students

You should also contact your local British Council office (**www.britishcouncil.org**) as we work closely with them in providing up-to-date information to students – they might be able to help you search for a UK course.

Regardless of how old you are, it's important not to rush your choice.

Mature students

Deciding on the right course is crucial if you're to make the most of higher education. Looking on Course Finder at **www.ucas.com** will help to differentiate one course from another, and will also provide links to university and college websites with information specifically for mature students. If you find that the entry requirement information is only tailored for school leavers, contact the admissions tutor for the course and find out whether your experience and qualifications would be suitable.

Students with disabilities

Concentrate first on what you want to study. Most subjects can be made accessible with the appropriate support. Don't be put off by people assuming that you can't do something because of your impairment.

- Visually impaired students take graphic design courses.
- People who are deaf or hard of hearing study music.
- People with dyslexia train to be teachers.

If you have very specific needs, you should visit all the institutions you're interested in. It's better not to waste one of your UCAS choices by finding out that an institution isn't suitable after you've applied. Many institutions welcome early, informal visits as they provide staff with an opportunity to discuss possible support arrangements with you.

Look at university and college websites and prospectuses

Once you have an idea of what you want to study, start to do some more detailed investigation into each university that interests you.

Uni and college websites and prospectuses should provide accurate info about the courses available, covering course content, structure, study style and career destinations. You can find links to uni and college websites on Course Finder, or look for copies of prospectuses in your local careers office.

Alternatively, you can order prospectuses directly from unis and colleges. Ask them to send you a copy of their undergraduate prospectus along with any additional course-specific leaflets, or they might have an option on their website to fill in your contact details to receive a prospectus or view a copy online. But remember prospectuses also act as advertisements to encourage students to apply particularly to that uni or college – so make sure any courses you're interested in are definitely right for you.

Student tip:

'Try to gather information from people already studying or working in areas you're interested in. Then research every course in depth – the core units, the structure, available work placements, scholarships and opportunities for studying abroad.'

Attend a higher education convention

These are excellent opportunities to meet representatives from unis and colleges who will tell you more about their institution. UCAS higher education conventions are held throughout the UK and run between March and July in England, Wales and Northern Ireland and between August and October in Scotland. Exhibitors also include further education colleges, Connexions, gap year organisations, student support services, professional bodies, student travel firms and student finance.

Outside of the UK, events are held throughout the year – including many hosted by the British Council. You can check the following website to see what events are being held in your country: **www.educationuk.org/uk/events**. You could also ask the institutions you're interested in if they will be visiting your country at any point.

Student tip:

'At the Education UK Exhibition in Hong Kong I gained great insights into UK universities, kind of compensating for the fact I can't visit the universities in person. Everyone was extremely helpful and enthusiastic.'

The events play a vital part in helping applicants decide what and where to study. Many of them also have seminars about topics like 'grants and loans', 'taking a year out', 'how to fill in your UCAS application' and 'entry into medicine, law and psychology'.

They're mainly designed for 16-17 year old students. Schools and colleges often make group bookings to attend – but you're also welcome to visit a convention as an individual on the day (for free and without booking beforehand). Check out the list of higher education conventions at **www.ucasevents.com/conventions**.

If you do come along it's a good idea to have questions ready to ask the unis and colleges. Have a look at some examples below.

Getting onto the course

- How many places are available for the course and how many applications are received each year?
- Are there any subjects or qualifications that aren't acceptable for your course?
- What qualities do you look for when considering applicants?
- What key skills do you look for and what evidence do you need?
- What special entry qualifications or other arrangements for mature students exist?
- For art and design courses, is an art foundation course necessary?
- Will I have to sit an additional test?

Interviews

- Is a formal interview part of the selection procedure?
- What proportion of applicants do you interview?
- What is the purpose of the interview, how important is it, and what form does it take?

The course itself

- How is the course assessed – by exam or continuous assessment?

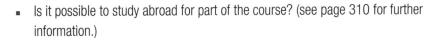

- Is it possible to study abroad for part of the course? (see page 310 for further information.)
- How flexible is the course? Is there scope to pursue special interests?
- How easy is it to change course or to study a subsidiary course?
- How is the course taught – through lectures, tutorials, seminars, laboratory work or other?
- How much contact time (in lectures, tutorials etc) is there each week?
- What is the staff to student ratio?
- Do departments give help or advice about gaining sponsorship?
- Will I be expected to buy materials or equipment?

Student tip:

'The UCAS fayre was fun, but there was a panic when we saw how many stands there were, from universities all over the country. I ended up bringing home so many prospectuses for absolutely no reason – but reading over each one I did eventually manage to whittle my choices down to just five.'

A year out

- Is taking a year out acceptable or encouraged? If so, is there any specific experience I should try to gain? See page 311 for gap year info.
- Should I apply during my final A level or equivalent year for deferred entry, or apply during my year out?
- What are the financial implications of taking a year out?

The university or college

- Is it based on one site?
- Do students live on site? Is there accommodation for all first year students?
- How far away is the accommodation from the institution?
- What is the typical cost of accommodation?
- Do I need to have personal transport? Can I keep a car or bike? If so, is parking available?
- Is public transport available from the halls of residence to lectures? If yes, what does it cost?

Student facilities

- Can you tell me about student services, the students' union, clubs, job shop, societies and sports and recreation facilities at your institution?
- What support services are provided, such as careers service, counselling, finance and medical?
- What support facilities exist for students with additional needs?

The future

- Where are graduates from this course likely to find employment?
- What exemptions does this course give with respect to professional qualifications?

Student tip:

'From going to a higher education event in my first year at college, I found out more about what universities have to offer, and also more about the information UCAS provides.'

Finding out more

- If I have any specific questions in the future, who should I contact at your institution?
- What are the arrangements for attending an open day or making a personal visit?
- Is there an alternative student prospectus? How do I get one?

Other recommended activities

- Attend uni and college open days. These will help you decide if the university or college is right for you, and help you avoid the disappointment of starting a course and finding it's not what you expected.
- Arrange an interview with your tutor or personal careers adviser to talk about any help or advice you might need.
- If you haven't already done so, create an information progress file to record your research.
- Draft a personal statement for your UCAS application.
- Establish a personal timetable for ongoing research and your application.

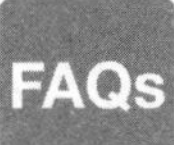

FAQs on conventions and exhibitions

What is a convention or exhibition?

Conventions bring together universities and colleges to inform and guide prospective students. There's a lot of higher education information available at conventions, as well as details about student finance and gap years.

Exhibitions tend to focus on particular subject areas such as art and design or media.

Where and when are they held?

There are a number of conventions and exhibitions run throughout the UK, usually taking place between March and October each year.

What use are they?

The conventions allow you to meet face-to-face with universities and colleges to gain info about the course you're interested in, and to find out what facilities, support and clubs the institution can offer. You'll also be able to ask any questions you might have.

How can I apply to go?

Tickets aren't needed for conventions, however invitations to book are usually sent out to schools and colleges before booking begins. You're also welcome to visit the convention on the day as an individual without booking.

You do need to book to attend an exhibition and you can do this online from the UCAS website.

Do I have to pay to come to an event?

No, all events are free of charge.

Choosing a university or college

There are lots of reasons why you might want to choose a particular university or college. The reasons will be personal to you, and the courses your friends choose

Student tip:

'I researched each university and found useful websites that classify universities according to each area of study, career prospects, employability after graduation etc, and I slowly cut down the list until only five choices remained.'

Student tip:

'I would recommend choosing your course before your university – as you want to be sure you'll enjoy three years of study. Next, find out which unis offer a version of your course you like the sound of, and through websites and open days decide which you prefer. Also make sure to pick unis with a range of different grade requirements.'

might not be right for you. Here are some of the questions you might want to think about.

- **Near or far?** You might need to look for a local course so you can stay with your family, or you might be happy to move to wherever you need to go to do the right course.
- **Town or country?** Would you like to live in the centre of a big city to be close to all the facilities it has to offer, or would you prefer a rural location?
- **Small or large?** Do you like the idea of studying at a major university with large lecture theatres and something for everybody, or would you prefer a small site where you can get to know everyone?
- **Campus or non-campus?** Would you like a campus with everything located on one site, or do you like the idea of travelling around different sites?
- **What are the study facilities, books and learning resources like?** This is very important if you're going to be spending a lot of time studying there.
- **Halls of residence or rented accommodation?** Does it have guaranteed institution-managed accommodation for first year students? What's the cost of staying in halls? How easy is it to find a student house to live in?
- **What activities, clubs and societies are there?** Many universities boast a vast array of clubs and societies, from rowing and tennis to debating and religious clubs, but some will be more active than others. Check with the Students' Union and ask students when you visit on an open day.
- **Nightlife and social life?** Can you be sure you'll find the social life you're after? Does it have an active Students' Union? What events does the Students' Union arrange? Are there clubs and pubs nearby you want to go to?
- **Male to female ratio.** Does it make a difference to you if there are more males or females?
- **What sports facilities are there?** Many unis have gyms, playing fields and swimming pools on site.
- **What's the university's reputation?** The reputation of a university or college can be very subjective, so it's important to choose a university that suits you

rather than trying to fit into one that might not. However, if you're thinking about your CV and the kudos a certain university will bring, then perhaps reputation is important for you. Maybe certain courses at specific universities are better regarded by an area of business or industry than others.

- **Does it have expert teaching staff?** What's the student to staff ratio? Are the academic staff experts in their field? How was the subject you were interested in rated in the latest Research Assessment Exercise (soon to be the Research Excellence Framework)? What teaching methods are used?
- **What's the general feel of the university and the university town?** What was it like when you visited? Do you feel safe and comfortable moving around the campus and town? Is it exciting or inspiring? Does it have the space and support you're looking for?

You can go to **www.ucas.com** to find a map showing all the unis and colleges. You can click into the ones you're interested in to find details about student numbers, campus info and accommodation arrangements.

International students
Check out the public transport around your chosen university so that you can fly in and get your luggage to the university easily!

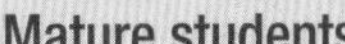

Mature students
Look as widely as possible to find a university and course which best suits you. If you're limited to a single local university or college, you might want to look at the full range of courses it offers to see if there's something which appeals that you didn't originally consider. Alternatively higher education courses, or segments of them, are available in further education colleges.

Groups of universities

When reading about universities in the paper or doing your research, you might hear people referring to a specific group or category of university. Here's an explanation of each term.

1994 Group – a group of 19 internationally renowned, research-intensive universities established to promote excellence in research and teaching and enhance student and staff experience. It includes universities such as University of

Bath, Lancaster University and University of St Andrews. Find out more at **www.1994group.ac.uk**.

Million+ Group – a university think tank which uses research and evidence-based policy to solve complex problems in higher education. It aims to develop and shape public policy to enable people from every walk of life to access universities that excel in teaching, research and knowledge transfer. It includes universities such as Kingston University London, Teesside University and University of the West of Scotland. Visit **www.millionplus.ac.uk** for more info.

Red brick universities – an informal term for six universities, originally civic colleges which achieved university status by the early 1900s. They are the universities of Birmingham, Bristol, Leeds, Liverpool, Manchester and Sheffield. More recently, due to their similar characteristics, universities such as Reading, Queen's University Belfast, Nottingham and Hull, among others, have also been classed as 'red brick'.

Russell Group – represents 24 leading universities committed to 'maintaining the very best research, an outstanding teaching and learning experience and unrivalled links with business and the public sector'. It includes universities such as Queen's University Belfast, Cardiff University, University of Edinburgh and University of Oxford. See **www.russellgroup.ac.uk** for a full list.

Post-1992 universities or new universities – an informal term referring to former polytechnics or colleges of higher education that were given university status from 1992 onwards. Examples include the universities of Coventry, Worcester, Portsmouth, Glamorgan, and Glasgow Caledonian.

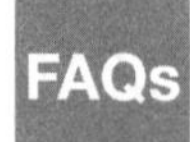

FAQs on choosing a university or college

Which institution is best for my chosen course?

Different places suit different people, so it depends what you're looking for. There are different guides and league tables that can help you, but check the source as it may be biased – some universities post league tables on their websites which show their courses at number one.

For information and impartial advice check the *Times Online* or *The Complete University Guide*, (an interactive site where you can enter your preferences and create your own unique table).

How can I find universities and colleges in my area that offer the course I want to do?

The Course Finder facility on the UCAS website allows you to search for the subject you're interested in and then narrow your search down by geographical region.

Also on the UCAS website there's a university and college map which shows you the locations of all institutions across the UK.

Where can I find out more about the student experience?

There are several different places you can go to speak to current students and get tips on the application process and going to university. Attending an open day will mean you get to meet current and prospective students to share your thoughts, questions and any worries you might have.

You can also use social network sites such as Twitter or Facebook – we have a UCAS adviser on both who can answer your questions, and you can chat to other students as well.

Parent tip:

'Don't make a choice based on just websites and league tables. We visited many universities (probably too many!) with my son, but that helped him confirm various factors, such as that he wanted a city centre site and a year abroad in industry.'

Visit the Unistats website to compare universities

Here you can search, review and compare unis, colleges and subjects so that you can choose the best course for you.

It includes results from the National Student Survey – more than 220,000 students giving their views about the quality of their higher education experience.

Go to **unistats.direct.gov.uk** to compare a range of uni statistics from:

- Student satisfaction
- Employment and accreditation
- Cost and accommodation
- Study information
- Entry information.

Student tip:

'I went to loads of open days. Some unis weren't as impressive as I thought they'd be but some were far more impressive than I ever anticipated. They definitely changed my mind about where I want to study.'

Student tip:

'I went to the open day and spoke to some tutors – they're really nice and spoke to us about the course, how we will be studying and how the course is assessed – ie coursework, group posters and assignments!!'

This is a great way to easily compare stats and feedback for the unis and colleges you're interested in. It's worth checking through these before you go to open days. Then if you read anything you're unsure of you can ask questions about it while you're touring the uni.

Open days and visits to universities and colleges

Visiting your chosen universities or colleges is a must if you want to be sure you end up in the right place for you. You'll get a taste of university life, seeing lecture theatres, labs, libraries and IT suites, as well as student catering facilities, bars and halls of residence. You'll also get an idea of the distance between the facilities you'll be using, where they are, how close you are to other public services and how far it is from home.

It's a good idea to visit all the universities and colleges you're interested in before applying, and definitely before you reply to your offers. This way you can make sure you avoid the disappointment of starting the course and finding it's not what you expected.

Remember, if you're planning to visit a number of universities around the UK it might be worth getting the 16-25 Railcard or the Young Persons Coachcard. The 16-25 Railcard saves you a third off rail fares across Britain for a year – you can get one if you're 16-25 years old, or in full-time education and over 26 years old. See **www.16-25railcard.co.uk** for details. The Young Persons Coachcard saves you up to 30% off National Express coach fares for a year – again you need to be between 16 and 26 or a full-time student. See **www.nationalexpress.com/coach/Offers/StudentCoachDeals.cfm** for details.

International students

Sometimes international applicants or offer holders are not invited to open days because the university assumes it will be difficult for the student to get there. If you do want to attend it's worth contacting the university to make sure you don't miss out.

If you can't visit, use video guides instead. **UCAS.tv**, **YouTube** and **unionview.com** all have really useful video clips to help you choose the right uni for your needs, and to see its location.

FAQs on open days

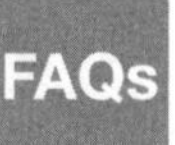

What is an open day?

An open day is a chance to visit a uni or college to make sure you're happy to go there before you apply.

When are the open days?

Each uni and college will have its own dates for open days. Check our open days and taster courses search at **www.ucas.com**. You can search by university, month, region, town or city, or subject. You'll find uni contact details, dates and times, further information and booking details.

Parent tip:

'We started going to open days for my daughter last summer term, but found that many were held on the same day and many others were on weekdays. So we ended up going to four open days in one weekend... I would advise you start going to open days as early as possible so you can get a better idea of the universities on separate days.'

What do they involve?

Usually you'll be shown around the campus, accommodation and student union. You'll also be able to meet current students and ask them any questions you have about the course and the university or college. Watch the UCAStv Open Days video at **www.ucas.com** for tips on how to make the most of your visit.

Are they worth going to?

Attending an open day helps you to confirm you feel right about that uni and that course. You need to make sure it's what you want before agreeing to study there. Visiting a university will help you do that and give you a taste of uni life.

How do I register to attend?

This depends on the university or college – contact them directly to confirm whether you need to register. If so, you'd usually be able to register on their website.

I can't make the official open day – can I still visit the university or college?

Probably. Although it's unlikely the university or college will be able to offer the normal tour and so on, you will be encouraged to see the institution before accepting a place. Contact the uni or college directly to discuss an individual visit on a day that suits you both.

Case study

Name: Jenny Vowles
Parent of an A level student

We were quite nervous about going to the university Open Day. For me it was a very significant marker in my son's journey towards adulthood and for him it was a first injection of reality into his dreams of studying his favourite subject - philosophy.

We were welcomed at the door by a current student, who seemed almost as nervous as ourselves. He had clearly not been given a script and was therefore able to describe his own experience of arriving at university and what everyday life there was all about. This is what my son needed to hear and the conversation between them was free-ranging and quite humorous, which released some of the nerves!

The programme for the day was well organised and we followed it carefully, though there was also plenty of opportunity to have one-to-ones with academic, administrative and pastoral staff. We began with an introduction to the college by the head administrator and then four lecturers each gave a half-hour talk. These were incredibly varied and again, we were quite convinced that no party line had been agreed apart from a freedom to peddle whatever each contributor thought would be attractive and engaging - thus we had a history of the college from 17th to 21st centuries; an interactive and fairly juicy lecture on different kinds of love; a presentation of one professor's latest research paper on the challenges of an evil god; and a more general introduction to the study of theology at degree level and beyond. This gave us insights into not only the subject matter of the college but into the cooperation between the various philosophical interests of the staff: contributing greatly to our feeling that this was a place where my son could prosper academically if he put his mind to it and was able to make the grade.

After a snack lunch we divided into groups and were shown round the on-site accommodation for students, which was very reminiscent for me of student days long ago, though back then it was unusual to have so much technology in your room – how things have changed! (But communal kitchens never change, it would seem.) The tour was led by a current student who, again, was obviously winging it and not at all sure where she was meant to take us, but by asking we also got to look at the student union facilities, libraries and computer suites as well as the gardens. Sports facilities existed but were unfortunately rather out of the way and not possible to view. My son asked about whether tennis courts were available and the student's eyes lit up and she said that if he got in they should set up a tennis club together – funding was available for such activities – and she had no doubt this would be really popular.

Indoors again it was time for more information-gathering about how subjects could be combined, what opportunities could be found to take a year abroad, what pastoral support was offered, what results were like and what graduates did after leaving the college.

We learnt an incredible amount and feel this set a standard for other universities to aspire to – and are off to our second open day soon. The nerves about open days are dispersed. But we've moved on to nerves about exams and the process of applying – it is never-ending, but we'll get there!

Visit www.ucas.tv and watch case studies

Our UCAStv video site at **www.ucas.tv** is a great place to go if you're still not sure about what's important to you. It has different case studies you can watch – ordinary students describing their experience of choosing a uni or college. We've also put together some 'how-to' guides which explain each element of applying so you can get to know the process.

Go to the site and click on 'students' to find all the videos relating to you. Good starting points are the 'how-to' guide for choosing courses and the 'how-to' guide on attending events.

International students

At **www.ucas.tv** you can watch videos about choosing courses, our 'how-to' guides and case studies for international applicants.

The information about league tables in this chapter has been contributed by Dr Bernard Kingston, author of *The Complete University Guide*.

Mayfield University Consultants has been compiling university league tables since 1995 and launched *The Complete University Guide* wholly online in 2007. The website is comprehensive and impartial and aims to help students to decide what to study where. It is free to access and a third of its users are based overseas. The interactive league table enables individuals to create their own unique university rankings. Visit **www.thecompleteuniversityguide.co.uk**.

Look at league tables

As part of your research for choosing what to study, you might want to consult one or more of the league tables published on the web and elsewhere. This section outlines their background, insights into how they're put together and suggestions as to when and how to use them.

The tables

The compilers of these tables are trying to define the quality of the uni experience you might expect and its outcome. They pull together a huge amount of info about unis and courses and collate it into an at-a-glance summary. League tables can't help you in the same ways prospectuses or open days can, but they can be useful in forming a list of unis and colleges that meet your needs. Remember there's no such thing as 'the best university' – only the best university for you – not for your friends, teachers or parents. It should be your own personal choice.

The higher education landscape is wide, diverse and complex – not always easy to navigate. League tables can help you by giving an overview and simplifying the search. They don't tell the whole story but they're good for signposting in the right

Student tip:

'I consulted online newspapers for university league tables, which did influence my decision somewhat. Other influences included the distance from my home, and the course modules and specialities.'

direction. Their coverage isn't comprehensive – typically the main table has all the unis and university colleges but not the specialist institutions.

The subject tables, on the other hand, do include the specialist colleges and institutes of agriculture and food science, art and design, and drama. These tables are based on the same data as the main table but some subjects use fewer measures.

The tables are mainly aimed at full-time, first degree applicants – so mostly for students planning to do undergraduate courses.

There are a variety of league tables from different sources, so how can you tell if they're fact or fiction? The first test has to be credibility – how impartial or independent are they? Most are tied to specific newspapers and possibly reflect their readerships, but it's doubtful any editorial influence would be exerted on the compilers of the tables. On the other hand, there could be conflicts of interest if the compilers come from within unis appearing in the tables. Then there's the issue of openness and transparency. All publish the methodology they use but some are easy to understand while others are complicated and difficult to understand. See for yourself if you can follow how the data is turned into the final rankings. If you can't understand what it all means, don't be afraid to ask questions.

First rule: approach the tables with caution, look at them with a critical eye and try to understand the assumptions behind the rankings.

Next, never rely solely on them – don't use them as the deciding factor.

Much of the data comes from the unis themselves, mostly from the Higher Education Statistics Agency (HESA). Many of the measures are common to all the compilers so that they're consistent, comparable and preferably audited. However, there are time lags and fluctuations from one year to the next, and these are then countered in some tables by averaging over two or three years. This results in even greater time lags, so it's worth remembering these limitations when you read the outcomes. Most datasets are available at the beginning of the calendar year and this determines the earliest time the tables can be published. By spring or early summer all league tables are published, apart from *The Sunday Times* supplement which appears in late summer or autumn.

The compilers

The producers of the four main university league tables of interest to undergraduate applicants are listed in Table 1, and the scope of their offerings in Table 2. Three are overseen by national newspapers and the other is completely independent.

Table 1 The compilers of the tables (university league tables published in 2011)

League table	Website	Compiled by
The Complete University Guide	www.thecompleteuniversityguide.co.uk	Mayfield University Consultants
The Guardian	www.guardian.co.uk/education/universityguide	Intelligent Metrix
The Times	www.thetimes.co.uk/gug	Exeter Enterprises
The Sunday Times	www.thesundaytimes.co.uk/universityguide	Alastair McCall and Munro Global

Table 2 The scope of the tables (university league tables published in 2011)

	The Complete University Guide	The Guardian	The Times	The Sunday Times
No. of institutions	116	119	116	122
Measures used	9	8	8	8
No. of subjects	62	46	62	39
Measures used	4	8	4	6

UCAS has over 300 member institutions, so these league tables are by no means exhaustive. They can, however, be used to gauge the effectiveness of an institution across a variety of different criteria.

There's some similarity in methodologies between *The Times* and *The Complete University Guide* tables – this is because Mayfield University Consultants used to oversee *The Times* league tables before it was taken over by Exeter Enterprises (a subsidiary of the University of Exeter). But since then these methodologies have grown apart year by year.

Sometimes a lower ranked university may have a good record for student satisfaction and graduate employment but have lower entry grades or a lower profile research environment. Websites such as The Complete University Guide allow you to rank according to the criteria that matter to you.

In 2007 Mayfield University Consultants joined with Constable & Robinson to publish *The Complete University Guide* as an independent web-based uni guide. The league tables here are interactive and allow you to put together your own tables based on your preferences. This is a great feature – and the other league table compilers are developing their own websites to take advantage of these online benefits.

There is sometimes a cost to see these tables. *The Times* guide book has always been priced, but more recently its website and *The Sunday Times* website have added a cost to viewing their tables online. However *The Guardian University Guide* website and *The Complete University Guide* are free.

Methodology

League tables aren't an exact science, but they try to be logical and compromises have been made to improve the quality of the outcomes. Plus the university sector itself has improved the quality of the data they send to HESA. Most of the compilers have also established expert groups – mainly from a variety of unis and colleges – who offer advice on methodologies.

The raw source data from the unis is manipulated in a number of different ways, leading towards a uni receiving a final score and ranking. Compilers sometimes decide themselves which measures are more important – so it's definitely worth customising your own table so you can see the best results for you.

The main table ranking all the unis is usually the one in the headlines, but most experts would agree the subject tables are as important if not more so. It's definitely worth checking these as well, because although main rankings are useful, some academic departments might have their own national (or even international) reputations. It's also worth not paying too much attention to unis climbing or falling in the rankings – often this is a result of universities being closely bunched together with similar scores.

As such there's often not much movement at the top of the table, much more movement lower down and interesting changes in the middle where many new unis are overtaking old ones.

Measures

The measures used in the rankings published in 2011 are summarised in Table 3. Confusingly, these are usually referred to as the 2012 tables because they're aimed at applicants planning to go to university in 2012. Go to the individual websites for detailed descriptions of the methodology and measures used by each compiler. Some such as Entry Standards are input measures whereas others like Completion Rates look at output. Most rely on data from HESA and the National Student Survey (NSS) and Research Assessment Exercise (RAE) commissioned by the Higher Education Funding Council for England (HEFCE), although in a few cases directly from the individual universities.

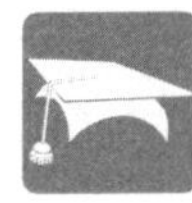

Adviser tip:

'Explore all the functionality and options within the league tables to really get the most out of them and to help hone your choice of what to study and where.'

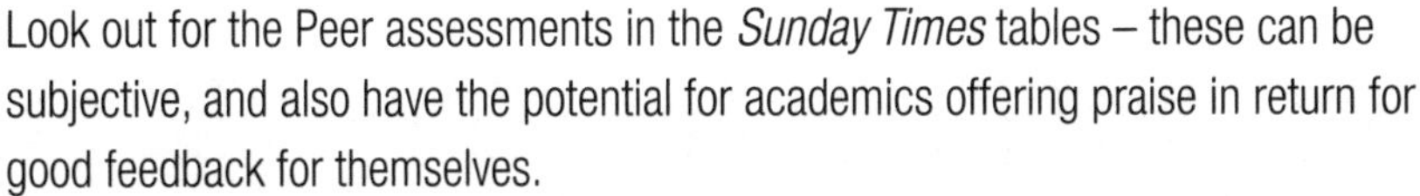

Look out for the Peer assessments in the *Sunday Times* tables – these can be subjective, and also have the potential for academics offering praise in return for good feedback for themselves.

Table 3 The measures used in the tables (university league tables published in 2011)

	The Complete University Guide	The Guardian	The Times	The Sunday Times
Student satisfaction	✔	✔	✔	✔
Research assessment	✔		✔	✔
Entry standards	✔	✔	✔	✔
Student:staff ratio	✔	✔	✔	
Spend on academic services	✔	✔	✔*	
Spend on student facilities	✔		✔*	
Good honours degrees	✔		✔	✔
Completion rates	✔		✔	✔
Graduate prospects	✔	✔	✔	✔
Peer assessments				✔
Value added		✔		

Note
*The Times combines the two figures in a single measure.

Student satisfaction

Source: the annual National Student Survey (NSS) of final year undergraduates

This gathers student opinion on their experience of teaching and learning. It's a measure of satisfaction not quality, and satisfaction is affected by many factors, including initial expectations.

The league tables use the survey results in different ways (see Table 4).

Table 4 The use of the National Student Survey's 22 questions (university league tables published in 2011)

	The Complete University Guide	The Guardian	The Times	The Sunday Times
The teaching on my course	✔	✔	✔	✔
Assessment and feedback	✔	✔	✔	✔
Academic support	✔		✔	✔
Organisation and management	✔		✔	
Learning resources			✔	
Personal development	✔		✔	
Overall satisfaction	✔	✔	✔	✔

Note

The Complete University Guide and *The Guardian* use 2010 NSS data, *The Times* uses 2009 + 2010 data, and *The Sunday Times* 2011 data. *The Guardian* uses three NSS sections to create three separate measures and the Sunday Times uses four to create two measures, whereas others use NSS sections as shown to produce a single measure of student satisfaction.

Research assessment

Source: the 2008 Research Assessment Exercise (RAE)

The RAE seeks to define the quality of a university's research and is an important source of university funding. Historically, The *Guardian* has always decided to omit any rating of research from its rankings.

Entry standards

Source: HESA Annual Survey

This is based on the full UCAS Tariff scores gained by new students – usually those under 21 years of age. It gives their actual results, but not the university offers made to them. Some unis have specific policies to accept students who have a wide range of entry qualifications in order to widen their intake – this tends to give them a lower score on this measure.

Adviser tip:

'Remember that you can focus on universities within a specific country or region, or those that score highly in a particular subject.'

Student:staff ratio

Source: HESA Annual Survey

The number of students per member of academic staff, except those solely involved in research activities. A low ratio is good but it doesn't guarantee the quality of teaching or how accessible the staff are.

Spend on academic services

Source: HESA Annual Survey

This is the spend per student on uni services like libraries and IT. The spend figure is often averaged over more than a year to allow for uneven expenditure.

Spend on student facilities

Source: HESA Annual Survey

This covers spending on student (mainly) and staff amenities such as the careers service, the health and counselling services, and athletic and sporting facilities. Again the figure is given as spend per student and averaged over more than a year.

Good honours degrees

Source: HESA Annual Survey

The proportion of graduates achieving a first or upper second class honours degree. Degree class is controlled to a large extent by the individual unis themselves and is the subject of considerable current debate. It has been argued, therefore, that it isn't an objective indicator of quality. However, it remains the primary badge of individual success and can often impact on graduate employment prospects.

Completion rate
Source: HESA Annual Survey
This shows the proportion of students projected to successfully complete their studies at the uni or to transfer to another one elsewhere.

Graduate prospects
Source: HESA Annual Survey
Most compilers take this to be the proportion of graduates who obtain a graduate job – not any job – or continue with postgrad studies within six months of graduation. If you want to read more about what constitutes a graduate occupation, see the classic study carried out by Peter Elias and Kate Purcell (Warwick Institute for Employment Research).

The Sunday Times uses graduate data on unemployment and those going into non-graduate jobs rather than the positive outcomes mentioned above.

Good employment stats are often quoted by unis in their publications, but be aware that some use all jobs, not just graduate jobs, in their figures.

Peer assessments
Source: Sunday Times Annual Survey
Academics were asked to rate departments in their own subjects for the quality of undergraduate provision. The level of response is not published but is reported to be 10-20%.

Value added
Source: HESA Annual Survey
The Guardian tracks new student qualifications on entry to unis, and compares these with the degrees awarded at the end of their studies. Value added is based on entry standards and good honours data (but remember the degree class debate) and assumes students with low entry qualifications find it more difficult to gain a first or upper second class honours degree.

Don't forget – use league tables alongside all the other information sources available to you, like prospectuses, student conventions and open days. You'll also find more tables on the web, including ones of interest to international students, on tuition fees, bursaries and scholarships, graduate salaries, safety and security, and sport and recreation.

League table checklist

- ☐ Never rely solely on league tables but only as part of wider research.
- ☐ Remember there is no such thing as 'the best university'.
- ☐ League table coverage is for full-time first degree study.
- ☐ Ask yourself how impartial or comprehensive any league table is.
- ☐ Remember there are inevitable time lags in the data used.
- ☐ Web-based tables have many advantages, including interactivity.
- ☐ The universities are given an opportunity to check their raw data.
- ☐ Tables are adjusted to allow for differing subject mix.
- ☐ The subject tables are at least as important as the main table.
- ☐ Movement by a few places in rank is usually statistically insignificant.

FAQs on league tables

What is a league table?

League tables are designed to help you compare universities and colleges by ranking them in order of specific categories. For example, the quality of teaching, graduate employment success, entry grades, student satisfaction or drop-out/completion rates. League tables are mainly compiled from Government data but unlike School/College or Sport League Tables there is no definitive single table ranking UK universities.

How important should a university's ranking on a league table be in my decision on where to go?

There are a lot of universities and colleges to choose from so it's important to think about what's important to you and where you will be happy. For example if you know you would like to stay close to home it's probably not a good idea to choose a university 200 miles away just because it is higher in a league table.

It's also important to check course content – students who rely on league tables alone may find that the course or subject is not right for them while other lower ranked courses may be more suitable. Don't forget to consider factors such as what the course specialises in, how it's assessed and if it involves sandwich placements, internships or year abroad opportunities.

Remember that different places suit different people and you should focus on which universities offer what you're looking for. Websites such as The Complete University Guide allow you to rank institutions according to your preferences. However, rankings do not at present include information on fees, scholarships, the cost of living, social life, clubs and societies.

How do I find out which university is best for the course I would like to do?
Looking at the different league tables is a good way to back up your research – or to give a starting point to the current top 30 or 40 in your subject. Then you can continue your research by looking at university websites, attending open days and speaking to teachers or advisers from your school or college.

Why is the course I'm interested in not listed in a league table?
It might be that the subject you're considering is more specialist so doesn't have a separate league table. The league table websites usually explain what other subject areas fit into each subject ranking. For example, marketing degrees may be included in the Business Studies table or French/Spanish may be included in Modern Languages. If in doubt, check with the university concerned.

In some cases the course may be too small or new, so might not have enough data to be included in a table. There are also some universities that don't allow their data to be used in league tables – these are listed on each league table website.

My chosen universities are in the bottom half of most league tables – are they worth going to?
Of course – there may be particular factors that attracted you to that particular course or university. Find out how it performs in the criteria that matter to you, ask questions on your open day visits and find out what the university is doing to improve both its position and the student experience.

Money: scholarships

Unis want to attract capable students, and some give huge amounts of money as scholarships. They'll all have their own individual schemes and application processes – some ask you to complete an application form while others automatically assess your UCAS information.

Some scholarships look at UCAS Tariff points only, but many look at other things like your ability to demonstrate a level of excellence and achievement above other students. This may be in any of a variety of areas, like the arts, sports or volunteering, for example.

For more details look at websites and ask at open days. Generally, if universities have an application process, you'll need to apply well before you start the course, because the basic idea of scholarships is to encourage you to go university 'A' rather than university 'B'.

What's the difference between a bursary and a scholarship?

Scholarships are usually awarded on merit (eg you demonstrate excellence in one or more areas), while bursaries are awarded on the basis of financial need (eg you might be dependent upon your family income).

You can find out whether the courses you're interested in have bursaries or scholarships available on Course Finder at **www.ucas.com**. Alternatively you can find out more on university and college websites.

Did you know?

The bursary comparison facility on Course Finder at **www.ucas.com** allows you to select bursaries and scholarships from up to six courses to view and compare them on a single page.

Summer schools and taster courses

Summer schools are taster courses held at unis and colleges which give you a taste of university life. They tend to be held during the summer after students have gone home so that the halls of residence can be used for residential programmes and lectures, and other facilities are also available.

Student tip:

'Summer school was genuinely brilliant – the week built up my confidence and belief that I could get into university.'

Some are subject specific while others are broad ranging, with an emphasis on introducing you to uni life and giving you an idea of what it might be like studying there. Subject-specific summer schools and taster courses are designed to help you decide if your chosen subject is a suitable education and career choice. They also help you decide which element of a subject you want to focus on, so if you know you like engineering, is it chemical, mechanical, civil or electronic engineering you should study?

There are week-long residential summer schools or one-day taster courses. Some cost, some are free to all and some are free but are only available to a specific group. For example, the Sutton Trust holds free summer schools for young people from non-privileged backgrounds. Many unis and colleges run short taster courses and, understandably, they're incredibly popular, so book early if you'd like to go.

Many summer school organisations accept applications in January in preparation for programmes running in summer, but some organisations like Villiers Park Educational Trust run courses throughout the year.

You don't have to want to study at the university hosting the summer school, you just need to think that you might want to do a higher education course in the future. Summer schools are aimed at learners from Year 9 (age 13) through to prospective mature students.

Your school should be able to tell you about possible summer schools or you can find them listed on university websites. Look at our open day and taster course search on **www.ucas.com** to find when and where they are available. In addition, here are a few websites which will get you started and help explain what's involved.

Headstart courses: **www.headstartcourses.org.uk**
The London Taster Course Programme: **www.london.ac.uk/tasters**
The Sutton Trust: **www.suttontrust.com**
UNIQ Summer Schools: **www.ox.ac.uk/uniq**
Villiers Park Educational Trust: **www.villierspark.org.uk**

Case study

Name: Sara Dalton
Studying: Natural Sciences
At: St Catharine's College, University of Cambridge

When I began my A level studies I had considered applying to Cambridge, although I was quite undecided. Fortunately, I was able to attend a Sutton Trust Summer School at Cambridge, which really gave me the confidence to apply. We spent a week living in college, attending lectures and practicals, as well as experiencing other aspects of Cambridge – including punting and an outdoor Shakespearean play! I was able to speak with academics and students, and their honesty and enthusiasm really inspired me to apply.

Having a supportive family was always very important, and through helping me research courses and having full confidence in me, I was sure that Cambridge was somewhere that I would love to study, and I was determined to apply.

The best thing about Cambridge for me is not only that everyone here is so enthusiastic about their chosen degrees, but that there are so many other aspects of Cambridge life to get involved in – sport, singing, drama and volunteering just to name a few. Cambridge is full of people from all backgrounds! I have met many amazing and like-minded people whilst studying here – as soon as I arrived I was made to feel welcome, and I knew from that day that Cambridge was the place for me.

From my own experience I have found that there are many students who would thrive in a university setting, but who often do not receive enough correct information when they are considering applying, and as a result are discouraged from doing so, on the basis of what typically are misconceptions about the university. However the right kind of support from school or parents can really help give students the confidence to pursue a degree.

Admissions tests

What is an admissions test?

It's a timed unseen written test – either paper-based or online – normally taken in the academic year before admission to a university or college. The results can then be used by that uni or college as one element in decision-making about an application.

Less that 1% of higher education courses require an admissions test – but for those that do it's an important part of the application process.

The type of test used depends predominantly on the course and the attributes deemed appropriate for the professional, vocational or academic discipline. They can be aptitude tests, essay writing exercises, problem solving tests, critical thinking assessments, subject specific tests, cognitive and non-cognitive tests. Many tests are designed to enable a correlation to be made between test results and degree success – that is, they're designed to be predictive as well as testing aptitude. Whether evidence can be presented to support this will require long-term study and analysis.

The tests take place in the academic year before admission or at interview: normally from November onwards. A test can be a uni's own devised test or a test

Adviser tip:

'Take a look at the website of the admissions test you are taking – research the information available and use any practice tests you can find.'

devised by another uni or a group or consortium of institutions with one or more testing or awarding bodies. A test might used by one uni for one or more subjects or may be used by many unis for the same subject.

What are tests used for?

A number of unis and test bodies argue that the use of a test can assist in assessing your potential regardless of your background. As all applicants sit the same test it's an element everyone can be judged on equally. However, there may be issues around access to familiarisation or practice sessions which would weaken this argument.

Some unis use admissions tests to help differentiate between the most able applicants. A test score in this context has become more significant because of concerns about the large numbers of candidates who achieve high grades in entry level qualifications, eg the increasing number of A grades at A level.

Tests could also focus on skills and aptitudes that are not assessed through academic attainment.

Student tip:

'Admissions tests can be stressful and worrying, but thankfully practice exams are available and prepare you for what to expect and the sort of answers you should be aiming to write.'

University and college tests

In addition to the tests listed ahead, an increasing number of unis and colleges use a variety of filtering techniques to decide who to interview or make an offer to. These are tasks usually given with a deadline to meet.

Examples include:

- submission of a sample essay from the student's A level coursework
- request to write 500 words on a set topic
- practical exercise based on use of statistics
- submission of a design brief.

While many unis mention in their course descriptions that you might need to complete a task, some don't – so it's worth being aware that something might come up.

International students

If English is not your first language (and also if it is!), practise and practise the tests that are used. You can often find examples on the admissions tests' and university websites.

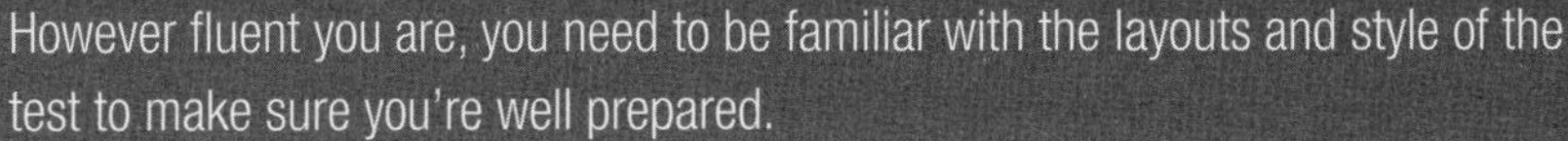

However fluent you are, you need to be familiar with the layouts and style of the test to make sure you're well prepared.

Examples of admissions tests

BioMedical Admissions Test (BMAT)	
Used for:	Entry to medicine, veterinary medicine and related courses
What it is:	The BioMedical Admissions Test (BMAT) is a subject-specific admissions test taken by applicants to certain medicine, veterinary medicine and related courses at the institutions listed below. The BMAT is owned and administered by Cambridge Assessment as well as produced and marked, and also an extensive worldwide centre network is provided at which candidates can sit the BMAT. BMAT was developed by Cambridge Assessment in response to a request by academics from some of the top medical and veterinary schools in the UK for an assessment that would: ▪ enable them to differentiate between applicants who appear to be equally well qualified and suited to the course ▪ provide a way of assessing the potential of students who have a range of qualifications. Cambridge Assessment has conducted research on data from previous years' BMAT sessions. The research shows that the BMAT: ▪ is a good predictor of performance at year one undergraduate level ▪ enables admissions tutors to screen out those candidates unlikely to take advantage of the best of higher education. The BMAT is a two-hour pen and paper test consisting of three separate sections. It does not require a great amount of extra study as it relies on skills and knowledge that candidates should already have.
Used by:	University of Cambridge, University of Oxford, Royal Veterinary College, University College London, Imperial College London
Entry method:	Through Cambridge Assessment – see the BMAT website **www.bmat.org.uk**
Duration of test:	2 hours
Other information:	BMAT website – **www.bmat.org.uk**

English Literature Admissions Test (ELAT)	
Used for:	Entry to undergraduate courses in English – except the joint course of English & history, for which candidates take the History Aptitude Test (HAT)
What it is:	The ELAT is a pre-interview admissions test for applicants to undergraduate courses in English at the University of Oxford. The test is designed to enable applicants to show their ability in the key skill of close reading, paying attention to such elements as the language, imagery, allusion, syntax, form and structure of the passages set for comment. ELAT is a 90-minute test and candidates write one essay comparing two or three passages. This is not a test of wide reading, nor is it based on the assumption that there are certain texts that all students should have read by this stage in their education. Marks will not be awarded for reference to other texts or authors, nor will candidates be expected to try to apply any theoretical frameworks to their essay. The test will be only one of the elements admissions tutors use to decide whether to invite a candidate for interview. Candidates will be given six poems or passages from prose and drama. The prose may include fiction and non-fiction. The six passages will be linked in some way, and this link will be made explicit in the introduction to the passages.
Used by:	University of Oxford
Entry method:	Through Cambridge Assessment – see the ELAT website **www.elat.org.uk**
Duration of test:	90 minutes
Other information:	ELAT website – **www.elat.org.uk**

Graduate Medical School Admissions Test (GAMSAT)	
Used for:	Graduate entry to medicine and dentistry
What it is:	GAMSAT is a professionally designed and marked selection test developed by the Australian Council for Educational Research (ACER) for medical schools offering graduate-entry programmes open to graduates of any discipline. Applicants are selected for admission into the graduate entry programmes on the basis of three criteria. The schools may apply these criteria in different ways. The criteria are: ▪ undergraduate honours degree ▪ GAMSAT scores ▪ interview. Non-school leaver applicants are selected into the Peninsula medical programme on the basis of performance in GAMSAT and in an interview. Performance in GAMSAT constitutes the only necessary information on an applicant's academic aptitude for the purpose of entry to Peninsula. Applicants who reach the threshold level in GAMSAT are invited to interview for assessment of non-academic attributes. Neither performance in a prior degree nor performance at secondary school will be considered. The programmes all build on the diverse interests and talents of the students admitted. Graduates of the programmes will have the skills and knowledge to practise effectively as pre-registration house officers under supervision, and to develop their careers through subsequent entry into further vocational training. Effective communication with patients and colleagues is seen as crucial. Teamwork and an awareness of community concerns will be stressed. In recognition of the fact that medical knowledge continues to expand and that doctors and dentists will continue to learn throughout their lives, self-directed learning is a major focus of the programmes. GAMSAT results are passed directly to the relevant institutions by UCAS, ensuring invisibility of choice is maintained.
Used by:	St. George's University of London, University of Nottingham, Plymouth University Peninsula Schools of Medicine & Dentistry, Swansea University and University of Exeter
Entry method:	Online via **www.gamsatuk.org**
Duration of test:	5½ hours
Other information:	On ACER website **www.gamsatuk.org**

History Aptitude Test (HAT)	
Used for:	Entry to history or a joint honours degree involving history
What it is:	The colleges of the University of Oxford have introduced a History Aptitude Test (HAT) for use in the selection of candidates for all degree courses involving history. This test, which aims to examine the skills and potentialities required for the study of history at university, gives an objective basis for comparing candidates from different backgrounds, including mature applicants and those from different countries. It is designed to be challenging, in order to differentiate effectively between the most able applicants for university courses, including those who may have achieved or can be expected to achieve the highest possible grades in their examinations. The HAT is a two-hour test, which requires candidates to read two extracts and answer a total of four questions about them. One of the extracts will be from a work of history; candidates will be asked questions to test their comprehension of the arguments and ideas in it, their capacity to apply those ideas to historical situations they know about, and their ability to think and make judgements about the extract as a piece of historical writing. The other extract will be from a primary source, and candidates will be asked to offer thoughtful interpretations of its content without knowing anything about its context. The HAT is a test of skills, not of substantive historical knowledge. It is designed so that candidates should find it equally challenging, regardless of what period(s) they have studied or what school examinations they are taking.
Used by:	University of Oxford
Entry method:	Through Cambridge Assessment – see the HAT website **www.hatoxford.org.uk** Most UK candidates in full-time education will be able to take the test at their own school or college. Mature candidates may take the test at the University of Oxford or at a regional test centre of their own choosing. International candidates will normally be able to take the test in their own school or similar institution, but may need to contact a local test centre.
Duration of test:	2 hours
Other information:	See Cambridge Assessment's website – **www.hatoxford.org.uk**

Health Professions Admissions Test (HPAT)	
Used for:	Entry to certain health profession courses at the University of Ulster
What it is:	The Health Professions Admission Test (HPAT-Ulster) is a professionally designed and marked selection test developed to assess aptitude for study in the allied health professions. It has been designed in consultation with the University of Ulster to assess a range of attributes considered important to the study and later practice of the health professions. It is designed to complement academic achievement, by providing assessment of skills in the areas of reasoning, understanding and working with people, and written communication. These skills have been identified as important for a competent health professional. HPAT-Ulster is not based on any curriculum or body of knowledge and presumes no particular field or discipline of prior study. HPAT-Ulster has a strong focus on general skills and personal abilities. It does not test knowledge of the basic sciences. HPAT-Ulster is available to any candidate whose educational level at the time of sitting the test is final year of secondary schooling or higher, and who is capable of meeting the academic entry requirements (including prerequisite subjects at A level or equivalent) set by the University of Ulster.
Used by:	University of Ulster
Entry method:	Through HPAT – **www.hpat-ulster.acer.edu.au**
Duration of test:	3 hours
Other information:	HPAT website – **www.hpat-ulster.acer.edu.au**

The National Admissions Test for Law (LNAT)	
Used for:	Entry to law and some combinations of law and other subjects
What it is:	The LNAT is a test run by a consortium of UK universities (LNAT Consortium Ltd) in partnership with Pearson VUE, the computer-based testing business of Pearson Education. The test helps universities to make fairer choices among the many highly qualified applicants who want to join their undergraduate law programmes. The test is professionally written and calibrated by Edexcel for Pearson VUE. The LNAT is a 2¼ hour test in two parts: a multiple-choice element (95 minutes) and an essay element (40 minutes). The multiple-choice element consists of 12 argumentative passages, with three or four multiple-choice questions on each, making 42 questions in all. The questions are designed to test powers of comprehension, interpretation, analysis, synthesis, induction and deduction. These are the verbal reasoning skills at the heart of legal education. The questions do not test (and do not require) knowledge of any subject except the English language. This part of the test is machine-marked and the results are passed in numerical form to (only) those LNAT-participating universities to which the candidate has applied. Candidates will receive their marks after the admissions process is over. The essay element gives the candidate a choice of questions on a range of subjects. Although these typically require some rudimentary knowledge of everyday subjects, the point is not to test that knowledge. The point is to test the ability of the candidate to argue economically to a conclusion with a good command of written English. This part of the test is not centrally assessed. Instead the essays are passed unmarked to (only) those LNAT-participating law schools to which the candidate has applied. The essays will be used by each university in the way that best suits its own admissions system. The whole test is conducted on-screen.
Used by:	University of Birmingham, University of Bristol, University of Durham, University of Glasgow, King's College London, University of Manchester, University of Nottingham, University of Oxford, University College London
Entry method:	Through LNAT: see **www.lnat.ac.uk**
Test date:	Is booked during registration
Duration of test:	2¼ hours
Other information:	See the LNAT website **www.lnat.ac.uk**

Modern and Medieval Languages Test (MML)	
Used for:	Entry to modern and medieval languages
What it is:	This written test will be taken by applicants, in the college by which they are being interviewed, while they are at the University of Cambridge for their interviews. (Applicants with disabilities or special learning needs are asked to inform the College so that they can take the test in an appropriate form.) There is no expectation that applicants will have practised this kind of exercise before. The test has been designed so that anyone who has already practised it will not be at any great advantage. The test forms just one small part of the overall assessment of applicants (based on the written application, school and college record, interviews, etc); even if an applicant does not do particularly well at this written test, it is perfectly possible for them still to be offered a place. Applicants are asked to read a brief passage in English (300-350 words) and then to answer two or three questions about it. They will write their answer in a target language that they are studying at A level (A2) or equivalent and that they are applying to study at the University of Cambridge. The questions will contain an element of comprehension but will also invite applicants to add ideas of their own. In other words, the exercise is a combination of comprehension and free composition. The purpose is to see how applicants write in the foreign language; it assesses their grammar, accuracy, ability to express ideas, and their vocabulary, although they are not expected to know the exact foreign-language term for each English term in the passage.
Used by:	University of Cambridge
Entry method:	Applicants need do nothing special about entering for the test, as colleges will inform applicants of all admissions requirements.
Duration of test:	45 minutes
Other information:	For more information about the test go to **www.mml.cam.ac.uk/prospectus/undergrad/test.html**

Sixth Term Examination Papers (STEP)	
Used for:	Entry to mathematics
What it is:	STEP is a well-established mathematics university admissions test, which is used to help select very academically able students for courses which are usually oversubscribed. STEP was originally administered by OCR (Oxford, Cambridge and RSA Examinations). However, in 2008 STEP was transferred from OCR to its parent Cambridge Assessment which has a specialist team that manages assessments relating specifically to university entrance. STEP has been designed to test candidates on questions that are similar in style to undergraduate mathematics. It is used by the University of Cambridge as the basis for conditional offers. The University of Warwick also includes STEP in its undergraduate mathematics offers. There are also a number of candidates who sit STEP papers as a challenge. Other universities may ask candidates to take STEP as part of their offer; candidates should consult their university regarding which papers to take. Cambridge Assessment is responsible for producing and marking STEP. It consists of three 3-hour examinations, STEP I, STEP II and STEP III. Candidates are usually required to sit either one or two of the examinations, depending on the requirements of the universities they have applied to. It is not possible to take STEP I and STEP III in the same year. The syllabuses for STEP I and STEP II are based on A level content while the syllabus for STEP III is based on Further Mathematics A level. The questions on STEP II and STEP III are of the same difficulty and harder than those in STEP I. Candidates are only expected to have knowledge of topics within the A level syllabus. Candidates who are not studying further mathematics will not be expected to sit STEP III.
May be used by:	University of Cambridge and University of Warwick
Entry method:	Applications to take STEP should go through a school or college, in the same way as GCE A levels. The papers must be taken at a recognised centre.
Duration of test:	3 hours per examination
Other information:	See **www.stepmathematics.org.uk/**

Thinking Skills Assessment (TSA Cambridge)	
Used for:	Mainly politics, psychology and sociology (PPS), computer science, natural sciences, engineering and economics
What it is:	The University of Cambridge has been using the TSA (designed, developed and extensively researched by Cambridge Assessment) since 2001. The TSA is a 90-minute multiple-choice test consisting of 50 questions. These measure an applicant's critical thinking and problem-solving skills. However, the version used for politics, psychology and sociology (PPS) contains critical thinking questions only.
Used by:	University of Cambridge
Entry method:	To find out whether you will need to take the TSA you are advised to look at the exact entry requirements for a particular course.
Duration of test:	90 minutes
Other information:	For further information go to **www.tsa.cambridgeassessment.org.uk**

Thinking Skills Assessment (TSA Oxford)	
Used for:	Entry to philosophy, politics & economics (PPE), economics & management (E&M), geography, experimental psychology (EP) and each of the courses within psychology, philosophy & linguistics (PPL)
What it is:	The TSA (University of Oxford) is a pre-interview admissions test. Admissions decisions are complex because candidates come from a wide variety of subject backgrounds, and the study of the undergraduate courses listed above requires a range of abilities. The TSA will help tutors to assess whether candidates have the skills and aptitudes that are required to study these subjects. It is a 2-hour pre-interview test consisting of two sections: ▪ Section 1: Thinking Skills Assessment (TSA) ▪ Section 2: Writing task.
Used by:	University of Oxford
Entry method:	Through Cambridge Assessment – see the TSA website **www.tsaoxford.org.uk**
Duration of test:	2 hours
Other information:	TSA website – **www.tsaoxford.org.uk**

Thinking Skills Assessment (TSA UCL)	
Used for:	European social and political studies
What it is:	The TSA is a 90-minute multiple choice test consisting of 50 questions. These measure an applicant's critical thinking and problem-solving skills.
Used by:	University College London (UCL)
Entry method:	The TSA is used as part of the interview process for candidates applying to UCL. Any candidate needing to take the TSA will have their test sitting arranged for them by UCL when they come for their interview.
Duration of test:	90 minutes
Other information:	For further information go to **www.tsaucl.org.uk**

UK Clinical Aptitude Test (UKCAT)	
Used for:	Entry to medical and dental schools
What it is:	The UKCAT Consortium consists of 26 medical and dental schools which require the test to be taken by candidates applying to their medical and dental programmes. The test helps universities to make more informed choices from among many highly qualified applicants. It ensures that the candidates selected have the most appropriate mental abilities, attitudes and professional behaviour required for new doctors and dentists to be successful in their clinical careers. Candidates are required to take the test in the year before their intended year of entry, or two years before for deferred entry. The test is designed to be a test of aptitude. It is therefore not possible to revise for the test as you would for other examinations. However, candidates should familiarise themselves with the type of questions and the time restrictions in the test. The UKCAT website includes two fully timed tests to assist candidates in preparation. UKCAT does not endorse commercially available preparation courses or books and candidates should note these may contain misleading information. The test is run by the UKCAT Consortium in partnership with Pearson VUE, a global leader in computer based testing and part of Pearson plc. It is delivered on computers worldwide through Pearson VUE's high street centres. The test lasts for 2 hours and consists of four separately timed subtests: ▪ Verbal reasoning – assesses logical thinking about written information and ability to make reasoned conclusions ▪ Quantitative reasoning – assesses ability to solve numerical problems

continued overleaf

UK Clinical Aptitude Test (UKCAT) continued	
What it is (cont'd)	▪ Abstract reasoning – assesses ability to infer relationships from information by convergent and divergent thinking ▪ Decision analysis – assesses ability to deal with various forms of information, infer relationships, make informed judgements, and decide on an appropriate response. In 2012, items were trialled testing non-cognitive ability. These items did not contribute to candidate test scores. Candidates may require additional time for the test (eg for dyslexia) and in this case will sit the UKCATSEN which provides a standard 20% additional time. Information regarding taking this version of the test can be found on the website. Candidates in financial need may apply for a bursary to cover the full test costs.
Used by:	University of Aberdeen, Brighton and Sussex Medical School, Barts and The London School of Medicine and Dentistry, Cardiff University, University of Dundee, University of Durham, University of East Anglia, University of Edinburgh, University of Glasgow, Hull York Medical School, Keele University, King's College London, Imperial College London, University of Leeds, University of Leicester, University of Manchester, University of Newcastle, University of Nottingham, University of Oxford, Plymouth University Peninsula Schools of Medicine & Dentistry, Queen's University Belfast, University of Sheffield, University of Southampton, University of St Andrews, St George's University of London, Warwick University
Entry method:	Online registration only, through **www.ukcat.ac.uk**
Duration of test:	2 hours
Other information:	UKCAT website – **www.ukcat.ac.uk**

UCAS Card

If you're in Year 12, S5 or equivalent and thinking about higher education, then the UCAS Card scheme is designed for you. You can sign up for a UCAS Card online, at UCAS higher education conventions or through your school if they're participating in the scheme.

There are many benefits you can take advantage of:

- discounts in your favourite high street shops
- regular info about the courses and unis you're interested in
- free monthly newsletters providing application advice, reminders and tips
- expert help from our UCAS advisers including reminders about important deadlines, hints and tips
- the chance to sign up for the yougo app, the UCAS student network on facebook.

As well as great discounts, by choosing to register for a UCAS Card you'll also receive regular email bulletins which are full of advice, including info to help you decide whether uni is right for you, reminders on key UCAS deadline dates and guidance about filling in your application.

It's important to remember you're not alone. Thousands of students talk about taking the step up into higher education on yougo. Chat with other students and make new friends by signing up on the UCAS Facebook page.

How do I register?
To register, visit **www.ucas.com/ucascard** and fill in the application form.

Need some help?
If you get stuck or have a query you can call 0871 468 0 471 for advice or email us at ucascard@ucas.ac.uk.

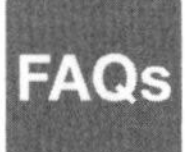

FAQs on the UCAS Card

What is a UCAS Card?
The UCAS Card can be used as a discount card on the high street. The list of on and offline shops where you can get a discount is on **www.ucas.com/ucascard.**

Who can have a UCAS Card and when can I sign up?
You're eligible for a UCAS Card if you're in Year 12, S5 or equivalent. You can register online from October through to August each year.

What is yougo?
yougo is the UCAS student network on Facebook. It's an app you can sign up for on the UCAS Facebook page, and a great place to make friends before you make the move to uni.

I've already signed up. How long until I get my UCAS Card?
Once you've registered online, you can expect your card to arrive within a few weeks.

How do I change my contact details?

There's an option to edit your details on the website. Just log in to the UCAS Card area of the site using your UCAS Card number, email address and password. Alternatively you can call the UCAS Card helpline on 0871 468 0 471 for assistance.

I've forgotten my password. What should I do?

There's a link on the login page where you can enter your email address and your password will be sent to you.

Chapter checklist

These are the things you should be doing in Step 1 of your applicant journey:

- ☐ Explore different career paths to ensure you choose the right subject and qualification. Research the resources available in careers centres, Connexions and websites.
- ☐ Use Course Finder on **www.ucas.com**. Check the entry requirements and the course descriptions.
- ☐ Look at the case studies on **www.ucas.tv**.
- ☐ Visit unis and colleges on their open days, or make your own arrangements to visit.
- ☐ Visit a UCAS student convention and start thinking about your personal statement (see Step 2 Applying).
- ☐ Use prospectuses and uni websites. Focus on your subject choices and possible career prospects.
- ☐ Check the results of the National Student Survey at **unistats.direct.gov.uk**.
- ☐ Check if there are any admissions tests you need to register for (eg LNAT, BMAT).
- ☐ Narrow down your choice of institutions – you can apply to a maximum of five courses.
- ☐ Look for available scholarships.
- ☐ Consider attending a summer school or taster course.

Applying

Step 2
Applying

Now you've done lots of research and decided on the course you want to study and where you want to study it, you need to start thinking about making your application to the universities and colleges. This section of the book guides you through the process, from those all-important deadlines, to how to apply for different types of courses, and how to complete your UCAS application. It also includes specific advice for Oxbridge applicants and those of you applying to medicine, dentistry, veterinary science and veterinary medicine.

Step 2 **Applying**

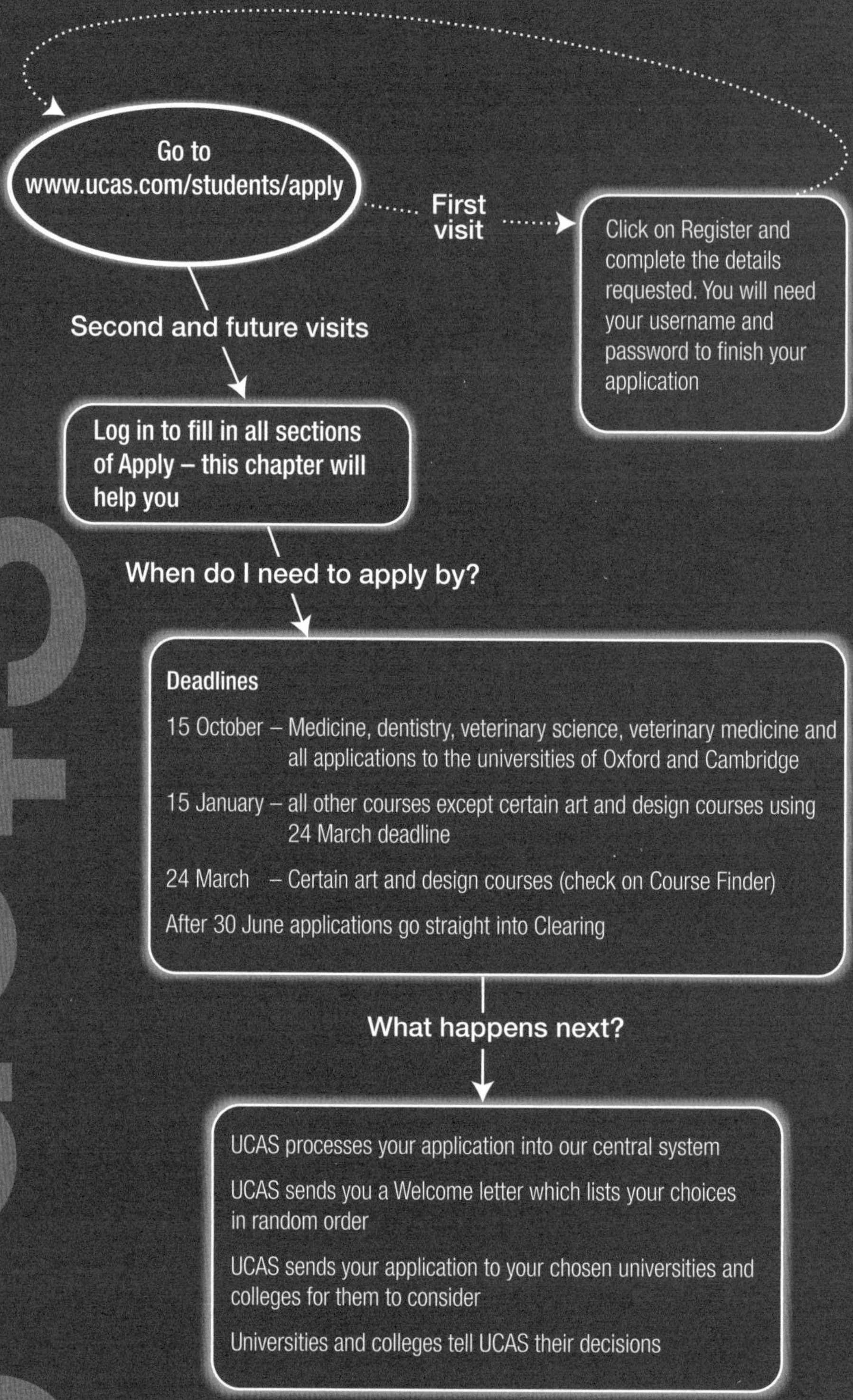

Go to www.ucas.com/students/apply

First visit

Click on Register and complete the details requested. You will need your username and password to finish your application

Second and future visits

Log in to fill in all sections of Apply – this chapter will help you

When do I need to apply by?

Deadlines

15 October – Medicine, dentistry, veterinary science, veterinary medicine and all applications to the universities of Oxford and Cambridge

15 January – all other courses except certain art and design courses using 24 March deadline

24 March – Certain art and design courses (check on Course Finder)

After 30 June applications go straight into Clearing

What happens next?

UCAS processes your application into our central system

UCAS sends you a Welcome letter which lists your choices in random order

UCAS sends your application to your chosen universities and colleges for them to consider

Universities and colleges tell UCAS their decisions

When to apply

Different application deadlines you need to know

Applying from the UK

There are three different application deadlines, depending on the course you are applying for. It's important to check the deadline for your chosen course(s) on Course Finder at **www.ucas.com**.

- **15 October** – application deadline for the receipt at UCAS of applications for all medicine, dentistry, veterinary medicine and veterinary science courses, and for all courses at the universities of Oxford and Cambridge.
- **15 January** – application deadline for the receipt at UCAS of applications for all courses except those listed above with a 15 October deadline, and art and design courses with a 24 March deadline.
- **24 March** – application deadline for the receipt at UCAS of applications for art and design courses except those listed with a 15 January deadline.

If you apply by the above deadlines, you're guaranteed to be considered by the universities and colleges. If your application is received at UCAS after the deadlines, up until 30 June, you'll only be considered by the universities and colleges if they still have vacancies for the course(s) you have chosen.

You can only send us one application in each year's application cycle. If you send a second application, it will be cancelled and you will not receive a refund.

Art and design courses: if you apply for art and design courses with different deadlines, you can submit your application before 15 January for courses with that deadline, then add further choices before the 24 March deadline using Track (as long as you haven't already used all five choices).

If you're applying through a school or college: they might set an earlier deadline – you need to send your application to them by this date so that they have time to write your reference and send your completed application to us before our deadline.

If you're applying as an individual: it is your responsibility to make your referee aware of any deadlines when asking them to provide you with a reference.

Adviser tip:

'Find out well in advance when your school is asking you to complete your application and stick to that deadline. It is not considered submitted until sent by your referee (to UCAS), after your qualifications and information have been checked and approved.'

Course start dates

Not all courses start in September or October – some start between January and May. Check the start dates for the courses you are interested in on Course Finder at **www.ucas.com**. For courses that start between January and May, you may need to apply before the three application deadlines above, as the universities and colleges will need time to consider your application.

Contact the university or college direct for advice about when they need your application. Although some will be happy to receive applications right up to the start of the course, be prepared to send your application early.

Please remember you do not have to apply for all your choices at the same time. You can add further choices, up to 30 June, as long as you have not used up all your choices and have not accepted a place.

International applicants

If you are applying from outside the UK or EU, whatever your nationality, you need to be aware of the three application deadlines, although many universities and colleges will consider your application up until 30 June. This does **not** apply to applications for the universities of Oxford and Cambridge, courses in medicine, dentistry, veterinary medicine or veterinary science. For all of these, you must apply by 15 October.

Universities do not guarantee to consider applications they receive after 15 January, and some popular courses may not have vacancies after that date. Please check with individual universities and colleges if you are not sure. You are advised to apply as early as possible.

Remember to allow enough time for entry clearance or immigration; also travel and accommodation arrangements, which can take longer during the summer when immigration departments are busy.

If you think you may be assessed as a 'home' student (UK or EU) for tuition fees, you should apply by the relevant deadline as shown in the 'Applying from the UK' section on page 121.

Several countries require their citizens to complete mandatory military or national service. If this affects you, check with universities and colleges in advance to discuss when you should apply. You can defer through UCAS for a maximum of one year. It would be useful to include information about your military or national service in your personal statement.

Taking a year out?

If you want to take a year out before starting your course, check with your unis that they will accept a deferred entry application. If you apply for deferred entry, you must still apply by the relevant deadline above, and meet the conditions of any offers by 31 August in the cycle in which you are applying, unless an alternative date is given by the university. If you accept a deferred entry place, you can't reapply through us in the following year's cycle unless your original application is withdrawn.

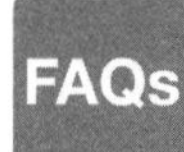

When to apply – FAQs

Why do universities have application deadlines?
Universities need a certain amount of time to consider the thousands of applicants who apply to them. Deadlines are set so that the universities have time to consider all applications.

How do I know what the application deadline is for my course(s)?
There are three major application deadlines – your deadline will be dependent on the subject you want to study and whether you are applying to an Oxbridge university or not. Deadlines for each course are listed on Course Finder at **www.ucas.com**. A university has no obligation to consider a late application, so we would always advise you to check this information to ensure you don't miss your deadline. More information about deadlines is shown on page 121.

Student tip:

'The UCAS application is pretty straightforward but it is time-consuming, so make sure you don't leave it to the last minute!'

I'm applying for a nursing course which starts next spring. Do I have a different deadline?
Most undergraduate courses start in September; however nursing diplomas and nursing degrees are often the exception to this rule. You may find that some universities offer either a January, February, March or April start, as well as an autumn start for these courses. If you wish to apply for a spring start, you must ensure that you submit your application as soon as possible, in order for the university to have time to shortlist and interview their applicants. Contact the university direct for advice about when they need your application. From September 2013, new entrants to the nursing profession will have to study a degree rather than a diploma. More information can be found on the NHS Careers website at **www.nhscareers.nhs.uk**.

Can I apply after the deadline?
All applications sent by the required deadline are given equal consideration by the universities. If your application is sent after the deadline, it will only be considered at the discretion of the university. UCAS processes applications and sends them to universities until 30 June; however there is no guarantee that the universities will consider a late application, or offer an interview or place. If you are applying after the deadline for your course(s), contact the unis first to find out if there are any vacancies and if they are happy to consider a late application from you.

How to apply

Full-time undergraduate courses: you apply through UCAS using our online service called Apply at **www.ucas.com**. You can only send us one application in each year's application cycle, but you can choose a maximum of five choices on your application.

Part-time undergraduate courses: we do not recruit for these – you apply direct to the universities and colleges. However, from July until September we provide a part-time course search at **www.ucas.com**.

Music courses: there are two ways to apply for music courses – the route you take depends upon the type of course you'd like to study. For full-time undergraduate music degree courses, you apply through UCAS.

If you'd like to study a practice-based music course, you apply through the Conservatoires UK Admissions Service (CUKAS), an admissions service for eight of the UK conservatoires. The Guildhall School of Music does not recruit through CUKAS: they accept applications direct.

If you can't make up your mind which music courses to apply for, why not apply through UCAS and CUKAS? You can then decide which course to take later in the year.

The courses offered by conservatoires are creative and varied. You can choose to study full- or part-time, take a postgraduate course if you have already completed a degree, and can specialise in one or more instruments. You can also apply through CUKAS for drama, dance, screen and production courses at participating conservatoires.

For more information about CUKAS, please visit the website **www.cukas.ac.uk** where you'll find a detailed list of available courses and the online application. You can access the courses available by clicking on the Course Search link and searching by various criteria, such as type of study (eg undergraduate, postgraduate) or by instruments and study areas.

Postgraduate courses: with the exception of the subjects detailed below, UCAS does not recruit for postgraduate courses.

If you are applying for a subject listed below, please read through the following information.

- **Medicine and dentistry:** for some postgraduate courses you apply through UCAS.
- **Nursing:** for diploma and degree qualifications (postgraduate and undergraduate) in nursing, you apply through UCAS.
- **Social work:** for degree qualifications (postgraduate and undergraduate) in social work, you apply through UCAS.
- **Teaching:** if you are applying for postgraduate teacher training courses in England, Scotland or Wales, you will usually need to apply through the Graduate Teacher Training Registry (GTTR) at **www.gttr.ac.uk**. If you are applying for postgraduate teaching courses in Northern Ireland, you normally apply direct to the university. Teaching courses at undergraduate level are processed through UCAS.

UKPASS: search for postgraduate programmes through UCAS' postgraduate application service, UKPASS (UK Postgraduate Application and Statistical Service) at **www.ukpass.ac.uk**. You can apply online to universities and colleges using the scheme and there are links to universities and colleges who use other online application systems. Contact details are provided for those without an online system, so that you can check how they would like you to submit an application.

How to apply – FAQs

What is UCAS' role?

We are the organisation responsible for managing applications to higher education courses in the UK. If you want to make an application to a full-time higher education course, you will need to apply through UCAS. Once you have completed your application and sent it to us, we forward it to the universities of your choice. It is then up to the unis to decide if they can offer you a place. UCAS is not involved with the decision-making process.

Which courses can I apply for through UCAS?

You apply through UCAS for all full-time undergraduate courses. You can also use it to apply for nursing diplomas and degrees, for some postgraduate medicine and dentistry courses, and for postgraduate social work courses.

For most postgraduate and part-time courses, you apply direct to the university or college. If you are unsure of how to apply, you should contact the institution for advice.

You may need to use a different admissions service to apply for your course. Use the table below to find out which system you should be using. If you are still unsure, contact the uni to check.

UCAS	GTTR	CUKAS	UKPASS
All undergraduate courses, including medicine courses. Postgraduate social work courses. Nursing courses (undergraduate and postgraduate). Some postgraduate medicine and dentistry courses. Undergraduate teacher training courses.	Full-time and part-time postgraduate teaching courses.	Practice-based music, drama, and dance courses at eight of the UK conservatoires.	Some postgraduate programmes, including part-time and distance learning, with the exception of those currently in the UCAS scheme.

Can I make more than one application in the same year?
No, you can submit only one UCAS application per academic year. You can apply for a maximum of five choices on your application.

If you contact us to cancel your application within seven days of the date on your Welcome letter, we'll give you a refund. You could then submit a second application for the same academic cycle if you wished, as long as the first application was cancelled within the seven-day period. If you cancel an application after the seven days have passed, you cannot send another application.

Where can I find information about foundation degrees?
The study methods for foundation degrees can be very flexible, which means that they are available to people already in work, to those wishing to embark on a career change, and to those who have recently completed level 3 qualifications (eg A levels, Advanced Apprenticeships or NVQ3). You can find more information about foundation degrees and research courses on the Foundation Degree Course Search at **www.ucas.com/students/choosingcourses/choosingcourse/foundationdegree**.

How to complete your UCAS application

To apply for a university or college place you use our online application service, called Apply. Apply is a secure web-based system, available 24 hours a day. You can use it anywhere that has internet access, so you can complete your application where and when it suits you. You do not have to complete your application in one go – you can start it and come back to it as many times as you like.

Student tip:

'Your UCAS application is not as scary as your teachers make out... it is really hard to make a mistake as it takes you through step-by-step. The quicker you embrace it the easier it becomes.'

At **www.ucas.tv** you can watch our video guide *How to apply* and our frequently asked question videos to find out more. There is also detailed help text throughout Apply and at **www.ucas.com** to help you fill in your application.

We provide an option to apply in Welsh, but only use the Welsh version of Apply if you're applying to Welsh universities and colleges or English universities with the resources to translate your application into English. If you're not sure, check with your universities and colleges before applying.

If you choose to receive correspondence in Welsh, any written communication from us will also be in Welsh.

Myth buster

Everyone completes the same UCAS applications

Everyone making an application uses the same link to access Apply, and registers and completes the same application. It makes no difference if you are making your first application or reapplying, applying as an individual or through a school, or if you are a mature applicant or an international applicant, there is only one link – **www.ucas.com/students/apply**.

This section gives you an overview of the different sections you'll need to complete in Apply.

Registration

This is the first step to applying. You'll need to add personal details, such as your name, address and date of birth, and you'll be asked to read and agree to the terms and conditions for using Apply. Once you've registered you'll be given a username and be asked to create your own password. **Keep these in a safe place as you'll need them every time you log in to your application.**

If you're applying as an individual: if you're not applying through a school, college or centre, you'll need to answer a few questions to confirm your eligibility before you can start your application. If you're applying from the UK and don't have access to a computer, you can use one at a local online centre. Search for your nearest centre at **www.ukonlinecentres.com**.

If you're applying through a school, college or centre: you'll need to obtain a 'buzzword' from the centre you're applying through. This 'buzzword' links your application to your centre so that your referee can write and attach their reference.

Personal details

The personal details you entered when you registered will be automatically transferred into this section. Check that your name, address, date of birth and contact details are correct.

International students: It is very important to make sure your postal address is up-to-date to ensure that UCAS and the universities you apply to can get in touch with you. If you're studying in the UK but live in another country and you enter your school as the postal address then you will receive post there. But you must remember to update the address when you leave in the summer. Make sure you add in your home address (or BFPO if your parents are in the armed forces) in your home country. You can update this information in Track.

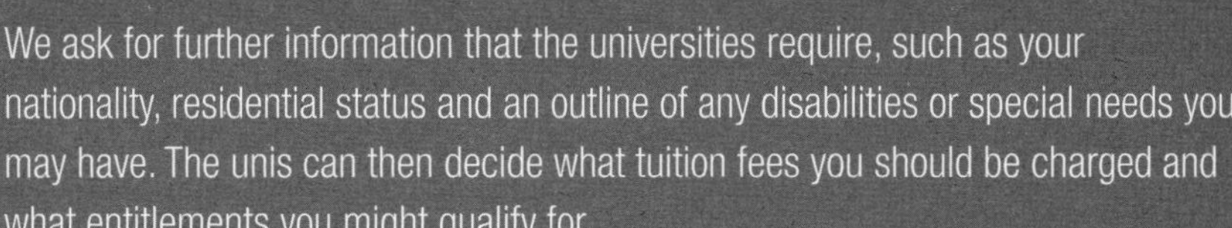

We ask for further information that the universities require, such as your nationality, residential status and an outline of any disabilities or special needs you may have. The unis can then decide what tuition fees you should be charged and what entitlements you might qualify for.

Fee code: you'll need to choose a code from a drop-down list to show the university how you expect to pay for your tuition fees. Most applicants from the UK, Channel Islands, Isle of Man and the EU will be in category 02. You should use that code if you are eligible for assessment under student support arrangements, even if you think your family income will be too high for you to receive support.

The options available to you are:

- 01 Private finance – entire cost of tuition fees is to be paid by private finance.
- 02 UK, ChI, IoM or EU student finance services – applying for student support assessment by local authority, Student Finance England, Student Finance Wales, Student Awards Agency for Scotland, Student Finance NI (Northern Ireland), Northern Ireland Education and Library Board, SLC EU Team, Channel Island or Isle of Man agency.
- 04 Research councils – contribution from a research council.
- 05 DHSS/Regional Health – contribution from the Department of Health and Social Security or from a Regional Health Authority.
- 06 UK Govt international award – international student award from the UK Government or the British Council.
- 07 Training agency – contribution from a training agency.
- 08 Other UK Govt award – contribution from another Government source.

Student tip:

'The online application wasn't hard to fill in and I could easily go back and change details as and when I wanted, so don't worry if you are unsure what to put or what UCAS is asking on the form, check with a teacher and then you can go back to it.'

- 09 International agency – contribution from an international agency, government, university or industry.
- 10 UK Industry/commerce – contribution from UK industry or commerce.
- 90 Other source – other source of finance.
- 99 Not known.

If you're applying to any of the authorities listed in fee code 02, they may assess your eligibility for any financial support towards tuition fees.

If you are applying for a mixture of courses involving more than one fee code, such as 02 and 05, enter the fee code that applies to most of the courses you have chosen.

If all or part of your tuition fees will be paid by an award from another organisation (for example, a National Health Service bursary, a company sponsor or a training agency), please choose the appropriate code. Bursaries for nursing courses are usually category 05. If you're applying for sponsorship, give the name of your first choice sponsor in your personal statement section. You can find out more about company sponsorship from a careers adviser. You should say in your personal statement if you plan to defer to the next academic year if your application for sponsorship this year is unsuccessful.

You should only use code 01 if you are paying all of your tuition fees from private finance and you are not eligible for assessment under student support arrangements.

A small number of universities and colleges don't receive public funding and their students may not get help towards tuition fees under the student support arrangements. These institutions are clearly marked in the Course Finder section of the UCAS website. Alternatively, please refer to their prospectuses for more information.

You can find out more about student finance on pages 49 to 56.

Students with disabilities or special needs: it is not compulsory but we would encourage you to enter details of any disabilities or special needs on your application. Universities and colleges welcome students with disabilities, and will try to meet your needs wherever possible. Don't be worried about disclosing your disability or special needs as the earlier the unis and colleges know, the easier it will be for them to get support put in place for you. This might include adapted accommodation, extra equipment, readers or interpreters or extra time to complete your course. If you do not know what facilities or support you need, please contact the disability coordinator at your chosen unis. You can find their contact details on the Disability Rights UK website at **www.disabilityrightsuk.org/disabledstudents.htm**, and you could also visit the university to make sure you are happy with their facilities. They may ask you for more details to help them plan for you, as well as explain to you how they will keep any information you give them confidential. You may be able to get extra financial support or help with care from Disabled Students' Allowances (DSAs); see page 54 for more information.

You might be unsure whether to tell people about your disability or wondering about the best time to do this. Although this may be the first time you've thought about 'disclosing', universities and colleges will have had many disabled students through its doors and are likely to have experience of supporting students with a similar impairment.

Disability Rights UK (**www.disabilityrightsuk.org/disabledstudents.htm**) has provided the following information to help you decide whether to disclose a disability, ongoing health condition, mental health condition or specific learning difficulty like dyslexia in your UCAS application:

Pros

- **Getting support set up**
  You may need additional support to attend an interview or sit an admissions test. If you need support on the course, such as a reader or an adapted computer, it is best to set it up as early as possible. If you need adapted residential accommodation, or if ramps, new signs or other building modifications have to be made, then work needs to start early, not the day you arrive. Staff may also need training, which can take time to arrange.
- **Supporting your application**
  You may have had an unusual academic career, perhaps sitting exams later than other people on your course. Without the knowledge that you have a

Watch our UCAStv video guides ***Students with disabilities*** and ***Advice from disability officers*** at www.ucas.tv.

Uni tip:

'If an applicant has indicated they have a disability, once their application is received we begin to contact them, to make sure everything is in place should they ultimately come to the university.'

disability or impairment, tutors might wonder why you took longer over some courses. Take advantage of any opportunities to describe your disability in a positive way. Your experiences may have provided you with skills that are useful for the course you've chosen.

- **The information will come from you**
  If you decide when to tell people about your disability, you'll have more control over the way it is seen. Disclosing the information yourself, and in a way you feel comfortable, may be preferable. This may be at the application stage or you might want to give this information at an interview. Alternatively, you could think about whether you are happy for the person who fills in your reference to mention your disability or impairment.
- **Confidentiality**
  Information about your disability is protected by the Equality Act and the Data Protection Act. It is sensitive personal information and cannot be passed on to anybody else without your permission. Universities and colleges have policies outlining which members of staff will be told about your disability.

Cons

- **Irrelevance**
  You may have a disability or impairment that you do not think will affect your study. However, it is important to remember that studying in higher education may be very different from studying at school, and you may need additional support.

  If you do not disclose your disability on your application, you can still tell the university or college disability adviser once you've been accepted onto the course. However, if the disability adviser is not informed before the start of the course, it may take longer to arrange the support or access requirements and these may not be in place as soon as you need them. Whether you disclose does not affect your right to Disabled Students' Allowances (DSAs), although in Scotland the disability coordinator or assessor needs to sign your DSAs application form. Recent research shows that disabled students who receive DSAs get better final grades than those who choose to go it alone, without asking for or accepting support.

- **Discrimination**
  It is unlawful for institutions to discriminate against you because of your disability or impairment. You may still feel, however, that an institution will discriminate against you, even if your disability or impairment will not affect your studies. In this case, you may choose not to tell the college or university. If you need support, you could tell the relevant staff once you have been accepted. However, it can take longer to make access arrangements or set up support if they are told after your course has begun. This is a risk you take if you do not inform someone at an early stage.

International students: if your permanent home is outside the UK, we collect applicants' passport information on behalf of universities and colleges, who need it for purposes of visa application and checks with the UK Border Agency (UKBA). For further details of UKBA please visit their website **www.ukba.homeoffice.gov.uk**. If you plan to change your passport before starting at university, enter the current details but be sure to update any changes direct with your firm and insurance choice universities.

If you are taking, or have taken, Test of English as a Foreign Language (TOEFL) you should enter your registration number in this section; for International English Language Testing System (IELTS), enter your Test Report Form (TRF) number. More information about English language proficiency tests can be found at **www.ucas.com/students/wheretostart/nonukstudents/englangprof**.

Student tip:

'I suggest you read through everything on the UCAS application so you don't miss anything.'

Criminal convictions: as part of their duty of care to all applicants and existing students, the universities will also need to know if you have any relevant criminal convictions. If you have a relevant criminal conviction that is not spent, you're required to declare this on your application. If you declare a relevant criminal conviction it does not mean you will be automatically excluded from the application process. More detailed information about the criminal convictions declaration is provided in Apply.

Nominated access: if you want to, you can choose to nominate someone who can discuss your application with us and the universities if you're unavailable. This could be, for example, a parent, grandparent, guardian or adviser.

Additional information (UK applicants only)

This section provides extra information required by the universities and colleges. It is only available in Apply to those applicants who are permanently resident in the UK. You're asked for the following details:

- **Ethnic origin and national identity** – your national identity reflects how you choose to classify yourself. It's different from ethnicity and nationality and can be based on many things, such as culture, language or ancestry/family history. You do not have to provide this information if you'd prefer not to.
- **Activities in preparation for higher education** – you can enter details of up to two activities, such as summer schools or taster courses.
- **Care** – this question is optional. If you have spent any time in local authority care, even for one day (this includes if you have been in public care and have lived in one or more of foster care, semi-independent living or residential care homes), you should select 'yes' from the drop-down list. Universities will treat this information in confidence and may contact you to discuss if you need any extra resources or support to undertake your chosen course. Selecting 'yes' to this question may also enable you to access additional financial support universities provide to young people who have been in care.
- **Parental education** – you'll be asked to indicate whether or not any of your parents, step-parents or guardians have taken a course at higher education level. This question is also optional.
- **Occupational background** – if you're under 21, you are asked to give the job title of your parent, step-parent or guardian who earns the most. If she or he is retired or unemployed, you give their most recent job title. If you are 21 or over, you're asked to give your own job title. If you prefer not to give this information, you can enter 'I prefer not to say' in the text box. This information will not be passed to your chosen institution until they have given you an unconditional offer that you have accepted as your firm choice. This information will be used for statistical monitoring only.

Student tip:

'Filling in the application is simple... with little help boxes next to every piece of information... telling you exactly what they want...'

Choices

- You can choose a maximum of five choices and there's no preference order – Apply will store your choices in alphabetical order.
- Your application is sent to all your chosen unis at the same time.
- Each uni will only see details of its course(s) that you've applied to. They won't see your other choices until you've received the final decision on your application.

Course combinations

You can apply for any combination of unis or colleges and courses that you want, with the following exceptions:

- a maximum of four courses in any one of medicine, dentistry, veterinary medicine or veterinary science courses
- you can apply to only one course at either the University of Oxford or the University of Cambridge. You cannot apply to both universities. The only exception to this is if you will be a graduate at the start of the course and are applying for course code A101 (graduate medicine) at the University of Cambridge. Then you can also apply to course code A100 (medicine) at Cambridge, in addition to being able to apply to course code A101 (graduate medicine) at the University of Oxford.

You can use your remaining choice(s) for any other subject. For example, if you apply to four medicine courses, you could still make one choice for veterinary medicine. However, be aware that your personal statement will be sent to all the universities and colleges that you've chosen. See page 167 for more information about applying to multiple courses.

More advice about applying to medicine, dentistry, veterinary medicine and veterinary science courses can be found on page 177.

There are different application deadlines for some courses, universities and colleges – see the When to apply section on page 121 for more information.

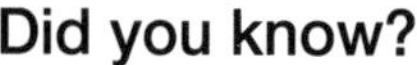

Did you know?

Choices are not sent in preference order

Your application is sent to your chosen unis at the same time, so it doesn't matter which order you add your choices. They'll be listed in alphabetical order in Apply, then we will generate a random order when we process your application.

Myth buster

You don't have to add five choices

There's space for five choices, but you don't have to use them all up – you can apply for just one if you know exactly where you want to go, or two, three or four if you want – it doesn't have to be five.

Only add choices you're sure about. If you wouldn't be happy going to one of them, see if there's somewhere else, or apply to fewer choices – you don't have to fill up the space for the sake of it.

If you apply to fewer than five choices, you can add more later if you want to (but be aware of the deadlines for adding choices – see page 214). This can be useful if you spot a new course after you've sent us your application. You can add another choice in Track if you have space (Track lets you see the progress of your application once we've processed it) and we'll send it to the university as normal.

Additional requirements

Admissions tests: some courses require an admissions test or tests. It's your responsibility to find out if you need to take one for your course(s), and to register by the deadline. Go to the admissions tests section on pages 101 to 114 for more information.

If you're applying for **medicine, dentistry, nursing, midwifery or certain other health courses**, UK health authorities recommend you should be immunised against Hepatitis B before you start training. Universities and colleges may also ask you for certificates to show that you're not infected. Check the immunisation and certification requirements with your universities and colleges.

International applicants for nursing or midwifery degrees: before applying please check the latest information at **www.ucas.com/students/wheretostart/nonukstudents/choosingacourse/nursing**.

Criminal convictions declaration: you will be required to declare whether you have any relevant unspent criminal convictions. The help text in Apply explains what is classed as a relevant unspent conviction. In addition, some courses have entry requirements which might require you to disclose further information regarding any past criminal activities, and may also require a criminal records check.

Education

Unless asked, don't send any exam certificates or other papers to us or to your unis.

Universities need to know where you've studied and which qualifications you're taking or have taken. You add your schools and colleges, then list your qualifications. You must include all schools, colleges and universities that you have attended since the age of 11, even if you withdrew from your course.

For each school and college, you provide details of:

- all qualifications for which you have accepted certification from an awarding organisation, even if you're retaking all or part of the qualification
- all qualifications for which you are currently studying or awaiting results.

Student tip:

'..it [the application] was organised in such a manner in which you can easily view, edit or even update information regarding your education or employment. The thing I found most useful was that you could go back to the information at any time.'

All qualifications must be entered, even if you received an unsuccessful grade, if you are still waiting to take the final exams or if you are waiting for the results.

Resits: If you're resitting a qualification you need to enter it twice: once as a completed qualification with the grade achieved and once as a qualification with the result 'Pending'.

All qualifications have to be entered manually – you can't copy and paste in transcripts.

More information about entering specific qualifications can be found at **www.ucas.com/students/applying/howtoapply/education/quals**

Your highest level of qualification: you'll be asked to select the highest level of qualification you will have before you start your course. This doesn't include the course you're applying to – it's just about the qualifications that you'll complete before starting the course.

Mature students: enter details for all your qualifications. If you're unsure of the awarding body for your qualifications, check the certificate or speak to the school or college where you obtained it. If you are currently studying for a qualification, ask your centre for the awarding body. There is a list of exam boards at **www.ucas.com/students/applying/howtoapply/education/examboards** which might help you. If you don't have any qualifications, you should still enter details for your schools. If you're hoping to enter higher education through the Accreditation of Prior Learning (APL) or the Accreditation of Prior Experiential Learning (APEL), you still apply through us, but you should contact your chosen unis first to discuss whether APL or APEL is acceptable and what evidence they'll need. Find out more about APL and APEL at **www.ucas.com/students/wheretostart/maturestudents/courses/apl**.

International students: check the suitability of your qualifications with the admissions offices at your unis before applying. A lot of schools outside the UK are not listed as a 'centre' in Apply. Don't worry, just enter the school name and country – there will be a warning message on the screen if you don't enter a centre number but this will not affect your application. When you apply, you must give full details of all your qualifications, including exams you took when you left school, exams you took to get into higher education, vocational exams and any other qualifications or awards. You should also include qualifications you are studying currently or planning to complete. If you are asked to enter modules on your application, these are the subjects which make up the overall result of your qualification.

Please do not try to give a UK equivalent. If your first language is not English:

- say whether or not your qualifications were completely or partly assessed in English

- enter details for any English language tests you have taken or plan to take.

UCAS has made it easy for international applicants to enter their qualifications. Many are listed by country and name. You can also find a listing for many English language exams and degrees (if you have already taken or are currently taking a degree course). If you cannot find your qualification, list as much information as possible under 'Other'. The unis and colleges will then contact you for further information about your qualification if required.

Student tip:

'Make a list of all your schools and colleges, international or national competitions and language certificates. Don't forget to add anything.'

Employment

In this section, you fill in the details of your paid work history and employers. If you've not had any jobs, you can leave this section blank, but you'll still need to mark it as complete to continue with your application.

Personal statement

The personal statement is your opportunity to tell universities and colleges why they should choose you. You need to demonstrate your suitability for the course(s), your enthusiasm and commitment, and above all, make sure you stand out from the crowd. Because this is such an important part of your application there is a separate section to help you with your personal statement, on pages 147 to 175.

Student tip:

Take as much time as needed to make sure that it (personal statement} contains everything that you consider relevant for your course, what makes you unique, what makes you different and most importantly, what makes you a suitable candidate for your course.'

Your reference

Your application needs a reference from a tutor, careers adviser or other professional who knows you well enough to write about you and your suitability for the course.

Applying through a school or college or other organisation: this section will be completed by your referee and you won't have access to it. Once you have completed each section, checked your application and marked all sections as complete, you pay for it and send it online to your referee. Your referee will then check and approve your application, write the reference and send your application to us.

Applying as an individual: if you're applying independently you will be asked to provide contact details of your referee. A request will then be sent by email to your referee asking them to complete and submit a reference through our secure website. Your referee can click on the help text links to read advice on what to include in the reference. We check that they are still able to supply your reference and ask them to confirm their identity. If they decline to give you a reference for any reason we will notify you. We notify you by email when the reference is complete and a red tick will be displayed next to the 'Reference' section in the left-hand navigation in Apply. You can then complete and submit your application. **It's up to you to ensure that your chosen referee is aware of any deadline you have and for you to make sure that you request a reference allowing adequate time for them to prepare and submit the reference.**

If you're applying independently but would like your reference to be written by a registered school, college or other organisation, you can request that the centre completes the reference for you in Apply. This means that the centre can write a reference for you but they won't be involved in the rest of your application. Once they have completed the reference, a red tick will be displayed next to the 'Reference' section in the left-hand navigation.

Who should write the reference?

- Your referee should know you well enough, in an official capacity, to write about you and your suitability for higher education.
- If you're at school or college, or left recently, ask your principal, head teacher, teacher or tutor.
- If you left school or college several years ago, ask your current or previous employer, or in the case of voluntary work your supervisor.
- If you've recently attended any training courses you could ask your training provider.

International students: you will probably need a teacher to write a reference for you, and it may be in a style that differs from the typical style of references in your country. Show this page on the UCAS website to your referee – **www.ucas.com/advisers/online/references.** References must be entered onto the UCAS application in English, although they can be translated. Make sure you keep a copy of both the original and translated reference, as your chosen institutions may ask to see a copy for verification purposes.

If you're in prison, your application must include a statement from the prison authorities, even if you're asking someone else to write your reference. The prison authority has to say whether you're suitable for a course of study, and whether you'll be able to accept a place for the start date chosen.

Who should not write the reference?

- It is not permitted for family, friends, partners or ex-partners to write your reference. If we find this to be the case, your application may be cancelled.

More information about the reference and a guide to writing references can be found at **www.ucas.com/students/applying/howtoapply/reference**.

Cost of applying

How much will it cost?

The fee depends on how many courses and universities you apply to. Please check **www.ucas.com** for up-to-date information about the application fee.

How do I pay?

If you're applying through a school, college or other organisation, they'll let you know how to pay. It will be either by credit or debit card online, or by paying your centre who will then pay us. If you apply to one course and pay the reduced application fee, and later add choices to your application after it has been sent to UCAS, you pay the additional fee to UCAS.

If you're applying independently, you pay online using a credit or debit card. The card doesn't have to be in your name, but you will require the consent of the cardholder. If you pay your fee using a credit or debit card that you do not have permission to use, we will cancel your application.

We accept UK and international Visa, Visa Debit, Delta, MasterCard, JCB, Maestro and Electron credit or debit cards. At the moment we do not accept American Express or Diners Club cards.

When do I pay?

You pay after you have completed your application and are in the process of sending it to us (or to your referee).

If you're paying by card, you'll be asked for your card details once you have agreed to the terms of the declaration and data protection statement.

Please remember that you can only complete one application in each cycle. If you send a second application, it will be cancelled and you will not receive a refund.

How to complete your application – FAQs

How do I apply for more than one subject?

You can apply for a maximum of five choices on your application. This could be five different universities for the same subject, or five different subjects at one university, or any combination. You can select any course you wish (with the exception of those courses detailed in the 'Choices' section on page 137).

Student tip:

'...the application on the UCAS website was very easy to complete, partly due to its structure and also because it had tips all over the application, in case I got a little confused about what was asked for.'

However, you can only submit one personal statement with your application. If you are applying for different subjects, you will need to try to write your statement more generally. This will be easier if the subjects are similar. If the subjects are quite different (for example, medicine and law) you can contact the university and ask if it is possible to send an amended version of the statement direct to them. If they agree, you can write the statement on your application specifically about one subject, and then write an amended version about the second subject. More advice about applying for multiple courses is given on page 167.

Will the universities I've chosen be able to see my other choices?

No. UCAS will keep this information private, so the universities will be not be able to see your other choices. However, once you have accepted your firm choice and your insurance choice (if you have one), then both of these universities will be able to see the other. They can also see whether they are the firm or insurance choice.

Can I reapply if I already have a deferred place?

No. If you don't want to attend the course you have accepted, you will need to discuss your options with your university or college. If they agree to withdraw your place and you had applied for the course in the previous application cycle, you can complete a new application.

How do universities and colleges view deferred entry applications?

The value of gap year activities is widely documented and most unis will allow you to apply for deferred entry, but check with them before applying. When you apply, include details of your proposed gap year in your personal statement to support your application.

A note for international applicants:
Several countries require their citizens to complete mandatory military or national service. If this affects you, check with universities and colleges in advance to discuss when you should apply. You can defer through UCAS for a maximum of one year. It would be useful to include information on your military or national service in your personal statement.

How do I link my application to my school or college?
You can do this in Apply. Go to the 'options' section and click on the 'link your application to your school/college/centre' link – enter your school/college buzzword and submit the request. Your school or college can then accept or reject your request – if they accept it, your application will then be linked to them and the 'reference' section of your application will disappear.

Once you have completed your application and sent it to your school or college, they will approve the application, enter the reference and send your application to us.

What happens when my application is sent to UCAS?
Once your application is completed and sent to us, we process it. If we have to query anything, we'll contact you for more information. Your application will then be sent to your universities and colleges to consider and we'll send you a Welcome letter. If your postal address is in the UK, allow 14 days for your letter to arrive. If your postal address is outside the UK, please allow 21 days. Find out more about what happens next in the Step 3 Offers section on page 195.

www.ucas.com

Personal statement

This is your opportunity to tell the unis why they should choose you. In your personal statement you'll need to demonstrate why you're suitable for the course, and show your enthusiasm and commitment. Above all, you'll need to ensure that you stand out from the crowd. Watch our UCAStv video guide at **www.ucas.tv** for help on how to start and what to include in your personal statement.

Look at our timeline overleaf to see when you need to start researching and writing your personal statement.

Adviser tip

'This is the most important and strangest piece of writing you will ever do. Make sure you start in plenty of time, get your friends to read it and see if it sounds like you. Get a person who doesn't really know you that well to read it – does it make them want to find out more about you?'

See when you need to start researching and writing your personal statement.

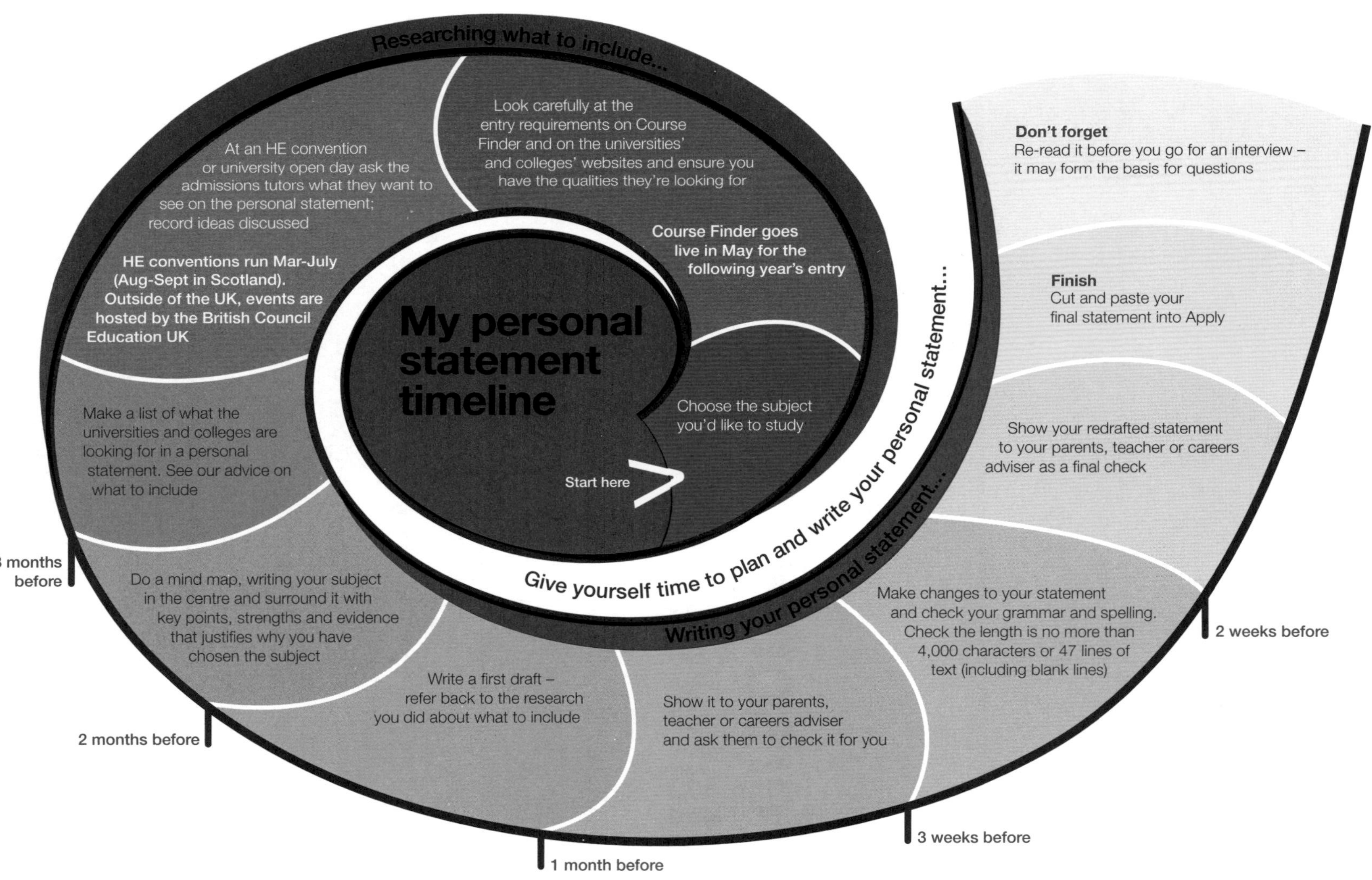

My personal statement timeline
Start here
Choose the subject you'd like to study
Course Finder goes live in May for the following year's entry
Look carefully at the entry requirements on Course Finder and on the universities' and colleges' websites and ensure you have the qualities they're looking for
Researching what to include...
At an HE convention or university open day ask the admissions tutors what they want to see on the personal statement; record ideas discussed
HE conventions run Mar-July (Aug-Sept in Scotland). Outside of the UK, events are hosted by the British Council Education UK
Make a list of what the universities and colleges are looking for in a personal statement. See our advice on what to include
3 months before
Do a mind map, writing your subject in the centre and surround it with key points, strengths and evidence that justifies why you have chosen the subject
2 months before
Write a first draft – refer back to the research you did about what to include
1 month before
Show it to your parents, teacher or careers adviser and ask them to check it for you
3 weeks before
Make changes to your statement and check your grammar and spelling. Check the length is no more than 4,000 characters or 47 lines of text (including blank lines)
2 weeks before
Writing your personal statement...
Give yourself time to plan and write your personal statement...
Show your redrafted statement to your parents, teacher or careers adviser as a final check
Finish
Cut and paste your final statement into Apply
Don't forget
Re-read it before you go for an interview – it may form the basis for questions

Structure and format

Think about the structure of your statement – it needs to look and sound good. A bad statement can say a lot, so make sure you get the grammar, spelling and punctuation right.

A representative from Ulster Business School told us:

> *'The presentation of the personal statement is of critical importance to demonstrate use of English language and grammar at a standard suitable for entry to higher education.'*

Adviser tip:

'The feedback I most often have on why a student was unsuccessful is that the student had NOT sufficiently researched the nature of that course at that university. As an example, history might be ancient history or modern history or US history or British history and so on. All are very different – make sure you clearly demonstrate that you know what you are applying for.'

How to provide your personal statement

You can enter up to 4,000 characters (this includes spaces) or 47 lines of text (this includes blank lines), whichever comes first. You don't have to use all the space provided. **We strongly recommend that you prepare your personal statement offline using a word-processing package and copy and paste it into the Apply system.**

Please note that you cannot use *italics*, **bold** or underlining in your personal statement – the system will automatically remove these when saved. This will not disadvantage your application.

If you want to, you can enter some European characters (such as à, ë, õ) in your personal statement. Not all universities and colleges can view these characters correctly, so a version with substituted English characters is also made available to them. You can find more information at **www.ucas.com/students/applying/howtoapply/overview**.

Student tip

'The best thing to do is to plan and get as much advice as you can from your tutors and the UCAS website. Don't leave writing it until too late; there's nothing worse than feeling as though you haven't left yourself enough time and having to rush it. Once you get started and you've planned it, filling in the gaps is straightforward. Also, redraft it. Then redraft it again and again. That way you can make sure that it is the very best that you could hope it to be.

'Look into some extra reading related to the course you are applying to, and then you can refer to it in your personal statement and hope it helps to impress those universities which you are so desperate to win the approval of!'

Student tip:

'I found that breaking it down into sections gave me a better idea of how to structure the personal statement. I used categories like work experience, skills and personal experiences to give myself an idea of what I wanted to talk about.'

What to include

This section gives you some suggestions of what to include in your personal statement, but these are only guidelines so don't worry if some of them aren't relevant to you. More detailed information and a UCAStv video guide to writing a personal statement are available at **www.ucas.com/students/applying/howtoapply/personalstatement.**

Firstly, check the entry requirements for the courses you're interested in on Course Finder at **www.ucas.com**. These explain what the unis are looking for in their students and the qualifications and experience you'll need for the courses. The entry requirements will give you some ideas about what to include in your personal statement.

Our mind map shown on page 152 summarises what you need to know about the personal statement, including preparation, presentation and what to include.

The worksheet overleaf has been designed to help you think about information you could include in your personal statement.

You can photocopy our timeline, mind map and worksheet from this book or download and print off PDF versions from **www.ucas.com/students/applying/howtoapply/personalstatement**.

Writing about the course

Two of the most important things to think about are:

- **Why you're applying for the courses you've chosen:** this is particularly important when you're applying for a subject that you have not studied before. Tell the university the reasons why that subject interests you, and include evidence that you understand what's required to study the course. For example, if applying for psychology courses, show that you know how scientific the subject is.
- **Why you're suitable for the course:** tell the universities the skills and experience you have that will help you succeed on the course.

Also think about:

- how your current or previous studies relate to the courses that you've chosen
- any activities that demonstrate your interest in the courses
- why you want to go to university.

Adviser tip:

'You can't believe how many first drafts begin "Since the age of 2...". Universities care about your current motivation and skills to study the course you've chosen. Don't spend your whole first paragraph reminiscing about your early childhood.'

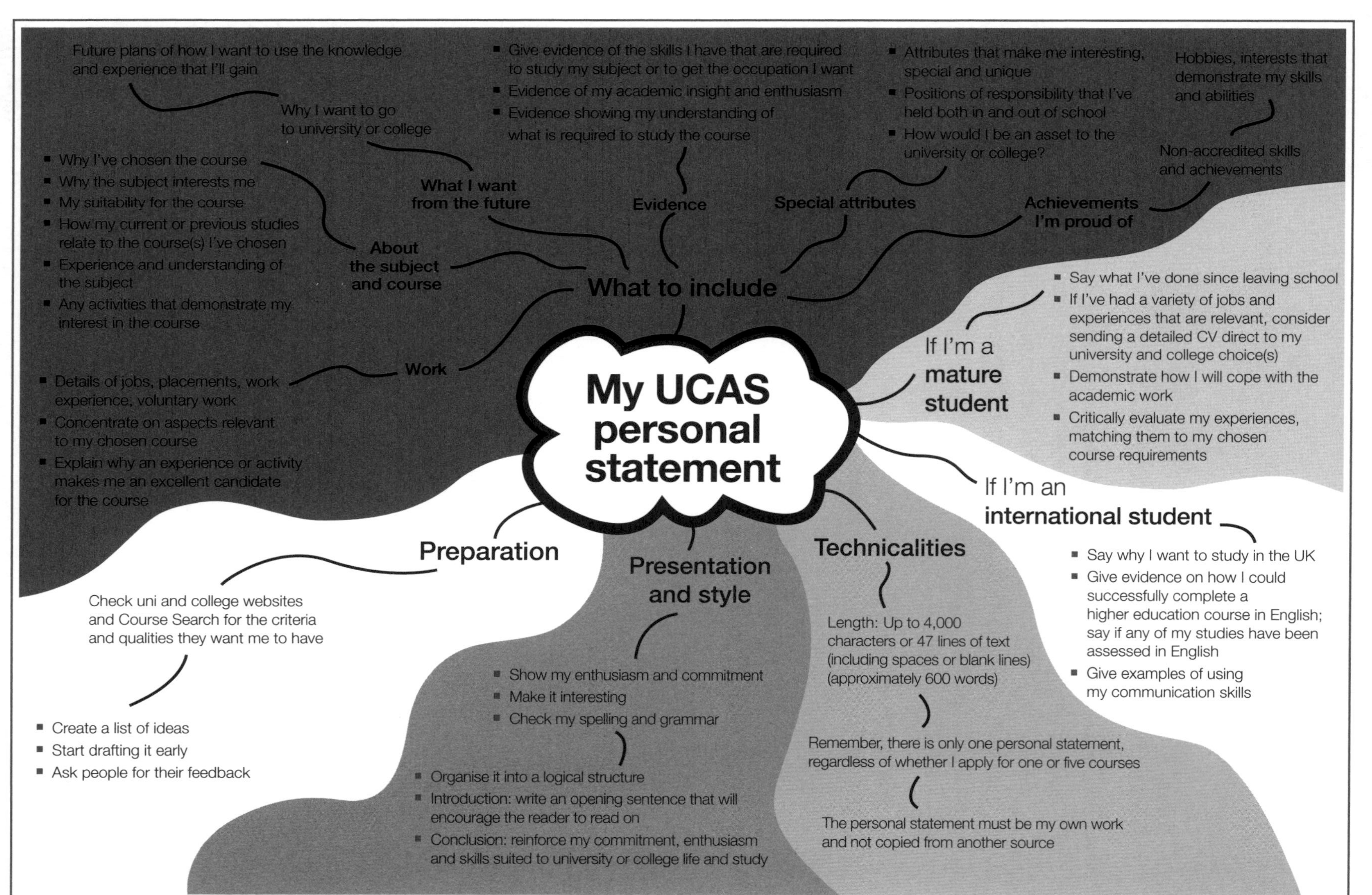
My UCAS personal statement
What to include
About the subject and course
Why I've chosen the course
Why the subject interests me
My suitability for the course
How my current or previous studies relate to the course(s) I've chosen
Experience and understanding of the subject
Any activities that demonstrate my interest in the course
What I want from the future
Why I want to go to university or college
Future plans of how I want to use the knowledge and experience that I'll gain
Evidence
Give evidence of the skills I have that are required to study my subject or to get the occupation I want
Evidence of my academic insight and enthusiasm
Evidence showing my understanding of what is required to study the course
Special attributes
Attributes that make me interesting, special and unique
Positions of responsibility that I've held both in and out of school
How would I be an asset to the university or college?
Achievements I'm proud of
Non-accredited skills and achievements
Hobbies, interests that demonstrate my skills and abilities
Work
Details of jobs, placements, work experience, voluntary work
Concentrate on aspects relevant to my chosen course
Explain why an experience or activity makes me an excellent candidate for the course
If I'm a mature student
Say what I've done since leaving school
If I've had a variety of jobs and experiences that are relevant, consider sending a detailed CV direct to my university and college choice(s)
Demonstrate how I will cope with the academic work
Critically evaluate my experiences, matching them to my chosen course requirements
If I'm an international student
Say why I want to study in the UK
Give evidence on how I could successfully complete a higher education course in English; say if any of my studies have been assessed in English
Give examples of using my communication skills
Technicalities
Length: Up to 4,000 characters or 47 lines of text (including spaces or blank lines) (approximately 600 words)
Remember, there is only one personal statement, regardless of whether I apply for one or five courses
The personal statement must be my own work and not copied from another source
Presentation and style
Show my enthusiasm and commitment
Make it interesting
Check my spelling and grammar
Organise it into a logical structure
Introduction: write an opening sentence that will encourage the reader to read on
Conclusion: reinforce my commitment, enthusiasm and skills suited to university or college life and study
Preparation
Check uni and college websites and Course Search for the criteria and qualities they want me to have
Create a list of ideas
Start drafting it early
Ask people for their feedback

Personal statement worksheet

1

This worksheet is designed to help you think about information you could include in your personal statement. We've included space for you to write down any thoughts you have as you go along. More detailed advice and guidance about writing your personal statement, including our UCAStv video guide, is available at **www.ucas.com/personalstatement**

Writing about the course

Why are you applying for your chosen course(s)?

Why does this subject interest you? Include evidence that you understand what's required to study the course, eg if applying for psychology courses, show that you know how scientific the subject is.

Why do you think you're suitable for the course(s)? Do you have any particular skills and experience that will help you to succeed on the course(s)?

Personal statement worksheet

Do your current or previous studies relate to the course(s) that you have chosen? If so, how?

Have you taken part in any other activities that demonstrate your interest in the course(s)?

Skills and achievements

Universities like to know the skills you have that will help you on the course, or generally with life at university, such as any accredited or non-accredited achievements. Write these down here. Examples can be found at **www.ucas.com/personalstatementskills**

Also think about any other achievements you're proud of, positions of responsibility that you hold or have held both in and out of school, and attributes that make you interesting, special or unique.

Personal statement worksheet

Hobbies and interests

Make a list of your hobbies, interests and social activities. Then think about how they demonstrate your personality, skills and abilities. Try to link them to the skills and experience required for your course(s).

Work experience

Include details of jobs, placements, work experience or voluntary work, particularly if it's relevant to your chosen course(s). Try to link any experience to skills or qualities related to the course.

Mature students

Explain what you've been doing since leaving education, and provide additional evidence to support your application. If you're not in full-time education, you should give details of any relevant work experience, paid or unpaid, and information about your current or previous employment.

UCAS

Personal statement worksheet

International students

Tell universities why you want to study in the UK and why you think you can successfully complete a course that is taught in English. Say if some of your studies have been taught or examined in English and if you have taken part in any activities where you have used English outside of your studies.

Future plans

If you know what you'd like to achieve after completing the course, explain how you want to use the knowledge and experience that you gain. How does the course relate to what you want to do in the future?

Dos and don'ts when writing your personal statement

- **Do** use your best English and don't let spelling and grammatical errors spoil your statement.
- **Do** show that you know your strengths and can outline your ideas clearly. Use words you know will be understood by the person reading your statement.
- **Do** be enthusiastic – if you show your interest in the course, it may help you get a place.
- **Do** expect to produce several drafts of your personal statement before being totally happy with it.
- **Do** ask people you trust for their feedback.
- **Don't** exaggerate – if you do you may get caught out at interview when asked to elaborate on an interesting achievement.
- **Don't** rely on a spellchecker as it will not pick up everything – proofread as many times as possible.
- **Don't** leave it to the last minute – your statement will seem rushed and important information could be left out.

How to make your application stand out from the crowd

We asked some universities what they were looking for in a personal statement to make it stand out. These are the answers they gave us:

Kingston University

'Individuality, concise history, anything unusual that students have been engaged in outside of their school or working life. We like to see evidence of personal engagement with the student's subject choice, relevant exhibitions, internships, their own opinions about the reasons why they would be a good candidate.'

The University of Nottingham

'We want to know what interests them about their chosen course. Applicants need to think about what interests them about the subject – refer to topics they've already studied and their wider interests in the area. It's also worth reflecting on any reading they've done on the subject, work experience and any extra-curricular activities they do.'

Bournemouth University

'Applicants need to explain to us what they do in their spare time and especially how that relates to their chosen area of study. Look at the details of the course they're applying for and link their interests and goals with the course content as much as possible. Mention any work experience, no matter how long or short, and ensure they list their key strengths – if they find this difficult why not ask another friend or family member to help. They need to sell themselves but also be true to themselves. Think hard about why they want to study in a certain area and explain future career goals or why they think they'll be successful on the course.'

We also received these longer responses:

University of Bristol

'We pay a great deal of attention to the personal statement, as it provides important indications of ability, motivation and potential. We look for evidence of your interest in the subject and make sure that this aligns with the kind of course we offer. We also take account of your extra-curricular interests and achievements, where these provide evidence of skills that will be relevant to the course.

'When it comes to writing your personal statement, you should make sure that it aligns with the selection criteria for the course. Everything in your personal statement should aim to show that you have the skills and qualities we are looking for, and convince us to offer you a place. If it doesn't do this, then leave it out.

'Before you write your statement, it's essential to understand why you want to study a particular subject. Whatever the reason, make sure your passion and enthusiasm comes across. Don't just tell us that you like something, show us that you do. What is it that interests you specifically? Why does it interest you? What have you done to pursue that interest?

'Similarly, when writing about relevant experience and achievements, make sure that you give concrete examples of the skills and qualities that they demonstrate. Don't be tempted to expand the truth, as it will catch you out in the long run!

'Finally, make sure that you have allowed enough time to check your work before you submit your application. It's useful to ask friends and family to help check the statement, but be careful that they don't try and force you to write it in the way they think it should be written. It is important that you write it in your own style rather than trying to conform to what someone else thinks is right, as there is no model way to write a personal statement. When it comes to spelling, however, there is only one "right" way.'

Durham University

'A personal statement is an opportunity for you to demonstrate why you think you would be a good student for the programme you're applying to, what you can contribute to the university and why the university should select your application over other equally excellent candidates. With many students applying with very strong academic results and predictions, the personal statement is crucial in helping admissions tutors identify students with the greatest merit and potential.

'Personal statements are used to help make a number of admissions decisions: including whether to invite an applicant to an interview, make an offer, or accept an applicant who's narrowly missed the conditions of their offer. Investing time into making sure your personal statement is as strong as it can be is therefore time well spent.

'Whilst there's no template we can give you for your personal statement – it should be personal to you – we do recommend that you answer three main questions in your personal statement in the following order and priority:

1. *Why do you want to study this subject?*
2. *What makes you someone particularly suitable to study the subject?*
3. *How will you contribute to the course and the university community and what makes you an interesting and unique individual?*

'At Durham University we particularly value personal statements that combine both an academic focus and consideration of your non-academic attributes and achievements. Other universities may be more interested purely in your academic achievements and potential.

'Stating any paid or voluntary work that you have done is a good idea if you can relate it to the programme you're applying for and/or to show your potential to contribute to the university community as a whole. The same is true for achievements in sport, music and the arts and involvement in any national or international competitions, including academic ones. Extra-curricular activities can provide proof of successful time management skills and a strong work ethic.

'Remember to draft and redraft your personal statement. Watch out for spelling mistakes (spellcheckers are not a guarantee) and missing or repeated words: doing this shows your commitment to the application and attention to detail. An admissions tutor will be impressed by the use of good English; a personal statement needs to be well written, in straightforward English, and laid out carefully. If you try too hard to impress with clever language you'll normally make your statement harder to read and your reasons for wanting to study a particular programme less clear.

'It can help to have someone else to look over your statement, to provide another opinion and to look for anything you may have missed, but don't lose your uniqueness by allowing others to write the statement for you or by copying what others have written.

'Make sure the personal statement is accurate. It is an academic statement for an academic programme of study so choose an appropriate tone. Attempts at humour are best avoided, as it doesn't always translate well in writing. Be enthusiastic and promote yourself. Do your research about the courses you want to apply to so you use your five UCAS choices wisely and your personal statement is tailored towards them.'

University of East Anglia

'After many years of reading personal statements and writing one myself (a long time ago) I know it can seem daunting, so here are my three tips to writing a good statement.

'Be bold: more often than not we're modest about our achievements. Don't be! What I like to see is some well thought out examples, and most importantly how they might relate to the subject you'd like to study at university. Make sure that you have clearly reflected on the skills and knowledge gained from your experiences. Concrete examples rather than a "wish" or a "dream" to study a subject will get you noticed.

'Structure: universities are reading a lot of personal statements and so I really like the first few lines to clearly outline the intended area of study and the reason why you want to study it. The end of your personal statement should also reinforce this. Although you are working in a restricted space I find it helpful when students use paragraphs so that the statement flows well and it's easy to identify key points. If you're going to be interviewed for a course, the interviewer will read the statement beforehand and may even refer to it during the interview, so a well-structured statement is imperative.

'Audience: it's very difficult to know who's going to read your personal statement. Indeed it's likely that a number of people in each university will and they'll have their own interpretation of what you're saying. Show your personal statement to as many people as you can and ask them if the key messages are coming through loud and clear. See if they can "paint a picture" of you from the words written down and use their feedback to refine the statement.

'A personal statement is your chance to promote yourself and the contribution you can make to a university. Look on it as a positive experience, giving you the opportunity to talk about the next steps in your life and career.'

The University of Manchester

'You should consider your personal statement as important as gaining the relevant entry qualifications for your chosen course. It's the only chance you get to express your personality alongside your academic abilities.

'A successful personal statement usually opens with positive intent and demonstrates a clear enthusiasm for the course in question. A common query from students is on what to include in their personal statement. The answer is a simple one, if it's relevant to your chosen course then include it and if it's not then leave it out.

'Quotes can be a useful way of demonstrating what has inspired you, whether that's an author of a book you've read or a famous philosopher. However, ensure the quote is relevant to a certain aspect of your particular course. It's also a good idea to write in the first person, this provides evidence of an individual personal statement and helps once again to portray your enthusiasm for the course you're applying for.

'If there's one key point to remember when writing your personal statement, remember the letters ABC! Activity, Benefit, Course! Universities want to see examples of the transferable skills you have obtained and how you plan to develop these skills at university. So, this is where ABC comes into play:

- *Activity – maybe you've volunteered in your local charity shop or played in a sports team.*
- *Benefit – what are the transferable skills you've acquired by doing this activity? For example, leadership, communication or self-motivation skills.*
- *Course – so you've done the activity and reaped the benefits, how does this relate to the course you're applying for? '*

'Good communication skills are vital for many university courses, especially during group work. You also need a lot of self-motivation in order to succeed on any undergraduate degree programme.

'Equally as important is a strong conclusion. Bear in mind, this is the last couple of lines in which you have to impress the admissions tutor. So make it count! Try to summarise your personal statement in a few lines and finish with a positive outlook on your future.'

Common errors

Apart from the obvious spelling and grammar mistakes (tip: don't rely on a spellchecker as it will not pick up everything and proofread your personal statement as many times as possible), these are the most common errors found by the unis we asked.

Kingston University

'It is too long, unfocused, uses bad grammar, names the institution they wish to progress to as it is not always the reviewer's university (eg I have always wanted to go to Camberwell when the reviewer is at Kingston University – immediate non-starter!)'

Robert Gordon University

'Not mentioning the course they have applied for. More and more, applications are being screened based on the personal statement. If there is no mention of the course or profession that demonstrates an understanding, then they are unlikely to be considered for entry.'

Bournemouth University

'Not explaining all the interesting (and relevant to the course) bits about themselves, and not linking their own interests, career goals, activities and skills specifically to the courses they're applying for. We aren't only interested in what they want to study and why – we also want to make sure that they're going to be happy and successful in their programme by choosing the one that most closely matches their intended outcomes and lifestyle.'

Your skills and achievements

Universities like to know the types of skills you have that will help you on the course, or more generally while you're at university. They also like to see if you've been involved in any accredited or non-accredited achievements. Include:

- non-accredited skills and achievement which you've gained through activities such as:
  - ASDAN (Award Scheme Development and Accreditation Network) awards, for example, Universities Award
  - CREST awards
  - Diploma of Achievement
  - Duke of Edinburgh Award
  - Millennium Volunteers Scheme
  - OCNW Level 3 Certificate in Personal Development for Progression (previously known as the Liverpool Enrichment Programme)
  - vfifty award
  - WorldWide Volunteering Certificate of Volunteering Achievement
  - Young Enterprise
- accreditation achieved for any activities in preparation for higher education, for example through the ASDAN Aimhigher Certificate of Personal Effectiveness (CoPE qualification)
- any other achievements that you are proud of, eg reaching grade 3 piano or being selected for the county cricket team
- positions of responsibility that you hold, or have held, both in and out of school, for example prefect or representative for a local charity
- attributes that make you interesting, special or unique.

Remember: your personal statement could be used as a basis for an interview, so be prepared to answer questions on it.

Student tip:

'State your achievements and how they've helped develop your qualities. Talk about your chosen subject, why you have chosen it, why you see yourself studying it and what past experiences you think make you suitable for the course.'

Hobbies and interests

Think about how your hobbies, interests and social activities demonstrate your skills and abilities. If there's anything that relates to your course or to the skills needed to complete a higher education course, include it – the more evidence the better.

The Assistant Registrar for Undergraduate Admissions from the University of Warwick says:

'The strongest applicants are those who can link their extra-curricular activities to their proposed course of study.'

Your statement will be more convincing and personal if you write about why an experience, activity or interest makes you a good candidate for the course. Include enough additional information to make it interesting and to demonstrate your own interest. Rather than making a statement such as:

'I enjoy badminton'

try to provide context and show what you have learnt:

'I play badminton twice a week with a club that plays in local competitions and I play in both singles and doubles matches. Doubles matches require good team working, an ability to support your partner, to devise a game plan but be able to adapt it as required and fast reactions. I enjoy the social side of the club and take responsibility for organising the social activities and fundraising events. This gives me an opportunity to develop my organisational and planning skills. Fitting in all these activities while keeping up with my academic studies demands good time management and I think I do that very well.'

Student tip:

'Getting a placement isn't always easy, but if you get the chance seize it, because it'll make your application stronger, as well as assuring you it's what you really want to do.'

Work experience

Include details of jobs, placements, work experience or voluntary work, particularly if it's relevant to your chosen courses. Try to link any experience to skills or qualities mentioned in the course entry requirements in Course Finder, university websites and prospectuses. For example, rather than just saying:

'I spent two weeks working at a department store. I enjoyed speaking to customers and helping them with their enquiries'

you could say:

'I spent two weeks managing customer enquiries at a department store. I learnt how to interact with customers and handle complaints. The experience

highlighted the importance of positive communication between a business and its customers, and taught me how to manage difficult enquiries effectively. I would like to develop this skill further by studying for a degree in public relations.'

If you are not in full-time education, you should give details of any relevant work experience, paid or unpaid, and information about your current or previous employment.

We asked some universities for their top tips about work experience:

The University of Nottingham

'A top tip would be for students to consider what they have gained from their work experience, what insight it has given them into their chosen profession, and how it impacted on their decision to study the course, rather than just focusing on what they did during their work experience.'

Bradford College

'We look for relevant work experience. This experience may be directly relevant to the course for which the student is applying, or the student may highlight in their personal statement what elements they have taken from their work that make it relevant.'

Kingston University

'We look for meaningful work experience in the student's chosen subject. It is interesting for us to see how the student secured a work placement. For example, "I had to write 50 letters and research every weekend so that I could gain relevant and valuable work experiences" rather than "my dad's firm wanted someone to help out so I spent a week with them".'

Student tip:

'I provided context to my previous studies: I mapped the skills from my job in IT management to my chosen humanities subject and the activity of studying, including the pace of working. I also included where my interest in the subject had arisen and further steps I would be taking prior to starting my course.'

Mature students

If you are applying as a mature student, use the personal statement to explain what you have been doing since leaving education, and provide additional evidence to support your application. We asked some universities if they had any specific advice for mature students when writing their personal statements.

'If you feel you've been out of education for a while and may appear rusty, why not explain how you have been keeping up with your reading or what other courses you have pursued in the gaps.' **Bournemouth University**

'Mature applicants should tell us about their prior experiences, particularly if they relate to their chosen field of study. They should tell us about how they plan to support themselves so we can see they have thought carefully about their career change.' **Kingston University**

'All students should emphasise their life experience and how it will help them on their chosen course. This is particularly pertinent for mature students who often have more life experience and may need to use this to compensate for a lack of recent academic experience.' **The University of Nottingham**

International students

If you're an international student, use the personal statement to tell universities why you want to study in the UK. Also try to answer these questions in your statement:

- How can you show that you can successfully complete a higher education course that is taught in English? Say if some of your studies have been taught or examined in English.
- Have you taken part in any activities where you have used English outside of your studies?

Personal statements may be in a different style to what you are used to in your own country, or for other countries you may be applying to. Make sure you read more about what should be considered when writing your personal statement at: **www.ucas.com/students/applying/howtoapply/personalstatement**

Here is some guidance offered by universities for international students.

'International students will need to show good command of the English language so best to get this checked by a family member or friend. However, don't be tempted to let them write it for you – it is often clear when parts of an application have been completed by different people, and it may be difficult to make an offer to a student when there is doubt over whether they have completed their own personal statement. This is especially true if you've used an agent – write your own personal statement first, then get them to look over it.' **Bournemouth University**

'International applicants should tell us why they wish to study in the UK and show that they have begun the process of visa application. They need to inform us of all language tests taken or pending, with dates and details of levels.'
Kingston University

'International students should include the same elements within their personal statements as all other students, with a focus on their chosen degree. They should also try to demonstrate why they are applying to study in the UK, and reference their ability to undertake university study in the English language.'
The University of Nottingham

Future plans

If you know what you'd like to achieve after completing a university course, explain how you want to use the knowledge and experience that you gain.

Don't be negative in your statement; put a positive slant on everything you can.

Applying to multiple courses

Remember that you only write one personal statement, so it will be used for all your choices. Try not to mention a university by name, even if you're applying to only one – your personal statement cannot be changed if you apply to a different place later.

If you're applying for a joint degree – explain why you are interested in both aspects of this joint programme.

If you're applying for different subjects or courses – identify the common themes and skills that are relevant to your choices. For example, both mathematics and law are subjects where you have to think logically and apply

Student tip:

'My advice would be to write down whatever you feel is relevant to your course and why. Don't worry if you do something that you feel isn't relevant; write it down anyway because it might be. For example, "I attended my school choir for five years" is probably not relevant. However, "I attended my school choir for five years, which has taught me to be committed" may be relevant.'

rules. You may like both subjects because you enjoy solving problems, using theory and natural or man-made laws to come to a correct conclusion.

If your chosen courses can't be linked by a common theme – think about your reasons for applying to such varied courses. It might be useful to speak to a careers adviser to get some guidance.

If you mention a subject in your personal statement and are applying to other courses, you may be asked by the university or college for additional information about why you have chosen alternative courses.

Attention-grabbing

Some statements start with quotes, some include jokes, some set out to be unusual or eye-catching. Sometimes it works, but it might have the opposite effect to what you hoped. The admissions decision-maker may not share your sense of humour so be careful when trying to make your statement stand out.

Write what comes naturally

In your personal statement you need to put your meaning across directly and simply. You can do this by keeping your sentences to an average of 12-20 words, and using English (or Welsh) in a way that is natural to you. Avoid sounding either over-familiar or over-formal and write to get yourself and your message across clearly. Check that each sentence adds something new, otherwise it is just adding to the word count rather than adding value.

The quality of your writing reflects the quality of your thinking. Show that you know your strengths and can outline your ideas clearly. Use words you know will be understood by the person reading your statement; you might find it easier if you imagine you are talking to them across their desk. In fact, you can sometimes spot where your statement doesn't work well by reading it aloud!

Dos and don'ts when writing your personal statement

Do create a list of your ideas before attempting to write the real thing.

Do expect to produce several drafts before being totally happy.

Do ask people you trust for their feedback.

Do check university and college prospectuses, websites and Course Finder (at **www.ucas.com**), as they usually tell you the criteria and qualities that they want their students to demonstrate.

Do use your best English/Welsh and **don't** let spelling and grammatical errors spoil your statement.

Do be enthusiastic – if you show your interest in the course, it may help you get a place.

Don't feel that you need to use elaborate language. If you try too hard to impress with long words that you are not confident using, the focus of your writing may be lost.

Don't say too much about things that are not relevant – if you think that you are starting to, take a break and come back to your statement when you feel more focused.

Don't lie – if you exaggerate you may get caught out at interview when asked to elaborate on an interesting achievement.

Don't rely on a spellchecker as it will not pick up everything – proofread as many times as possible.

Don't leave it to the last minute – your statement will seem rushed and important information could be left out.

Don't expect to be able to write your personal statement while watching TV or surfing the internet – this is your future, so make the most of the opportunity to succeed.

Student tip:

'It can't be stressed enough that you should begin your personal statement as early as possible! The best time is after AS exams so that you can get in a draft to your teachers and then work on their suggestions over the summer holidays.

'Make sure you give your personal statement to a range of people, like relevant subject teachers, family and friends. Once you've written your first sentence it usually flows from there. I actually found the very last sentence to be the hardest part and it has to be impactful without sounding too cheesy. But don't worry too much – eventually something will come to you!'

www.ucas.com

Similarity detection

We put all applications through similarity detection tests, which identify statements that have been copied from another source. The service we use, called Copycatch, finds statements that show similarity, works out how much of the statement may have been copied, and reports the findings. Don't be tempted to copy another person's application materials, or download your personal statement from a website. There could be serious consequences to using other people's work. If any part of your personal statement appears to have been copied, we will inform all the universities and colleges that you have applied to. They will then take the action they consider to be appropriate. We will also contact you by email.

What the Similarity Detection Service does

Each personal statement is checked against:

- a library of personal statements previously submitted to UCAS
- sample statements collected from a variety of websites
- other sources including paper publications.

Each personal statement received at UCAS is added to the library of statements after it has been processed.

What happens if a personal statement has similarities?

- Any statements showing a level of similarity of 10% or more are reviewed by members of the UCAS Similarity Detection Service Team.
- Applicants, universities and colleges are notified at the same time by email when an application has similarities confirmed.
- Admissions tutors at individual universities and colleges decide what action, if any, to take regarding reported cases.
- If you applied through a school, college or other UCAS-registered centre, we and the universities and colleges might, with your consent, communicate direct with the centre to seek further information on it.

Eliminated words: the Copycatch process ignores commonly used words that many applicants use in their statements such as 'and', 'so' and 'with'. Copycatch also ignores a selection of commonly used words and phrases including 'Duke of Edinburgh' and 'football'.

What are the most common opening sentences used in personal statements?

The table below details the most common personal statement opening sentences from the UCAS scheme in the 2011 application cycle:

Rank	Sentence	Number of statements
1	I am currently studying a BTEC National Diploma in ...	403
2	From a young age I have always been interested in ...	287
3	Nursing is a very challenging and demanding career ...	236
4	From an early age I have always been interested in ...	234
5	Nursing is a profession I have always looked upon with ...	211
6	"Fashion is not something that exists in dresses only"...	193
7	For as long as I can remember I have been fascinated with ...	164
8	I am an International Academy student and have been studying since ...	131
9	For as long as I can remember I have been interested in ...	129
10	Academically, I have always been a very determined and ...	129
11	I am applying for a place to study social work because ...	112
12	I am currently studying for a BTEC National Diploma ...	106

Applicants found to have a level of similarity of 10% or above

The figures in **bold** show those detected by the Similarity Detection Service (SDS).

Year of entry	UCAS applicants	GTTR applicants	CUKAS applicants	Total number of applicants	Applicants detected by SDS
2011	700,161	61,900	3,914	765,975	**29,757 (3.88%)**
2010	697,351	67,289	3,901	768,541	**29,228 (3.80%)**
2009	639,860	63,138	3,841	706,839	**20,086 (2.84%)**
2008	588,689	N/A	N/A	588,689	**17,811 (3.03%)**
2007	In a pilot study of 50,000 UCAS applicants, approximately **5%** were detected by SDS				

You can find further guidance about the UCAS Similarity Detection Service at **www.ucas.com/students/applying/howtoapply/personalstatement/similarity detection**.

Personal statement – FAQs

Does the word limit really matter?

Yes, it does. The limit is there for a reason and a key test of the process is to check whether you are able to explain your reasons for wanting to study in a clear and succinct way.

I'm not interesting or unique... what should I do?

Everyone has aspects to their personality that make them interesting; it is just a case of putting them into words. You might find it helpful to ask someone close to you such as a friend, relative or teacher. The hardest part of the process is getting started, so at first try not to confine yourself to a word limit or worry too much about the structure – just get your ideas down.

Student tip:

'Don't write things to make yourself someone you're not. It is a personal statement, not a fictional story! Think about what you want to do and incorporate that into your statement. It is no good telling them you're brilliant at balloon modelling when you are applying to be a dentist. Take the time to make notes and plan your statement. Dissect your life experiences into skills that you can use for university and in future life.'

What balance should I make between my course interests and my extra-curricular activities?

There's no clear rule for how much of the personal statement should be allocated to course-related interests and skills, and how much for hobbies and other activities. The importance placed on the information varies between universities, colleges and courses. What is important to remember is that a good personal statement will usually manage to link most activities back to your chosen degree.

Case study

Name: Emma Alexander
Applying to study Politics, Philosophy and Economics

The personal statement is, in my opinion, the most important thing about your application that can be easily influenced. You can have 50 A*s at GCSE, AAAAAAAA at AS, and still run the risk of being rejected by your universities if you submit them a piece summarising your life that makes you seem like the most boring stick-in-the-mud to ever walk the earth.

I started writing my personal statement in the summer and the first draft is pretty embarrassing. Having been afraid of plunging into the thing properly, I decided not to make it particularly serious and so the document began with 'PPE is my aim, my dream, blah blah blah'. In the margins I'd written, perhaps wisely, 'come back to this later...' Underneath that I listed my A levels. Perhaps I was worried I'd forget them? Underneath that was a thick paragraph of book titles I intended to read during the summer (but didn't); following on from that were the details of an essay competition I intended to enter during the summer (but didn't); and the rest consisted of doodles, repeated statements, and excuses regarding why I'd failed to flesh the thing out.

When I started writing my personal statement I didn't even use that bit of paper as reference material. I ended up preparing for my application by doing work experience during the summer. It was so much easier to get into a groove with that on my mind, instead of what was essentially a 'to do' list. Anyway, one thing I do know is that if I was as successful at trimming the fat in real life as I ended up having to be when writing my personal statement, then I wouldn't have to worry about binge-eating after completing a particularly successful trawl of the internet for rejection statistics.

I started out at 5,500 characters and I tell you this – it can be rescued when it's that long. I managed to cut it down to 4,000 without losing anything of value. Mostly by getting rid of 'nothing-words' like 'particularly', 'really', 'very' and 'relatively', as well as a useless joke about how, at the age of 7, I'd considered the words philosophy, politics and economics to be indicative of extreme boredom.

To anyone who has yet to write theirs, these are the most important things to remember. Firstly, utilise all 4,000 characters. There's an urban legend about a pupil applying for geography who made their personal statement into the shape of a tree using appropriate spacing. It's funny, but the content suffers. Also, instead of just listing your various achievements and endeavours, every university stresses how important it is to reflect on these experiences and really demonstrate what you gained from them that makes you a more prominent applicant. Particularly, show that you aren't just someone who is content to sit in lessons and not exhibit academic curiosity. Talk about your studies and reading outside class. However, it's still important to link your current studies with your future studies, and show how they stimulated your interest in the course.

If you're applying to different courses at different institutions (like me – I'm applying to one which does not involve philosophy), make sure the personal statement is entirely relevant for each, and that the courses are sufficiently similar so your application does not suffer on both fronts.

Most importantly, don't lie. You'll regret it later, and it's unfair for the thousands of others applying entirely fairly up and down the country. Most of all, enjoy it. It's an opportunity to show who you are academically and it gives you a chance to draw together everything you've done. It might end up surprising you – you may have done more than you think.

Applying for medicine, dentistry, veterinary science or veterinary medicine

Early deadline: If you're applying for medicine, dentistry, veterinary science or veterinary medicine you'll need to submit your application to UCAS by the early deadline of 15 October.

Admissions tests: For most medicine, dentistry, veterinary science or veterinary medicine courses you'll need to sit an admissions test for the course(s) you are applying for. You can check this in the entry requirements for your chosen courses on Course Finder at **www.ucas.com**. You can read more about admissions tests on pages 101 to 114 in the Choosing courses section.

Interviews: You'll normally be interviewed by the university before they decide whether to offer you a place or not. If they want to invite you for an interview, this will usually be displayed in UCAS Track. You can accept the invitation in Track, or if you are unable to attend, you can request that the university offers you a different date.

Medicine

We asked Imperial College some questions about making an application to study medicine with them. They offered the useful guidance below about what to include in an application and gave an insight into their selection process.

Personal statement

What are you looking for within a personal statement to make it stand out?
'To make a personal statement stand out, we advise that applicants demonstrate their suitability for the course. We want to see their skills and experience that will demonstrate their suitability because medicine is a very demanding subject. We want to be sure that applicants can show that they are motivated to study medicine. Applicants need to clearly explain why they are applying for medicine, and why they would be a strong candidate.'

What are the most common errors made in personal statements?
'The most common errors include saying too much in the statement about things that are not relevant.'

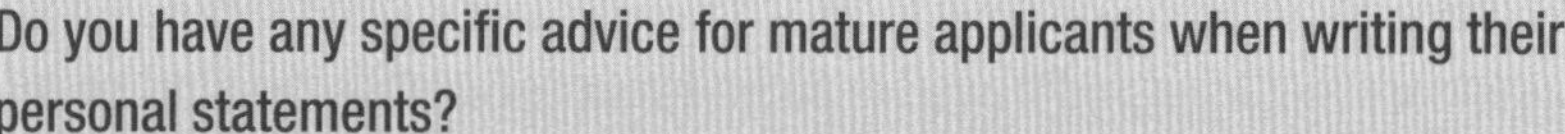

Do you have any specific advice for mature applicants when writing their personal statements?
'It would be beneficial for mature applicants to explain what they have been doing since leaving education, and provide additional evidence to support their application. If applicants are not in full-time education, they should try and give details of any relevant work experience, and information about their current or previous employment.'

Selection

Can you give a brief explanation of what happens to an application once it's received at your university?
'Admission for medicine at Imperial is highly competitive. For the six-year course, we generally receive well over 2,000 applications for entry and interview about 650 candidates. Approximately 500 offers are made, and 283 students will be admitted in October. For the four-year graduate entry course, we receive around

800 applications for our 47 places, so we interview around 100 candidates for those places.

'Once applications are received, a range of criteria will be used to assess applicants. The School of Medicine has a comprehensive admissions policy that ensures that all applications are dealt with in the same way. Applications are assessed to make sure that candidates fulfil the minimum requirements.'

What are your selection criteria when considering applicants?
'A range of criteria is used to assess candidates. They must meet the minimum academic requirements outlined in our entrance requirements.

'For the six-year undergraduate course, candidates must have obtained or be predicted to gain grades in GCSE, A level and AS, International or European Baccalaureate, or other acceptable qualifications that satisfy the School of Medicine's academic criteria.

'For the four-year graduate entry course, candidates must have obtained a minimum of an upper second in an acceptable biomedical subject. In addition, depending on the course, candidates must have the Biomedical Admissions Test (BMAT) or UK Clinical Aptitude Test (UKCAT) and apply by the deadline. Candidates must have high marks for sections of the relevant admission test. (See pages 101 to 114 for more information about admissions tests.)

'No offers are made without applicants attending an interview. The only exception is the biomedical science course, where offers are made without an interview.'

How do you decide which applicants to shortlist for interview or audition?
'If a candidate fulfils the minimum entry requirements and has scores in the top rankings for all three sections of BMAT, or has outstanding UKCAT scores, his or her application will be passed to an experienced member of the selection panel. The selection panel comprises of academics and clinicians with experience in the admissions process, who will decide whether to offer the candidate an interview. These decisions are ratified by one of the admissions tutors.

'The panel members look at the following criteria when assessing applications:

- *GCSE results*
- *A level and AS or equivalent predicted (or achieved) grades*

- *degrees (for the graduate entry course)*
- *BMAT or UKCAT scores*
- *motivation and understanding of medicine as a career*
- *community activities*
- *leadership and teamwork*
- *general interests*
- *the UCAS application reference.'*

Myth busters

'Common myths relating to the School of Medicine include:

- *There are no women on the course. In reality, the number of women on the medicine course is actually higher than men.*
- *Imperial is 'geeky' and there is a lot of hard work. Yes, the medicine course is very demanding and it entails a lot of hard work. However the School of Medicine is part of two active student unions; the larger umbrella Imperial College Union, and the Imperial College School of Medicine Student Union. The unions host a variety of clubs and societies with participation at every level.'*

Medicine and dentistry

Peninsula Schools of Medicine & Dentistry at Plymouth University offered the following advice and guidance to potential medicine and dentistry students.

What are you looking for within a student's personal statement which will make them stand out?
'Peninsula Schools of Medicine & Dentistry do not score personal statements as there is no evidence to prove that they have been written by the applicant. We prefer to assess applicants face-to-face at interview. We do, however, read all personal statements to ensure that the applicant has not said anything that would lead us to believe that they would not make a good doctor or dentist.'

What are your selection criteria when considering applicants?
'Peninsula Schools of Medicine & Dentistry select direct school leavers mainly on achieved GCSE grades and achieved or predicted GCE A/AS grades (or equivalent), together with UKCAT scores. Non-direct school leavers are selected on the basis of GAMSAT scores.'

Myth busters

'It is not easy to get into Peninsula Schools of Medicine & Dentistry at Plymouth University. Approximately 10 applications per place are received for medicine and seven applications per place for dentistry. Only one third of applicants are selected to attend an interview. However, both Schools will consider applicants who have not achieved all grade A or A at GCSE.'*

Work experience

If you're applying for medicine, dentistry, veterinary science or medicine, most universities will expect you to have gained some relevant work experience. We asked several universities what type of work experience they were looking for and how this can enhance an application.

University of Oxford

'For medicine, some work experience in hospitals is theoretical desirable, but we do appreciate that it can be very difficult to arrange and we therefore have no requirement for it. Some candidates are exposed to more opportunities in this area than others. Any form of voluntary work would be beneficial in the context of applying for medicine (such as helping out in a hospital, at an old people's home, St John's ambulance, or work with a charity or overseas agency).'

Peninsula Schools of Medicine & Dentistry at Plymouth University

'Peninsula Schools of Medicine & Dentistry are committed to widening access to medicine and dentistry. Therefore, we do not insist on work experience in a healthcare setting, as it favours those applicants who have contacts in the health profession. However, we do recommend that applicants undertake any work experience that may help them improve some of the personal qualities that we assess at interview, eg communication skills, team work and flexibility.'

Imperial College

We would like applicants to provide examples of jobs, placements, work experience or voluntary work, and to indicate how it might be relevant to the medicine course. For example, this could include placements in a healthcare setting, working with charities, and any form of volunteering.

'Work experience can enhance an application because it would show us the candidate has a realistic understanding of what is involved in a career in medicine and thus be a sound basis to decide whether such a career would suit them. Although we would like to see a sustained commitment, we understand that this is not always possible. Candidates should expect the interview panel to explore what they have gained from their work experience.'

The University of Nottingham

'Medicine, veterinary medicine [courses]... may require students to reflect on their relevant work experience in detail and identify what they have gained from the experience, including an insight into their chosen profession.

'We find that those applying for vocational subjects, such as medicine, are sometimes too descriptive about what they did during their work experience, rather than focusing on what they got out of the experience, what they observed (eg interaction between patient and carer, how individuals react differently depending on how we're feeling), and the impact it had on their decision to enter the profession.'

Veterinary science

The University of Bristol has offered information about how applications to its veterinary science undergraduate courses are processed; along with tips on writing your personal statement, and what to expect if you are invited to an interview.

'All applications are considered on an equal basis. Applications are not segregated by the type of educational institution attended. Applications are initially screened on the basis of educational achievements and predictions. A second screening ranks the student in terms of the following:

- *a realistic interest in veterinary science*
- *knowledge of the scope of careers in veterinary science*
- *work experience in veterinary practice, on farms and in other settings*
- *interests outside veterinary science*
- *school, college or community activities*
- *evidence of initiative and non-academic achievements.*

This information is obtained from the personal statement and the reference on your UCAS application.

Finally, the admissions tutor makes a judgment as to whether the application has been:

1. *Unsuccessful.*
2. *Successful - possibly interview.*
3. *Successful - definitely interview.*

Some applicants may be interviewed soon after selection, but others will be held for possible interview, dependent upon numbers of applicants. All students are informed of the admissions panel's decision in writing. The aim is to respond to all applicants within four weeks of receipt of application, in order to establish contact and inform them of the process to be followed.'

Interviews

'Interviews are held from November until March. Applicants are interviewed by two individuals (at least one of whom will have been trained in fair and effective recruitment techniques) using 20-minute interview slots. A third member of staff may be present in the room to observe the process. Interviews are undertaken in accordance with the university's policy on equal opportunities.

Each team of interviewers is asked to place the applicants within one of three categories:

- *exceptional*
- *acceptable*
- *unacceptable.*

The acceptable group is further broken down by order of merit (1 to 8).

After each day of interviewing, offers are usually made within 48 hours to all exceptional candidates. Applicants ranked as either 1 or 2 in the acceptable group will be informed that they are being held; all other candidates will be informed that they have been unsuccessful at this stage. The on-hold applicants will be monitored by the admissions tutor, with further offers being made if places are still available in February or March.

International applicants are treated in a manner similar to the above, taking into account the exam structure of the country they live in, but they may be offered a telephone interview.'

Personal statements and interviews

'Important criteria in your personal statement and, particularly, the interview include:

- *a proven interest in veterinary science and commitment to the subject and career*
- *evidence of work experience both with veterinary surgeons as well as with animals*

- *evidence of clear thinking and understanding, problem solving, scientific knowledge and analytical skills*
- *evidence of effective team working, interpersonal and communication skills*
- *evidence of commitment to others*
- *non-academic achievements and extra-curricular interests*
- *positions of responsibility; voluntary or paid work*
- *evidence of relevant reading or research beyond the school or college syllabus*
- *evidence of motivation and commitment; a self-propelled learner!'*

Thoughts from two professionals...

Junior doctor

Dr Nina Reeve, who works as a junior doctor in a general hospital, offered this advice to potential medicine students:

'It's a great job with so much variety. You can really find a speciality that suits your personality. You do have to work hard and work lots of nights and weekends. You also still have lots of exams to do after you qualify in order to progress to your chosen speciality. I like it because no two days are the same, you get to meet lots of people, both colleagues and patients, and so it is a very sociable job.

'There is also plenty of opportunity to travel and work abroad for a year. Most people do this after foundation training and before speciality training and usually end up in Australia and New Zealand. There are difficult times, and times where you think is medicine worth it, and these are the times that test you because to do medicine, you need to love it, otherwise you wouldn't be able to do it well.

'I absolutely love it and can't imagine doing a 9-5 and living for the weekends. Of course there is a life outside of medicine, but I think that you should love your job and that way both you and your employer get the most out of the situation. It is a big commitment and you have to miss things such as bank holidays and Christmas occasionally but when a patient and their family thanks you for what you have done for them, I promise it's worth it.'

Small animal vet

Small animal first opinion vet, Caroline Queen, had this to say to anyone thinking of studying veterinary science or veterinary medicine:

'If someone wants to do veterinary science or veterinary medicine then be single-minded and don't be put off! Be persistent, even if you are initially rejected. Get as much work experience as you can in as many different disciplines as possible, for example dairy farming, lambing, kennel work, small animal practice, equine practice, farm animal practice, abattoir work.

'My advice would be to work hard, play hard, and at the end of the course you'll have a good qualification, and have had the most carefree, fun years of your life!

'If you are sure it is what you want to do, then go for it! Don't do it if the reason is for financial gain as there are lots more higher paid, but less rewarding jobs. Being a veterinary surgeon is a lifestyle, and a profession. There will be times when you are exhausted, but extremely rewarded by the work that you and your colleagues are doing.'

Other websites you may find useful

Medschools online is a free information resource for people who are considering applying to study medicine in the UK: **www.medschoolsonline.co.uk**

Widening Access to Medical School – a resource for potential medical students: **www.wanttobeadoctor.co.uk**

New Media Medicine – an online community of doctors, medical students and applicants to medical school from around the world: **www.newmediamedicine.com**

British Medical Association – includes advice about careers in medicine and a guide to medical student finance: **www.bma.org.uk**

Dental Schools Council provides advice on education and research in UK dental schools: **www.dentalschoolscouncil.ac.uk**

British Dental Association offers advice about careers and education in dentistry: **www.bda.org**

NHS Careers gives information about working within the NHS: **www.nhscareers.nhs.uk**

British Veterinary Association has a 'Student centre' section on its website: **www.bva.co.uk**

'Emma the TV Vet' – this website includes advice about getting into vet school: **www.emmathevet.co.uk**

Applying for Oxford and Cambridge

Early deadline: the application deadline for all courses at the Universities of Oxford and Cambridge is 15 October.

Admissions tests: Depending on the course, you may need to take an admissions test or tests. It's very important to check this so that you don't miss any deadlines. More information about admissions tests is available on pages 101 to 114 and on the universities' websites.

If you're applying to the University of Cambridge, you may be required to complete one or more application forms in addition to the UCAS application. These forms should be sent to the university, not to UCAS.

- **If you're applying from outside the EU**, you must submit a Cambridge Online Preliminary Application (COPA) in addition to a UCAS application by 15 October (for courses starting the following year). This applies to all applicants who are living in a country outside the EU and is regardless of fees status or nationality. If you are an overseas student but are studying at a school in the UK you do not need to submit a COPA.

Official figures from the Higher Education Statistics Agency (HESA) show that, for 2009/10 entry, 59.3% of full-time first degree entrants to the University of Cambridge were from state schools or colleges; the figure for the University of Oxford was 54.3% *(Source: HESA Performance Indicators. Reproduced by permission of the Higher Education Statistics Agency Limited. HESA cannot accept responsibility for any conclusions or inferences derived from the data by third parties.)*

- **If you would like to be considered for an interview in a country outside the EU** where interviews are held, earlier deadlines usually apply for receipt of your COPA. You should consult the University of Cambridge website for details.
- **If you're applying for the Graduate Course in Medicine (UCAS code A101)**, you must submit a Graduate Course in Medicine Application Form by 15 October.
- **If you are applying for an Organ Award**, you must submit a Cambridge Online Preliminary Application. Earlier deadlines also apply.

See the University of Cambridge website at **www.study.cam.ac.uk/undergraduate/** for further details.

The University of Oxford does not require a separate application form, except for students applying for medicine course A101 (fast-track graduate entry only), or those applying for a choral or organ scholarship. For some courses you may need to submit written work to the university. Check the University of Oxford website at **www.admissions.ox.ac.uk** for more details.

In December, the Universities of Oxford and Cambridge hold their interviews for undergraduate applicants. See pages 223 to 233 for examples of interview questions you may be asked by the University of Oxford or the University of Cambridge.

University of Cambridge

We spoke to the University of Cambridge, who gave this useful information for those of you who are thinking of applying to them:

How important is the applicant's personal statement when applying to Cambridge?
'An applicant's personal statement is one of the many sources of information the University of Cambridge uses to assess an application. A personal statement should reflect why you want to study the course you have applied for and indicate any additional independent work you have done that further illustrates your interest and understanding of the subject.'

There are still misconceptions about the University of Cambridge. Here are some myth busters, provided by the university itself:

Myth 1: Cambridge is not for people like me, I won't fit in there.
There is no typical personality type at Cambridge and students come from all sorts of backgrounds. Cambridge is no different from any other university – you will always find plenty of like-minded people.

Myth 2: So many people apply, I have no chance of getting in.
The odds of getting a place at Cambridge are better than 1 in 5. Many other universities have far more applicants per place. There is no 'secret' to making a successful application. We are looking for students who have academic potential, are best suited to the course in question, and who will most benefit from what we have to offer, whatever their background.

University tip:

'More than 1 in 5 applicants are successful in gaining a place at Cambridge.'

Myth 3: Cambridge selects applicants who are good at everything.

We select on academic ability alone: enthusiasm, knowledge and interest in your subject is much more important than extra-curricular participation.

Myth 4: There's so much work you don't have time for any fun.
With many student societies, Cambridge students participate in a huge range of activities outside their studies.

University of Oxford

The University of Oxford give us an insight into the application process and its selection criteria:

Are your applicants required to complete any other forms in addition to the UCAS application?
'No, most students are not required to complete any forms in addition to the UCAS application. The only extra forms required are those for students who wish to apply for an organ or choral scholarship, or those applying for fast-track graduate entry medicine, A101.'

Student tip:

'Because I had decided to apply to Oxford my application had to be in a lot earlier than everyone else's. But this is no bad thing. Not only is all the pressure of making those life decisions off you, you can also relax over Christmas rather than trying to rush off a personal statement.'

What are you looking for within a personal statement to make it stand out?
'We are looking for evidence that students are really passionate about their chosen degree course, and committed to studying it. We're interested to know what inspires you about your subject, and why you want to study it at university.

'However, please do remember that the personal statement is only one aspect of the application that Oxford will consider: tutors here will also look at the grades you have already achieved, predicted grades for future qualifications, your academic reference, and performance in any written test or written work required for your course. If your application is shortlisted, you will be invited to Oxford for an interview, and your performance in that interview will also be considered.'

What are the most common errors made in personal statements?
'Sometimes students devote too much of their personal statement to information about extra-curricular activities. These activities are welcomed at Oxford, but please bear in mind that they will only strengthen your application if they help to demonstrate how you meet the selection criteria for your course. For more information please see ***www.admissions.ox.ac.uk/selectioncriteria****.'*

What work experience are you looking for and how can this enhance an application?
'Our tutors select students using the agreed selection criteria for each course. All candidates are free to refer to skills or experience acquired in any context when trying to address these criteria, which can certainly include reference to voluntary work and other extra-curricular activity. However, neither work experience nor extra-curricular activities are formally required, as many forms of evidence can help demonstrate to tutors that a candidate has researched their decision to study a particular course, and meets the selection criteria.'

(If you are applying for medicine at the University of Oxford, read what they said about work experience specifically for medicine applicants on page 182.)

Can you give a brief explanation of what happens to an application once it's received at your university?
'The first thing that we do is see how many applications there are for each subject at each college. We then look at all the students who have made open applications, and allocate them to colleges which have relatively fewer

applications for their subject in that year. This helps to make sure that colleges are considering roughly equal numbers of candidates for each place.

'Applications are then passed on to tutors, who will consider ***all*** *the information on the UCAS application:*

- *existing grades*
- *predicted grades*
- *personal statement*
- *reference*

as well as

- *your performance in any written test or tests*
- *written work required for your course*

and, for graduate applicants

- *the transcript of your first degree.*

'If you haven't done particularly well in any one of these areas, you may still be shortlisted. Tutors consider each application on its individual merits, and will take your personal circumstances into account, where these have been mentioned in your personal statement or academic reference. Some contextual data is also taken into account.'

What are your selection criteria when considering applicants?
'Tutors are looking for students with the academic abilities and potential to thrive at Oxford, and for those with passion and commitment for their chosen degree course. For further details please see ***www.admissions.ox.ac.uk/selectioncriteria****.'*

How do you decide which applicants to shortlist for interview or audition?
'During the shortlisting process, Oxford tutors will consider the personal statement and academic reference, grades already achieved and predicted grades for future qualifications as well as performance in any written test or written work required for the course. Some contextual data is also taken in to account.'

Myth busters

Myth 1: Many people seem to think Oxford's admissions process is designed to be as intimidating and confusing as possible but nothing could be further from the truth.

We go to huge efforts to be as open and transparent as we can, including offering videos of admissions interviews, putting sample interview questions on the web, and providing podcasts with further information. We even have a dedicated team of staff here specifically to answer questions from applicants, their parents, teachers and other advisers.

The university itself is also very different from the image sometimes presented in the media. Oxford students are very diverse, from all different backgrounds, from all parts of the UK and around the world.

In other sections of this book, you can find more information and advice from the Universities of Oxford and Cambridge (including specific guidance for disabled, international and mature applicants) about their admissions tests, selection process, interviews, bursaries, and what to expect if you start studying at the university.

Myth 2: Some students think that Oxford has quotas for state schools, independent schools and international students, or that we favour one type of student over another.

We have no quotas for the types of student that we will admit: each application to Oxford University is assessed on its individual merits. We do look at some contextual data, to help tutors understand the circumstances in which your qualifications have been achieved, but the most important aspect of our selection process is that we want to recruit the very best and brightest students, whatever their background.

(The one exception is for medicine, where there is a Government-imposed quota which allows us to admit a maximum of 14 students who are classified as international students for fees purposes.)

Applying for Oxford and Cambridge – FAQs

Which college should I choose?

For admission to Oxford or Cambridge, it is necessary to be accepted by a college. Under 'Campus code' in the Choices section of your application, select the appropriate campus code to denote your choice of college. Applications may be submitted without a nominated college by selecting the 'Open application' option.

You can contact the universities direct for information about all of their colleges. Try to visit the college if possible, or arrange to attend an open day. This will help you decide if you feel comfortable with the college and with the university.

Can I apply to both Oxford AND Cambridge?

You can apply to only one course at either the University of Oxford or the University of Cambridge. You cannot apply to both universities. The only exception to this is if you will be a graduate at the start of the course and are applying for course code A101 (graduate medicine) at the University of Cambridge. Then you can also apply to course code A100 (medicine) at Cambridge, in addition to being able to apply to course code A101 (graduate medicine) at the University of Oxford.

Chapter checklist

These are the things you should be doing in Step 2 of your applicant journey:

- ☐ Check the deadline for your chosen course(s) on Course Finder at **www.ucas.com**.
- ☐ Watch the UCAStv video guide *How to apply* at **www.ucas.tv**.
- ☐ Register on Apply at **www.ucas.com** and **keep your username and password in a safe place**.
- ☐ If you have a disability or special needs watch our UCAStv video guides *Students with disabilities* and *Advice from disability officers* at **www.ucas.tv**.
- ☐ Check if you need to take an admissions test for the course(s) you've chosen.
- ☐ If you're applying to the University of Cambridge check with them if you need to complete an additional application form.
- ☐ If you're applying for medicine, dentistry, nursing, midwifery or certain other health courses, check the immunisation and certification requirements with your unis.
- ☐ Look at our personal statement timeline and plan when you need to start researching and writing it.
- ☐ Check uni prospectuses and websites, and **www.ucas.com** – you'll find info about the criteria and qualities they're looking for in personal statements.
- ☐ Use our personal statement mind map and worksheet to help you think about what to include.
- ☐ Watch the UCAStv video guide to writing a personal statement at **www.ucas.tv**.
- ☐ Check the spelling and grammar in your personal statement. Don't rely on a spellchecker as it will not pick up everything – proofread as many times as possible and ask other people to read it for you.

Step 3
Offers

This section explains what happens after you've sent your application to us and it's been processed. It provides advice on preparing for and attending interviews and auditions. It describes the different decisions unis can make and explains the difference between conditional and unconditional offers. You'll also find out about replying to offers and when you can accept a second offer as an insurance.

In this section you'll discover all the things you can do using our online Track service at ucas.com, including making changes to your application, finding out your unis' decisions, replying to offers and starting your student finance application.

If you don't receive any offers, you'll find out how you can apply for further courses.

Step 3 **Offers**

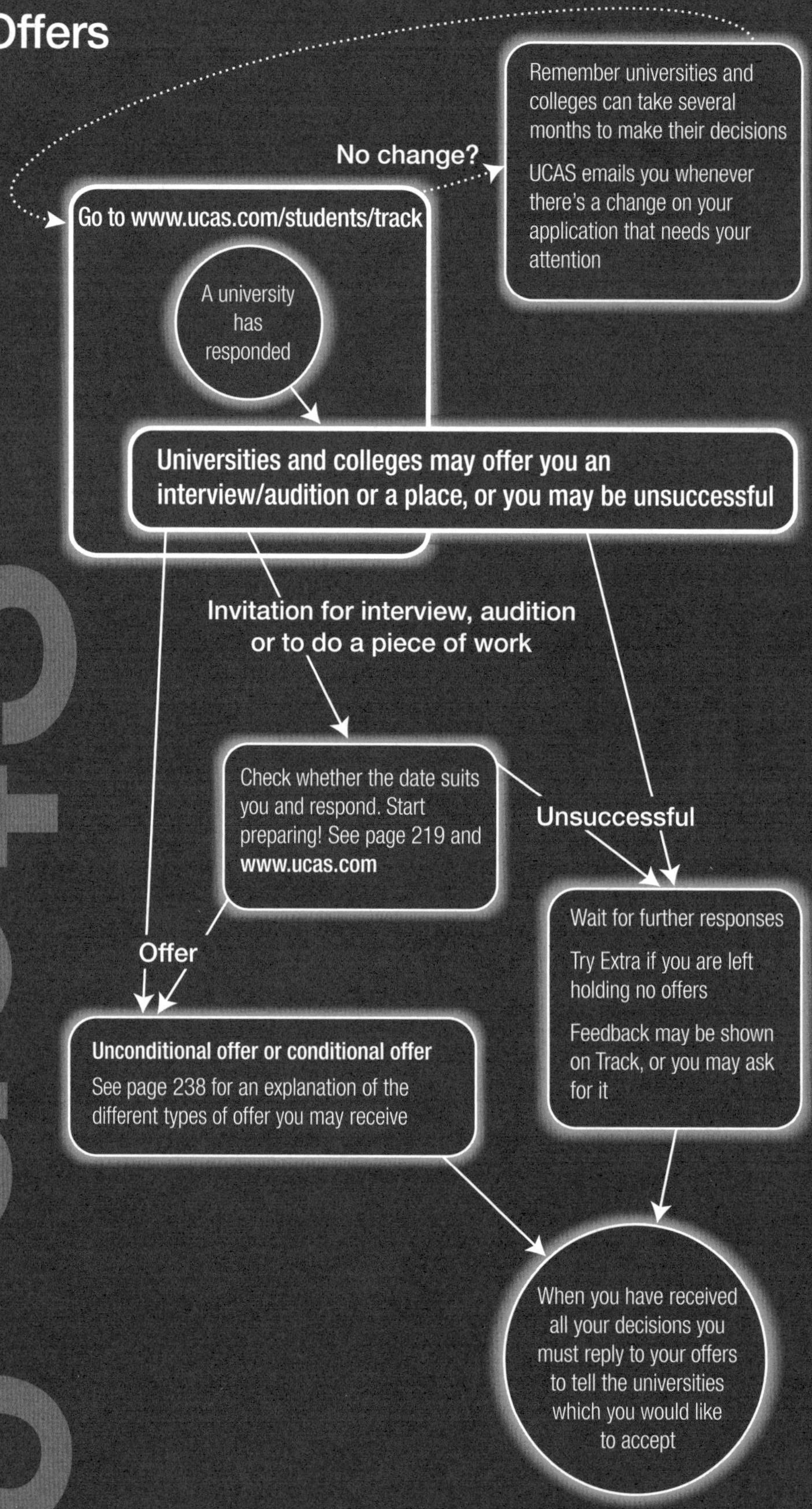

Go to www.ucas.com/students/track

No change?

Remember universities and colleges can take several months to make their decisions

UCAS emails you whenever there's a change on your application that needs your attention

A university has responded

Universities and colleges may offer you an interview/audition or a place, or you may be unsuccessful

Invitation for interview, audition or to do a piece of work

Check whether the date suits you and respond. Start preparing! See page 219 and **www.ucas.com**

Unsuccessful

Wait for further responses

Try Extra if you are left holding no offers

Feedback may be shown on Track, or you may ask for it

Offer

Unconditional offer or conditional offer

See page 238 for an explanation of the different types of offer you may receive

When you have received all your decisions you must reply to your offers to tell the universities which you would like to accept

Step 3

After you apply

What happens next?

After we've received your completed application, the following things happen:

- We process all the information you've provided and if we need to query anything, we contact you for more details.
- After processing your application, we send you a Welcome letter that lists your choices. We ask you to check your personal details and choices carefully and let us know immediately if anything is not correct. We also ask you to contact us if you don't receive your Welcome letter within 14 days of sending your application to us.
- You will have researched your chosen unis and courses thoroughly before you applied, so there should be no need to change your choices. However, you may make changes in Track for seven days from the date on your Welcome letter, provided it's before 30 June.
- You can view your application in our online Track service using your Personal ID and the same username and password you used to apply. We print your Personal ID and username on your Welcome letter. To find out about our Track service see page 201.

- Once your application is processed, unis can access it online. They can view your application, but they will not see where else you have applied. They'll only see any other choices after you have replied to your offers. Unis may contact you to tell you that they are considering your application. Not all of them do this, so don't worry if you don't hear from some of your choices.
- The unis consider your application against their own admissions requirements. Each has their own way of working, so you can expect to hear from them at different times. You may be contacted quite quickly or it may be some months before you hear anything.
- They decide whether or not to offer you a place and send their decision to us. Decisions are displayed in Track as soon as we receive them. For information about decisions, see page 237.
- If you have one or more offers and you've received decisions from all your unis, we'll ask you to reply to your offers. See page 247 for information about replying to offers.

Messages from UCAS

Throughout the application cycle, you'll receive messages from us about changes to the status of your application. After we have processed your application and sent it to your unis, we send you a Welcome letter and a *Your UCAS Welcome Guide* booklet, which explains the next stages of the application process. We ask you to check all the information in your Welcome letter and let us know if anything is wrong.

Each time we receive a decision from one of your unis we send you an email asking you to log in to Track to look at the change and read our online letters. When the last uni makes a decision, it's time to reply to any offers you've received.

After you've replied to your offers, we send you a Status Check letter to confirm that we've recorded your offer replies correctly. You need to contact us if any replies on the letter are wrong.

We send you a Confirmation letter when you accept an unconditional offer or when a uni confirms your place after your exam results are published. This letter will tell you whether or not you need to take any further action.

If you've received no offers or you don't have a confirmed place from the offers you accepted, we send you a New Options letter, which explains what you might do next.

If you or the unis tell us that you want to withdraw your whole application, we send you a Complete Withdrawal letter.

You can view your letters online in Track. These will be in Welsh if you requested correspondence from UCAS in Welsh when you applied.

Applicants with disabilities

You may have discussed your disability and requirements with unis before deciding where to apply. However, if you still have any doubts about how your unis will meet your needs or you want to see the facilities for yourself, contact the admissions officer or the head of department for your course. They will be used to arranging visits and will welcome enquiries from disabled students.

During your visit ask tutors about different course options and the number of assignments, lectures and seminars. Talk to them about how your individual needs can be met. Find out what kinds of adjustments the uni will make so you can complete your course. If you'll need flexible exam arrangements, discuss these as well. If a uni agrees to adapt buildings and/or elements of your course, ask them to put this in writing.

Most unis have a disability coordinator who should be able to help with disability-related questions and tell you about the uni's services for disabled students, including accommodation and support arrangements. You may also be able to meet accommodation staff and try out the facilities in halls.

The disability coordinator may be able to arrange for you to speak to students who are on the course you are interested in and other disabled students at the uni. Students will be able to tell you about the level of work expected and any difficulties they have had. Disabled students can tell you how good they find the support arrangements and what life is like there.

If the people you meet are not able to answer your questions, ask to speak to someone who can or ask for information to be sent to you. If you have further questions after your visit, don't be afraid to ask.

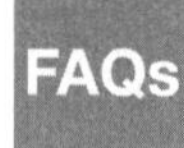

After you apply – FAQs

What happens to my application after I've sent it to UCAS?
When we receive your application we validate the information you have provided. We check whether or not you have already applied in the current application cycle and whether any of your personal statement has been copied from another source. We then send the application to your chosen unis for consideration.

When will I receive my Welcome letter?
We send you a Welcome letter after we've processed your application and sent it to your chosen unis. If you haven't received this letter within 14 days of sending your application to us, call our Customer Contact Centre.

I've sent my application to you. Why can't I get into Track?
You will only be able to log in to Track after we have fully processed your application and you've received your Welcome letter.

When will I hear from my unis?
If we receive your application by 15 January, unis must make their decisions by early May, but you could hear from them much earlier.

Why are the unis on my Welcome letter in a different order to my application?
The order of your universities was changed when we processed your application. The order does not indicate any preference because your application is sent to all your unis at the same time.

Why is my Welcome letter in Welsh?
When you applied you must have ticked the box to receive correspondence in Welsh. You need to call our Customer Contact Centre to amend your application.

Track

When you receive your Welcome letter, you can follow the progress of your application using the online Track service on the UCAS website. You log in to Track with your Personal ID and the username and password that you used when you made your application. We print your Personal ID and username on your Welcome letter. For security reasons your password is not printed on this letter. Don't worry if you can't remember your login details; Track has a 'Forgotten login details?' service.

When you've logged in to Track you see the 'Welcome' screen below with links to the different sections for entering or changing information.

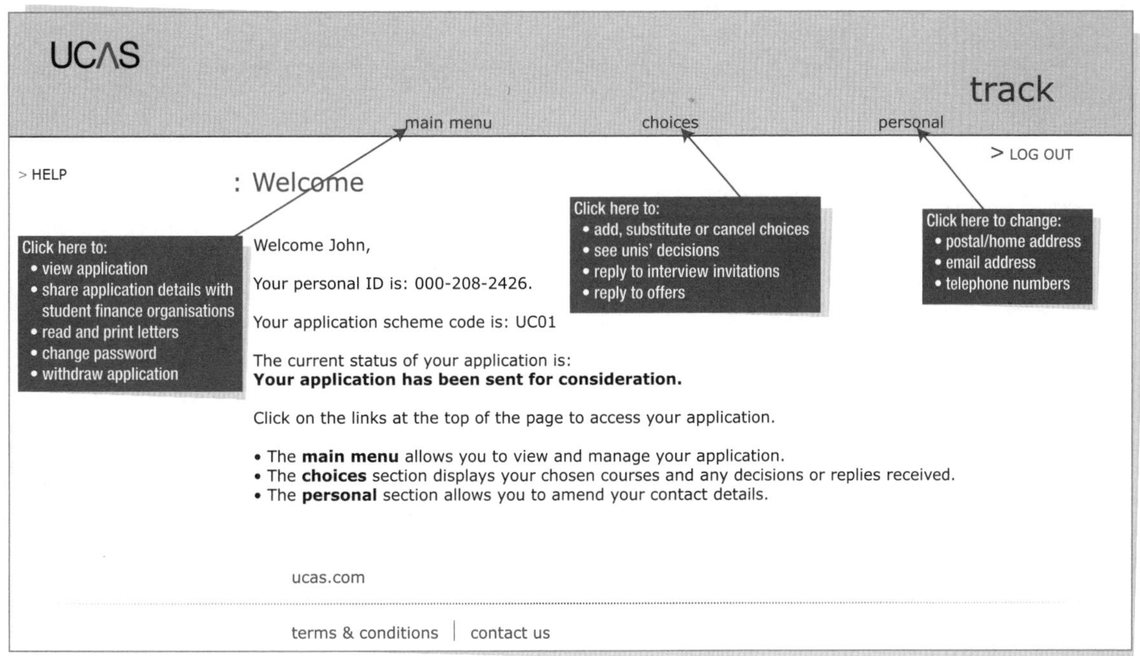
UCAS
track
main menu
choices
personal
> LOG OUT
> HELP
: Welcome
Click here to:
• view application
• share application details with student finance organisations
• read and print letters
• change password
• withdraw application
Click here to:
• add, substitute or cancel choices
• see unis' decisions
• reply to interview invitations
• reply to offers
Click here to change:
• postal/home address
• email address
• telephone numbers
Welcome John,
Your personal ID is: 000-208-2426.
Your application scheme code is: UC01
The current status of your application is:
Your application has been sent for consideration.
Click on the links at the top of the page to access your application.
• The main menu allows you to view and manage your application.
• The choices section displays your chosen courses and any decisions or replies received.
• The personal section allows you to amend your contact details.
ucas.com
terms & conditions | contact us

When you look at your choices on Track, they may be displayed in a different order to what you expected because we generate a random order when we process your application. Don't panic – the displayed order doesn't indicate any preference order; we send your application to all your chosen unis at the same time.

Whenever a uni makes a decision about your application, the details will be shown on Track. If you supply a valid email address on your application, we'll email you each time a decision has been made. To protect confidential information, the email doesn't contain the actual decision; you still need to go to Track to check the details.

You can also use Track to:

- change your postal address, telephone numbers and email address
- add and remove choices (depending on your circumstances)
- reply to interview invitations
- reply to your offers of a place
- send your application to a uni in Extra (see page 255)
- register for Adjustment (see page 295)
- send your application to a uni in Clearing (see page 299)
- help you apply for student finance (see page 204).

Track is normally available 24 hours a day, seven days a week.

Here's what some of our applicants said about Track...

'The Track feature was something that I found especially valuable. It set a lot of my nerves at rest to be able to see the progress of my application, and it was very easy to use.'

'I sometimes logged on [to Track] 3 or 4 times a day because I was so excited. The choices page is set out clearly to show exactly where you stand with your universities of choice, so it only took a quick flash to see if anything had changed.'

'The next thing I wanted to know was how my application to the different universities was going. This was effortless with the tracking feature that UCAS provides.'

'UCAS Track was really useful in the process. I love the fact that they email you when your application has been updated.'

'Logging onto UCAS Track is possibly the most exciting thing about applying to university. My heart races every time I wait for the web - page to load.'

Using Track to help with your student finance application

If you live in England, Northern Ireland or Wales and you chose not to allow UCAS to share your details with the student finance organisation in your country when you applied, you can still opt in to sharing this information in Track when you receive your Welcome letter. If we can give your details to your student finance organisation in advance, it will help them to process your finance application quicker and more efficiently. When you start your application for student finance, you will find that some of your details have already been entered.

Unfortunately, if you live in Scotland and you chose not to allow UCAS to share your details with the Student Awards Agency for Scotland (SAAS) when you applied, you cannot use Track to opt in to sharing this information with the SAAS.

We transfer your application details to your student finance organisation using a secure network, so the information is safe. The student finance organisations will only use your data for your finance application. They won't give your details to anyone else.

Tips for using Track

- Use Internet Explorer version 5 or higher, or Mozilla Firefox version 2.0 or higher to access the service. Older versions of browsers can cause problems with secure websites.
- Don't save your password using a facility within your internet browser. This prevents anyone else from logging in to Track and viewing your details.
- When you've finished using Track, log out by clicking on the 'log out' button and then close down your browser. This prevents anyone else from accessing your details. For security reasons, Track times out after five minutes of user inactivity.

UCAStv

Watch our video about how to use Track on UCAStv at www.ucas.com for more information.

Here's what the Track choices screen looks like just after we've processed your application...

UCAS

track

main menu   choices   personal

> HELP

> LOG OUT

: choices

university / college	course	starting	decision	your reply	updated	preference
University of Cambridge campus: 4 entry point: 1	A100	07-Oct-2013			10-Oct-2012	-
University of Birmingham campus: - entry point: 1	C100	23-Sep-2013			10-Oct-2012	-
Keele University campus: - entry point: 1	A100	30-Sep-2013			10-Oct-2012	-
The University of Nottingham campus: - entry point: 1	A100	07-Oct-2013			10-Oct-2012	-
The University of Sheffield campus: - entry point: 1	A100	07-Oct-2013			10-Oct-2012	-

Add choice   Reply to offers   Payment

Please make sure you have checked the details of your choices **before** making replies. Click on the course code in red above to access the choice details.

application processed by UCAS : 10-Oct-2012
last log in : 11-Oct-2012

ucas.com

terms & conditions | contact us

www.ucas.com

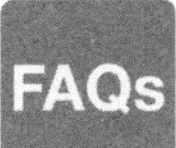

Track – FAQs

Why can't I log in to Track? My details aren't accepted.
You cannot use Track until we've received and processed your application. If your application has been processed, you must make sure that you enter your Personal ID exactly as it appears on your Welcome letter, and enter the username and password you used to apply. Your username and password are case sensitive.

If the fields are reset after you click on the 'log in' button, this usually means that incorrect details have been entered.

I've forgotten my Track username and password. What should I do?
You can find out your Personal ID, Track username and password by using our 'Forgotten login details?' service.You can access this service from the Track page on our website or from the Track login screen. If you've entered and verified an email address on your application, you just need to enter it in the 'Forgotten login details?' service and we'll email the requested details to you.

I've been locked out of Track. What can I do?
If you have three failed attempts to log in to the service in one day, you'll be 'locked out' of the system for 24 hours. If this happens, you need to contact our Customer Contact Centre and if you can answer the security questions, we'll unlock your account.

Track has timed out. What should I do?
Track automatically times out after five minutes of inactivity, for security reasons. You need to go back to the Track gateway page on our website and log in again.

How quickly is information updated on Track?
When you or universities provide updates, the changes are shown on Track almost immediately.

Money: apply for student finance

Don't wait until your exams, or (worse still) your results, before applying for your student funding. Making an early application will ensure your funding will be sorted before your course starts. If for any reason you change your course or uni, you can update your information, so there's no need to delay.

If you live in England, you can apply for your funding online by going to **www.gov.uk/student-finance**.

If you live in Wales, you should visit **www.studentfinancewales.co.uk** or **www.cyllidmyfyrwyrcymru.co.uk**.

If you live in Scotland, you should visit **www.saas.gov.uk**.

If you live in Northern Ireland, you should visit **www.studentfinanceni.co.uk**.

If you live in Guernsey, Jersey or the Isle of Man, you should visit **www.education.gg**, **www.gov.je** or **www.gov.im**.

The way you apply and the deadline dates to guarantee your money will be in place for the start of term will depend on in which country in the United Kingdom you normally live. All of this information is available from the GOV.UK website. Read it and commit it to memory!

To complete the student finance application successfully you will need:

- information about your parents' income – such as their P60s
- your National Insurance number – don't guess it or you won't be paid
- your bank details – the money will be paid into your bank account
- your passport if you have one – make sure it hasn't expired.

Get all this together before you start to complete the application and it will be much easier and quicker to do.

Did you know?

If you live in England, Northern Ireland, Scotland or Wales, you can opt to allow UCAS to share your details with the student finance organisation in your country when you apply. If we can give your details to your student finance organisation, it will help them to process your finance application more easily. If you live in England, Northern Ireland or Wales, you will find that some of your details have already been entered when you start your student finance application.

When you apply you can also ask us to send you an email reminder about applying for student finance when the service in your country goes live. The services in Wales, Northern Ireland and Scotland usually go live in the autumn and the service in England is normally available early in the following year.

After you submit your application you will be assessed and receive written confirmation of what you can expect (your entitlement). It is really important that you understand this, as it sets out exactly how much money you will have to live on for the whole year. You should also keep this document safe because you will need it when you enrol at uni. You may also need to show your bank or Jobcentre Plus a copy if you wish to apply for a student account or any benefits.

Funding for students on health-related courses

Students on health-related courses, such as medicine, physiotherapy, nursing, midwifery and occupational therapy, are funded differently from other students. The NHS has introduced revised financial support arrangements for new students starting health - related courses from 1 September 2012. For full information about NHS funding, visit **www.nhsbsa.nhs.uk**.

From September 2013 all entrants to nursing training will have to take a degree course. Universities and colleges will no longer offer diploma courses.

Tuition fees

As long as you meet the residency requirements and have not been funded by the NHS previously, you will not have to pay the tuition fees yourself. The NHS will pay these fees direct to your uni.

Living costs

If you are starting a health-related degree, you will be eligible to apply for a means-tested NHS bursary and a reduced rate student loan. This means that the NHS will look at your parents' or partner's income when they assess your living costs. In addition, you may be eligible to claim means-tested support for children or other dependants.

To apply for a reduced rate student loan, visit **www.gov.uk/student-finance**. The reduced rate loan is not means tested for NHS students; it is repaid at the end of the course once you are earning more than a certain amount.

How do I apply for an NHS bursary?

When your uni offers you a provisional training place, they will advise the NHS Student Grants Unit. The NHS will then send you a letter of confirmation, which will give you your unique student reference number. This letter will also tell you how to download the form from their website. You should return your completed form and supporting documentation to them. They will assess your application and let you know if you qualify for an award.

Unlike student loans that are paid in three termly instalments, NHS bursaries are paid to students monthly. If you are going to move into student accommodation, you should check the payment dates on your accommodation contract before you sign it. In some cases, it may be possible for you to pay this in line with your bursary payments.

International students

If you live outside the European Union, you cannot currently apply for a loan but your chosen universities may offer bursaries or scholarships that are worth applying for – check the finance section on their websites. If you live in the EU but not in the UK, call the Student Finance Services European Team on +44 (0) 141 243 3570 for student finance information.

Making changes

After you've sent us your application you may need to change some of the details you've provided or supply additional information. This section summarises the changes or additions you can make to your application when you receive your Welcome letter. Unfortunately, you can't make any changes to your personal statement or reference.

You're happy with the uni, but not the course, start date or point of entry

You need to contact the uni and not us if you still want to apply to them but want to change:

- your course
- your start date, for example to the next year if you decide to have a gap year
- your point of entry. You may have applied to start the course in the first year (year 1 entry) but later decide that you need to do a foundation year (year 0

entry) or find out that you have the qualifications to start the course in the second year (year 2 entry).

If the uni agrees, they will tell us about the change. If we have already sent you an offer for your original choice, we will change it and the new offer will be displayed in Track.

You want to change a choice of uni

You can change a uni choice in Track within seven days from the date on your Welcome letter, as long as it's before 30 June. You cannot normally change your uni choices after seven days. If there are exceptional reasons, like a change in your family circumstances or any personal problems, you need to ask your referee to write to us, explaining the situation and recommending that you are allowed to make the change. Your referee should include details of the proposed change(s) in the letter.

You've applied to one uni only and want to apply to others

If you only apply for one course and pay the reduced application fee, you can add up to four more if you pay an additional fee, as long as you have not already accepted or declined an offer. You can add choices and pay the additional fee in Track until 30 June.

You've made fewer than five choices and you want to make more

If you initially applied to fewer than five choices, you can add more choices as long as you have not accepted or declined your offers. You can add further choices in Track until 30 June.

Cancelling a choice

You can cancel an individual choice as long as the uni has not sent us a decision. You do this in Track.

Address and phone number changes

You can change your postal address, home and mobile phone numbers in Track and we let your chosen unis know. If you change your postal address and you're expecting any urgent letters from your unis, you should also tell them yourself. Remember to get your mail redirected so that you receive any letters that have already been sent.

If you're using a different address during term time, make sure that you change your postal address to your home or your new address at the end of the summer term.

Email address change

You can change your email address in Track. We send an email containing a verification code to the new address. You then enter this code into Track to confirm that the email address is correct.

Changes in exams and course arrangements

You must write to us immediately if your exam subjects, modules or units, exam board, centre number or any other details change. You must also tell the unis where you have offers or those that are still considering your application.

Unis usually base their conditional offers on your exam details. If your details change, they may change their offers or decisions.

If a uni cannot confirm your exam results because they do not have enough information, they may not be able to offer you a place. You need to tell us and the unis immediately if anything changes.

Accident, illness or personal problems that affect your exam results

If you suffer an accident, illness or personal problems that affect your exam results, write to each uni that is considering your application to explain. You need to include a supporting letter from your school or other authority and, in medical cases, from your doctor. You should send the details as soon as possible after the problem has arisen. Do not wait until you receive your exam results.

Cancelling your application

If you want to cancel your application and receive a refund of your application fee you must call our Customer Contact Centre within seven days from the date on the

Welcome letter, which we send to you when we have processed your application. You cannot cancel your application in Track.

Withdrawing your application

If you decide you don't want to go to uni this year, you can withdraw completely from the UCAS scheme. You should tell us as soon as possible, preferably by mid-September before courses start, so that the places can be offered to someone else. We will let your chosen unis know that you have withdrawn. If you want, you can reapply in the following year.

If you have withdrawn from the scheme but, for exceptional reasons, you want to re-enter it, you need to contact our Customer Contact Centre for advice.

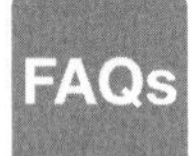

Making changes – FAQs

How do I change my address, phone number or email address?
You can change your postal address, email address and phone number using Track. We will then send your new details to your unis. If you are expecting correspondence from a particular uni you may wish to contact them direct to give them your new details.

Can I change my personal statement?
You cannot update your personal statement through UCAS. If you have additional information relevant to your application which you think your unis would find useful, you should contact them direct.

How can I change my year of entry?
You need to contact your unis direct. If they agree to change your year of entry, they will tell us and we'll show the change in Track.

Can I change my choice of uni?
You can change your choice of university or college within seven days from the date on your Welcome letter, depending on the time of year. After that, you can only make choice changes if your chosen course is no longer running or you have exceptional circumstances. To change a choice due to exceptional circumstances, we will need a letter of support from your referee, detailing the change you want and your reasons for requesting the change.

If you wish to change the course details at your chosen uni, you should contact them direct. In this situation, you do not need to contact us. If they are happy to change your course, they will tell us and we'll show the change in Track.

I haven't used all my five choices. Can I use the others now?
You can add further choices to your application using Track up to 30 June as long as you have not replied to any offers that you've received.

If you only had a single choice and paid the reduced application fee, you will also have to pay an additional amount. You can do this in Track.

Can I cancel my application and reapply?
You can cancel your application for seven days from the date on your Welcome letter by calling our Customer Contact Centre. After we have cancelled your application, you will be able to register on Apply again to make a new application.

After seven days from the date on your Welcome letter you can withdraw your application at any time, but you cannot reapply in the same application cycle.

www.ucas.com

Interviews, portfolios and auditions

Interviews

Many unis (particularly popular ones, running competitive courses) want to meet you and find out whether you'd cope with the demands of your chosen course before making you an offer. More and more are inviting potential students for interview before making a conditional or unconditional offer of a place.

Policies vary greatly and some unis interview only selected or borderline applicants and some do not interview at all. If you're invited for interview, there are lots of things you can do before, during and after interviews to get the most from the experience.

Some unis will contact you direct to invite you for interview and others will send online invitations to you in Track. If the interview invitation is made in Track, you can accept the invitation, turn it down or ask for another day online. The Unis' decisions section on page 237 gives more information about interview invitations.

Preparation

There's lots you can do to prepare for the big day – from having a mock interview to arming yourself with information about the uni and the course.

Top tips

The whens and wheres: Make sure you know where you need to be and when, and make any necessary travel and accommodation arrangements in advance. Visit the uni's website for maps and directions and make sure you know exactly where on campus you need to be. If you need more information, get in touch with the uni.

Knowledge is power: Be sure to read the prospectus and look on the uni website – the more you know about the uni and the course you have applied for, the keener you'll seem. Make a list of questions you'd like to ask, perhaps the kind of things the prospectus and website don't tell you.

Know your application: Make sure you're familiar with what you put in your application – this is all your interviewer knows about you, so he or she will probably ask you about some of the things you've mentioned.

Be familiar with 'hot topics' in your subject area: You may well be asked about them, and don't forget to read the newspapers too. Interviewers commonly ask for your views on the issues of the day.

Practice makes perfect: A mock interview might be a good idea. Typical things you might be asked are:

- Why did you choose this course?
- What do you enjoy most on the course you are currently studying?
- Why did you choose this uni?

Ask a teacher or careers adviser to run through a mock interview with you.

Get a good night's sleep: You won't perform your best without one!

At interview

Interviews are always nerve-wracking as you don't know what you're going to be asked. Just be yourself, be enthusiastic and be sure to 'sell' what you have to offer as a student on your chosen course.

Interviewers are looking for students who show an interest, who can think independently and consider new ideas. They are looking for students who will thrive well on their course and enjoy a varied academic life alongside their outside interests.

Top tips

Dress appropriately: Although you probably won't need to wear a suit to interview, show your interviewer you are taking things seriously by dressing smartly.

Arrive in good time: Take any contact numbers just in case the worst happens and you get delayed on the way to your interview.

Body language: Be aware of your body language in the interview room – don't slouch or yawn; sit up and look alert. Make sure you are giving out all the right signals.

Stumped?: If you don't understand a question ask for it to be repeated or rephrased. Make good guesses or relate your answer to something you do know something about.

Expect the unexpected: While interviewers aren't trying to trick you, some will want to see how you react under pressure. A surprise test or exercise isn't unheard of, so stay calm and think clearly.

Ask questions: While your interviewer needs to find out about you by asking lots of questions, you'll come across as enthusiastic if you ask appropriate questions too. Use the interview as a chance to find out answers to your questions that weren't answered on the website or in the prospectus.

Next steps

An interview is as much a chance for you to check out a uni, as it is for them to check you out, so take some time to reflect and consider how things could have gone better.

Top tips

Make notes: While the questions and your answers are still fresh in your mind, make some notes. If you're going to other interviews similar questions may crop up and it will be useful to compare responses.

Self-appraise: Think about what went well and what you can improve on. Start thinking about what you felt comfortable answering and what left you struggling. Come up with some answers that you are confident in, should similar topics crop up next time.

Sit back and wait: Once we've heard from the uni, we'll let you know in Track if you were successful or not. If you receive an offer, it may be conditional on you achieving certain exam grades.

Applicants with disabilities

Think about how you're going to get to the uni and the room where the interview will take place. You may want to arrange for help from your parents or other people such as a personal assistant or an interpreter.

Your application should be judged on your academic ability and experience. Therefore, your disability and associated requirements shouldn't be discussed during your interview, even if you have provided information on your application. Ideally, you will have discussed your disability and requirements with the uni's disability coordinator before you applied, but if you haven't already done this, make sure you find out the disability coordinator's name and contact details at interview so you can contact them later.

If your interviewer asks you questions about your impairment and special needs, just say that you have already discussed these matters with the uni's disability coordinator or that you would like to discuss them separately with this person after the interview and ask for their name and contact details.

What will they ask me at interview?

If you receive an interview invitation, you'll almost certainly ask yourself this question. Here are some example interview questions that the Universities of Oxford and Cambridge have asked applicants and what interviewers were looking for in the answers.

University of Oxford's interview questions

Subject: Biological sciences
Interviewer: Owen Lewis, Brasenose College

Q: Why do lions have manes?

A: Some of the best interview questions do not have a "right" or a "wrong" answer, and can potentially lead off in all sorts of different directions. Applicants might have picked up ideas about the function of a lion's mane from independent reading or from watching natural history documentaries. That's fine – but I'd follow up their response by asking how they would test their theory. When I've used this question in interviews I've had all sorts of innovative suggestions, including experiments where lions have their manes shaved to investigate whether this influences their chances with the opposite sex or helps them win fights over territory.

Q: Ladybirds are red. So are strawberries. Why?

A: Many biological sciences tutors use plant or animal specimens – often alive - as a starting point for questions and discussion, so applicants shouldn't be surprised if they are asked to inspect and discuss an insect or a fruit. Red can signal either "don't eat me" or "eat me" to consumers. I'm interested in seeing how applicants attempt to resolve this apparent paradox.

Subject: Computer science
Interviewer: Brian Harrington, Keble College

Q: A group of seven pirates has 100 gold coins. They have to decide amongst themselves how to divide the treasure, but must abide by pirate rules:

- ***the most senior pirate proposes the division.***
- ***all of the pirates (including the most senior) vote on the division. If half or more vote for the division, it stands. If fewer than half vote for it, they throw the most senior pirate overboard and start again.***

- ***the pirates are perfectly logical and entirely ruthless (only caring about maximising their own share of the gold).***

So, what division should the most senior pirate suggest to the other six?
A: This is a standard logic problem and is a good example of the type of question that could be asked. I like to see how students can take directions, and if they can break problems into smaller subsets, and work through a complex concept applying a solution in an algorithmic way. If students have any questions, I want them to ask – not to sit in silence feeling stuck!

Stumped? You can find the solution on University of Oxford's website.

Subject: Engineering
Interviewer: Byron Byrne, Department of Engineering Science

Q: How would you design a gravity dam for holding back water?
A: This is a great question because the candidate first has to determine the forces acting on the dam before considering the stability of the wall under the action of those forces. Candidates will probably recognise that the water could push the dam over. The candidate would then be expected to construct simple mathematical expressions that predict when this would occur. Some may also discuss failure by sliding, issues of structural design, the effects of water seeping under the dam, and so on. The candidate will not have covered all the material at school so guidance is provided to assess how quickly new ideas are absorbed. The question also probes the candidate's ability to apply physics and maths to new situations and can test interest in and enthusiasm for the engineered world.

Subject: English literature
Interviewer: Lucinda Rumsey, Mansfield College

Q: Why might it be useful for an English student to read the Twilight series?
A: There are several reasons I might ask this one. It's useful in an interview to find some texts the candidate has read recently and the Twilight books are easily accessible and popular. Also, candidates tend to concentrate on texts they have been taught in school or college and I want to get them to talk about whatever they have read independently, so I can see how they think rather than what they have been taught. A good English literature student engages in literary analysis of

every book they read. The question has led to some interesting discussions about narrative voice, genre, and audience in the past.

Subject: Geography
Interviewer: Lorraine Wild, St Hilda's College

Q: If I were to visit the area where you live, what would I be interested in?
A: The question gives candidates an opportunity to apply concepts from their A level Geography course to their home area. They might discuss urban planning and regeneration, ethnic segregation and migration, or issues of environmental management. The question probes whether they are able to apply 'geographical thinking' to the everyday landscapes around them. It reveals the extent to which they have a curiosity about the world around them. By asking specifically about their home area the question eliminates any advantage gained by those who are more widely travelled and have more experience of a variety of geographical contexts.

Subject: History
Interviewer: Ian Forrest, Oriel College

Q: Is violence always political? Does 'political' mean something different in different contexts?
A: This pair of questions allows the interviewer to deal with historical material from any period the candidate is studying or knows about from more general reading. It could also be answered extremely well from contemporary current affairs knowledge. The aim of the question is to get the candidate to challenge some perceived notions about what constitutes politics, and to think about how political history might be studied away from the usual kings, parliaments etc. A good candidate would, with assistance, begin to construct categories of when violence looks more and less political. A very good candidate would, with assistance, begin to construct a useful definition of 'political', but this is challenging. The main aim would not be to solve these problems, but to use them to find some new interest in a subject that the candidate already knows something about.

Subject: Law
Interviewer: Ben McFarlane, Faculty of Law

Q: What does it mean for someone to 'take' another's car?
A: There is no right answer to this question. For example, can you take a car without driving it, or even without moving it? Our focus is on the candidate's reasoning – how he or she formulates an initial definition, and how he or she then applies and refines that initial definition in response to hypothetical examples provided by the interviewers. One example might be: I am walking along the street when it starts to rain. I open the door of an unlocked car and sit there for 15 minutes until the rain passes. Have I 'taken' the car? The aim of the interview is to give the candidate a chance to show his or her application, reasoning ability, and communication skills.

Subject: Materials science
Interviewer: Steve Roberts, St Edmund Hall

Q: How hot does the air have to be in a hot air balloon if I wanted to use it to lift an elephant?
A: When I actually used this question in interviews, no-one actually got as far as an actual "X degrees C" answer, in the ten minutes or so we allowed for it, nor did we expect them to. We use this sort of question to try to find how applicants think about problems, and how they might operate within a tutorial. We make this clear to interviewees before even giving them questions of this type. Things we are looking for include how readily they can see into the core of a problem (what's the essential physics in this? – what concepts and equations might be useful?); how they respond to hints and suggestions from us (can they take a hint or two and run with it, or do they have to be dragged through every step?); their approach to basic concepts (how does a hot air balloon work, anyway? What else operates like one?); estimates (typical size of balloon, weight of elephant) and sorting out what's important (what about the weight of the balloon itself?); and how they use "rough maths" to get a quick idea of the likely sort of answer, using sensible approximations in working through formulae, and keeping track of units.

Subject: Medicine
Interviewer: Robert Wilkins, Department of Physiology, Anatomy and Genetics

Q:Why does your heart rate increase when you exercise?
A: The simple answer, which all students can provide, is because you need to deliver more oxygen and nutrients to muscles and remove metabolic products. But follow-up questions would probe whether the student appreciates that there must be a way for the body to know it needs to raise the heart rate, and possible ways for achieving this. Answers might include sensing lowered oxygen or raised carbon dioxide levels. In fact, gas levels might not change much, so students are further asked to propose other signals and ways in which those possibilities could be tested. This probes selection criteria such as problem-solving and critical thinking, intellectual curiosity, enthusiasm, and the ability to listen.

Subject: Modern languages
Interviewer: Stephen Goddard, St Catherine's College

Q: In a world where English is a global language, why learn French?
A: I might use this question early in an interview in order to set the candidate thinking, and to elicit some idea of their motivation before moving on to more specific questions. Given the nature of the modern languages course, I would be interested in responses about the French language as a 'window' into French culture, literature and history; a knowledge of which is valuable in itself and essential to understanding today's world. I would also be happy to see candidates investigate some of the assumptions underlying the question: Is English a global language? What about Mandarin Chinese, Spanish, etc.? Can we not in fact still consider French a global language? And so on.

Subject: Psychology
Interviewer: Dave Leal, Brasenose College

Q: Why do human beings have two eyes?
A: This question may result from a more general discussion about the human senses. It can develop in a number of different directions, partly depending upon the knowledge and expertise of the interviewee. For example, two eyes are important for three dimensional (3D) vision. Why can we still see in 3D when only looking through one eye? What determines the optimum position and distance

between the two eyes? Why is it that we see a stable view of the world even though we are constantly moving our head? How can an understanding of mathematics, physics and biology help us explain 3D vision? The discussion may develop into a consideration of the different senses and the role they play in us interacting with our environment, including interacting with other people, and the nature of perceptual experience.

University of Cambridge's interview questions

Subject: English

Q: Which of the literary works on your A level (or equivalent) syllabus have you most enjoyed studying? Can you tell me what qualities in it you most enjoyed, and analyse in a bit more detail why you think they work so well?
A: The purpose of this question is to measure how far applicants can reflect on what it is they find pleasurable in a literary work and explore the criteria which they use to assess literary works. An interviewer will want to know whether this pleasure is gained from the applicant's appreciation of the ways in which the writer has composed the work or if they just enjoy the subject matter. Further to this, can the applicant identify what specifically in a text creates that pleasure – is it a matter of style, of fidelity to reality, of psychological truth?

(After reading a previously unseen literary text)
Q: Are there any formal qualities to this poem/prose extract/dramatic excerpt which support or enhance its meaning? If so, show me where and how they work.
A: Questions like this enable assessment of the applicant's understanding of what is going on in the text being considered, and their willingness to engage in analytical thinking. Applicants should acknowledge that there might be an issue of plain sense, but also recognise nuances of meaning that need further exploration beyond the dictionary definition of words. An interviewer is looking to see if the applicant can understand why certain texts are written in certain ways. Further questions may emerge about the function of rhyme and metre in verse, or sentence structure and vocabulary in prose, or use of colloquialism in a dramatic extract, or any of these elements.

Subject: History

(About a piece of work submitted before the interview)
Q: If you were doing this piece of work over again, what, if anything, would you do differently? Please explain why.
A: This is an introductory question which is designed to gain an insight into whether the applicant has the capacity to reflect on what they have done, to move their thinking along in the light of new material, and to connect material in some work to other aspects of their studies. This question can also provide a starting point for further prolonged discussion as a result of the applicant's response.

(About a text read just before the interview)
Q: What are the main arguments within the piece you have just read?
A: Here we are looking to test an applicant's ability to read critically and to offer analytical criticism of what has been read. The question also provides evidence of how flexibly an applicant thinks. Interviewers are looking for applicants to identify evidence which supports their view and ability to recognise alternative interpretations.

Subjects: Engineering or physics

Q: From what height H must a roller-coaster car be released if it is to successfully travel around a loop of radius R without falling off at the top of the loop?

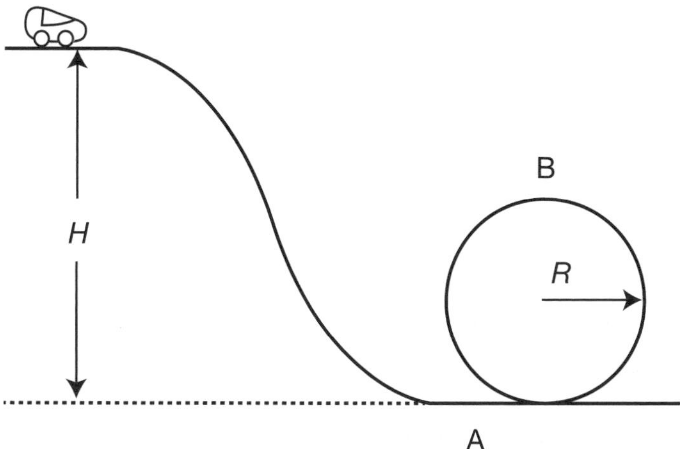

A: This question seeks to discover how well an applicant can link various concepts from physics and mechanics to solve a problem. It also tests some basic mathematical skills.

The discussion at interview breaks this down into a sequence of questions: having satisfactorily resolved one, perhaps with some help and prompting from the interviewer, we move on to the next.

1. *Assuming frictional forces can be neglected, if the car is released from rest at height H, how fast will it be moving when it reaches point A?*

   This can, perhaps with a hint from the interviewer, be answered using the principle of the conservation of energy – potential energy is converted into kinetic energy as the car descends the track: $V_A = \sqrt{2gH}$ *where g is the acceleration due to gravity.*

2. *If the car follows the track to the top of the loop at B what then is its speed?*

   This too can be answered using the principle of the conservation of energy. A very alert applicant will realise they can use the previous result but replacing H with the net change of height from the start to B (H – 2R): $V_B = \sqrt{2g(H-2R)}$

3. *When the car is at B what forces are acting on it and in what directions?*

   Here we are looking to see how well the applicant understands the physical origin of forces. If frictional forces are still neglected, the only forces acting are the car's weight and the reaction from the track on the car – both of which act straight downwards.

4. *What is the acceleration of the car at B and in what direction?*

   The applicant will hopefully recognise that this is an example of circular motion. If they cannot remember the expression for centripetal acceleration (V^2/R) *we would tell them this result (without penalty). If the applicant has not yet covered circular motion (rare) we would briefly explain the key points needed to make progress on the question.*

5. *How are the forces acting on the car at B and its acceleration linked?*

   This requires the applicant to recognise that Newton's Second Law ($F = Ma$) *can be applied to this situation. If all goes well, they will reach the result:*

$M\dfrac{V_B^2}{R} = N + Mg$ in which N is the reaction from the track on the car and M is the car's mass.

6. *Under what circumstances will the car lose contact with the track at B?*

   Here we hope the applicant will recognise that the car will lose contact if the reaction N falls to zero, which will happen if the car is not going fast enough at that point.

7. *So, from what height must the car be released if this is not to happen?*

   Pulling together the preceding analysis the applicant can show that $H > \frac{5}{2}R$ if the car is not to lose contact with the track at B.

   If an applicant does all of the above well and quickly then the question can be extended further by asking them to think qualitatively about how the situation changes if the object on the roller-coaster track is a ball bearing rather than a car, so it gains both translational and rotational kinetic energy as it descends the track.

Subject: Chemistry

Q: How does the structure of salt (sodium chloride) influence its properties?
A: The discussion breaks down into a series of questions of increasing difficulty: having satisfactorily resolved one, perhaps with some help and prompting from the interviewer, we move on to the next. The order of the individual questions might vary somewhat, and the number that might be completed depends on how fluently the applicant is responding.

1. *What is the formula of sodium chloride?*

   Everybody knows the answer to this, and so this is just to get things going.

2. *What is the structure of solid NaCl?*

   A regular arrangement of cations (Na^+) and anions (Cl^-), in a six coordinate structure. Perhaps a sketch of the three-dimensional structure might be given.

3. *NaCl has a high melting point solid, why is this?*

Here we are looking for statements about the high lattice energy, which prompts supplementary questions about the nature of the interactions which lead to the high lattice energy. Some discussion of the interaction between charges would follow, and perhaps on how this varies with distance and charge.

4. *In the structure a given positive ion is surrounded by six negative ions, but if you move further out the next ions you encounter are positive, and there are more than six of them. Comment?*

   What we are looking for here is a realisation that although the interactions with these positive ions are unfavourable, they are further away than the first set of negative ions. This leads to a discussion of how successive shells of positive and negative ions, at different distances, gives an overall favourable interaction.

5. *If the applicant is taking physics as well, they might be asked whether or not there is a force on each of the ions.*

   The point here is that although there are interactions between the ions, these are in balance so there is no net force. This leads to a discussion of what these balancing forces might be – repulsions at short distances.

6. *Does solid NaCl dissolve in water?*

   Of course, yes, easily.

7. *Given that the lattice energy is so large, why does NaCl dissolve in water?*

   Here we are looking for an understanding that the interactions between the ions and the solvent water are strong enough to overcome the interaction between the ions. There are many directions this discussion can then take depending on the ideas put forward by the applicant: we might discuss dielectric constants, entropy effects or solvation energies, for example.

8. *Why doesn't NaCl dissolve in organic solvents, such as hexane?*

   Here we are looking for a discussion of the fact that the interactions between the ions and hexane are rather different to, and weaker than, those between the ions and water. Again, the discussion can taken many directions at this point.

9. *Now a change of direction: why do greases and oils dissolve easily in hexane, but not in water?*

   With some help, it should be possible to tease out the idea that the inability of water to dissolve oils is a result of the strong interactions between water molecules – but this is a difficult point to get straight away.

Subject: Biology

Q: How does DNA interact with proteins?
A: Discussion builds through a series of questions. The aim is to start with a simple question that everyone can answer and then develop discussion from there. The question can develop in a variety of ways, depending on the response of an applicant. Knowledge base should not be a problem, as we are looking for the applicant to develop ideas based on their basic knowledge of the structure of macromolecules. How far we get will depend on the applicant.

1. *What is the structure of DNA?*

   A simple question that all biologists can answer, often drawing a diagram as part of their answer. Discussion about the linear molecule follows.

2. *How does DNA fit into a nucleus?*

   Applicants give various replies about packaging. This leads to discussion of the other molecules present in a nucleus and thus to proteins, either directly or indirectly.

3. *With reference to a chart of amino acid side chains: which amino acids might the proteins involved be rich in? Or what properties would you expect of amino acid side chains in these proteins?*

   This leads to discussion about which part of the DNA molecule is interacting with the proteins (the negatively charged backbone). So, we are looking for positively charged amino acid side chains.

What applicants say

Here are some comments from our applicants about interviews.

'Reminding yourself of what you wrote in your personal statement is a good idea, as you are likely to be asked about things you have written. Staying calm and relaxing during the interview is important. But they expect nerves. Just have fun, and show them what you've got!'

'Don't try and fake your personality, be yourself. Even if you're the shy type, show the universities that you're good and willing to learn. You won't be perfect and 100% knowledgable yet, which is why you're applying for the course. Never panic and just relax.'

Portfolios

If you've applied for courses in art or design subjects and you're invited for interview, unis will usually ask you to present a portfolio of your work as part of their selection process.

Top tips

Here are some top tips from Central Saint Martins College of Art and Design, University of the Arts London about putting together your portfolio.

- **Preparation** – be prepared to adapt the portfolio according to the course you are applying to (just like you would a CV or personal statement).
- **Sequence** – the portfolio should be well organised, so that whoever looks through it understands how you move from one idea to the next.
- **Scope** – show the range of what you can do, concentrating on recent work. Include visual and other background research, sketches, models and prototypes – not just the finished work.
- **Culture-wise** – your portfolio should show whatever interests you and influences your work: fashion, music, sport, environment.

- **Selection** – be choosy. Pick work that shows ideas, skills and media, which you want to explore further in the course that you would like to do. Don't include too much and avoid repetition of one kind of work just because you think you're good at it. Generally 15-20 items for a portfolio should be enough.
- **Identify yourself** – if you include work that was generated as a group project, highlight what your role was in the collaboration. If you are applying from a college or school, include a signed confirmation that the work included is your own.

Auditions

If you've applied for courses in performing arts, such as music, drama and dance, the unis may ask you to give an audition as part of the interview. They'll tell you in advance what you'll need to do for the audition, but you may be able to choose the piece or pieces you perform.

Top tips

Here are a few tips to help you get ready for your audition.

- Take advantage of any opportunities to perform in public or in front of other actors, musicians or dancers.
- Stage a practice audition with friends and family.
- If you're playing music, practise with an accompanist as often as possible.
- Practise your set or chosen pieces until you can perform them with confidence.
- Research the pieces you'll be performing so that you can talk about them and answer questions at interview.
- Practise relaxation and breathing exercises to help you handle nerves on the audition day.

Other things you may have to do

As part of the interview unis may ask you to:

- bring some pieces of written work with you
- write something on the day
- give a presentation
- take their own admissions test
- carry out a task on your own or in a group
- take part in a group discussion with other applicants.

The unis will tell you what you'll be asked to do at interview before the big day!

Whatever it is – be prepared and stay calm!

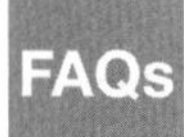

Interviews, portfolios and auditions – FAQs

How will I know if I have been invited for interview or audition?
Some universities will send all the interview or audition arrangements direct to you. Others will send an invitation to us and 'Invitation' will be shown alongside the choice in Track. These unis should also send full details direct to you.

If an interview invitation is shown in Track, you can accept or decline it online.

May I request a different interview or audition date?
If there is an invitation decision in Track, you can decline the interview or audition and request an alternative date online. You should contact the uni before you do this. If the interview or audition invitation is not shown in Track, you need to contact the uni direct to request a different date. Try to make the initial interview or audition date because unis may not be able to offer an alternative.

Unis' decisions

After a uni has considered your application, they decide whether or not to offer you a place. Some unis may be able to make a final decision using the information on your application, but others might ask you to attend an interview or audition, or to provide a portfolio of work, an essay or other piece of work. They can send this request direct to you or send it through us as an invitation.

Did you know?

Unis send their decisions at different times

Each uni considers your application against their own admissions criteria, so you'll hear from them at different times: it could be days, weeks or months before you hear anything, depending on where and when you apply and what you apply for. So don't worry if people you know have heard from a uni and you haven't – unis have years of experience and will contact you if they need information before they make a decision.

Invitations can be sent for any course. When a uni sends you an invitation, it will show on the choices screen in Track. If the invitation is for an interview or audition, you need to accept or decline it, or request an alternative time or date in Track.

If you need to change the time or date for an interview or audition, you also need to contact the uni. They can then update the invitation so that the revised details are shown on the choices screen in Track. You should try to attend on the date requested as it may be difficult for them to offer an alternative day. See pages 219 to 236 for tips and advice about preparing for and attending interviews.

If you need to attend an interview or audition, or send off a piece of work, after you've done this the uni will tell us if you've been offered a place or not, and we'll show its decision on the choices screen in Track.

You provide an email address and verify it when you apply so we can tell you when each uni makes a decision about your application. These emails do not provide details of the decision; they ask you to log in to Track to find out this information.

If you've a question about a decision, you should contact the uni and not us for advice.

We give unis the following deadlines for making decisions, but you may hear from them much earlier.

Application received at UCAS	Unis' deadline for making a decision
By 15 January	Early May
From 16 January to 30 June	Mid-July
From 1 July to mid-September (Clearing applications – see page 299)	Late October

Here are the decisions that unis can make.

Decision types

Conditional offer

A conditional offer means that the uni will offer you a place if you meet certain conditions, which are usually based on your exams.

You may be asked to achieve particular grades or results in qualifications, for example:

- grades ABB in three A levels, including an A in biology
- AABB in SQA Higher grades to include an A in maths
- pass an Access course with 60 credits, including at least 45 at level 3 and the remainder at level 2.

You could also be asked to gain certain grades in the units that make up qualifications.

Sometimes unis will ask you to achieve a certain number or UCAS Tariff points, for example:

- 280 Tariff points from a BTEC National Diploma
- 200 Tariff points from 3 A levels.

You must meet the conditions of your offer by 31 August, unless otherwise agreed by the uni. If you're taking a winter exam, the offer might ask you to meet the conditions by an earlier date.

One or more of your offers may be a joint conditional offer. It could include different conditions for a degree and an HND course. When your exam results are published, the uni will decide which part of the offer is most suitable for you.

Each offer is specific to your qualifications and circumstances.

Here are some examples of conditional offers from letters in Track.

> This offer is subject to you obtaining
>
> GCE A level
> Grades ABB in any order in
> Classical Civilisation
> English Literature
> Religious Studies
>
> Pass in a fourth subject to at least AS.

This offer is subject to you obtaining

AABB in SQA Higher Grades to include A in Maths. This offer is based on information provided in your application. All subjects must be university approved subjects and taken in 2011/12 examination year.

This offer is subject to you obtaining

A minimum of 240 UCAS Tariff points

240 points must be obtained from a minimum of 2 GCE A level qualifications or equivalent

(Equivalent qualifications can include GCE Single or Double Award, BTEC and OCR Nationals, Scottish Highers and Advanced Highers but exclude AS awards.)

Please send non-GCE or VCE results to this institution.

If you chose to study at Leeds Met, please see www.leedsmet.ac.uk/accommodation for details of Leeds Met accommodation and for information about how to apply. You can apply online for accommodation from February 2013.

For details on visiting Leeds Met, please see www.experience.leedsmet.ac.uk

See www.ucas.com/students/ucas_tariff for Tariff notes.

This offer is subject to you obtaining

Access to Engineering Course with a minimum of 36 credits at level 3 and 18 credits at level 2 and GCSE at grade C or higher in English language.

> This offer is subject to you obtaining
>
> An English language qualification approved by this institution, for example IELTS overall 6 with at least 5 in each component.

Unconditional offer

An unconditional offer means that you have met all the academic requirements and the university or college is happy to accept you. They will contact you if they need proof of your qualifications. They might have other requirements, such as financial or medical conditions, that you need to meet before you can start the course.

If the offer is for a place on a course that involves working with children or vulnerable adults, such as medicine, dentistry, nursing, teaching or social work, the uni will ask you to have a criminal record check before you start the course. These checks are done through the Criminal Records Bureau in England or Wales or the Scottish Criminal Record Disclosure Service in Scotland. The uni will explain the procedure to you.

If you are not a national from an EU country, the uni may ask you to provide evidence that you can pay your tuition fees and living expenses while you are studying.

These sorts of conditions can also be included in conditional offers.

Please remember – conditional and unconditional offers are only official when our offer letter is shown in Track, even if you receive an offer direct from a uni.

Here are some examples of unconditional offers from offer letters in Track.

> **Unconditional Offer**
>
> This offer is subject to you obtaining a satisfactory Criminal Records Bureau – Enhanced Disclosure (Police Check), Medical Questionnaire and State Primary School Experience between January and July 2013.

Unconditional Offer

Early application for government student support advised.
Details of accommodation available from 020 7815 6417.

If you have a disability, please contact Disability & Dyslexia Support on 020 7865 5432 to discuss your needs.

Unconditional Offer

Your student information pack will follow shortly.
Early application for Tuition Fee Loan and Student Support is advised.
Term dates and/or further course details will follow.

Accept your offer online @ www.ucas.com (app enquiries)

UCAStv

Watch our video 'Make sense of your offers' on UCAStv at www.ucas.tv for more information.

Unconditional Offer

Provide a copy of your passport
Pay tuition fee deposit

This institution regards you as overseas for fees purposes and the offer has been made on this basis.

Withdrawn application

A uni can withdraw your application to them if:

- you tell them that you don't want to be considered for a place
- you don't respond to their letters or emails or you don't attend an interview or audition.

A uni cannot withdraw your whole application.

Unsuccessful application

This means that the uni has decided not to offer you a place on their course.

Unis can decide not to offer you a place for many reasons, one of which could be that the course is full, so the decision may not be based on the quality of your application. The uni may provide a reason for their decision either when they send the decision through, or at a later date. If no reason is shown in Track, you can contact the uni to see if they will discuss why you were unsuccessful.

Here's what a couple of our applicants have said about uni's decisions.

'It's always a great idea to go to as many open days as you can when you've received conditional offers. It gives you an opportunity to physically evaluate the university as well as its surrounding area before you put your 'Firm' and 'Insurance' replies through. Open days are also a brilliant opportunity to meet people who are going to the same university and possibly even doing the same course as you are.'

'Be patient and don't panic! Whilst a few universities may reply relatively quickly, some will not reply for months, especially if they wait until after the 15 January deadline. I received my first offer exactly two weeks after applying but I had to wait almost four months for my final offer! There is really nothing you can do – best thing to do is get on with something else and just forget about it.'

An example of how a university selects their students

The University of Bristol provided the following information about how they select students for their drama degree course.

Things they look for in the application

- Evidence of a commitment to the study and appreciation of film and theatre, including an indication that applicants have read and viewed widely, beyond the requirements of an A level syllabus. Perhaps they have explored films from earlier periods and from different regions of the world, or developed an interest in experimental performance.

- Motivation and achievement in the fields of performance or media-related arts beyond the syllabus. This could be shown, for example, by participation in school or community drama productions, involvement in video production, or by attending summer schools or other courses. Applicants should show that they've made the most of any opportunities available to them and that they have initiative. The uni looks for evidence of potential, passion, maturity and focus rather than sheer quantity of extra-curricular activity.
- Appropriateness of the programme to the applicant's declared interests and ambitions. The programme is suitable if applicants are interested in both practice and theory. Applicants need to be interested in film, media and related arts, as the degree involves as much emphasis on film and television as on theatre.
- Does the applicant have any other relevant skills and passions, for example, in language, music, sports, or creative writing? What other experiences have shaped them? Applicants should show that they have reflected on these experiences, rather than simply enumerating them. What skills have they gained? The uni is looking for people with self-motivation, determination and breadth of knowledge, but also an ability to process their experience.
- Experience of having held positions of responsibility, especially where this provides evidence of maturity and of collaborative engagement with a wider community. It is essential that applicants are able to work with others, as the programme is taught primarily in groups, and some of the assessment involves working as part of a team.
- Clarity of expression, both written and oral. Applicants need to demonstrate this in their personal statement. They should avoid clichés, superlatives and generalisations. It would be useful if the reference indicates that they have good essay-writing skills.
- Evidence of intellectual rigour. Applicants need to be able to take a critical attitude to creative practice. The uni will be looking for evidence of independent thinking, curiosity and critical engagement in the applicant's personal statement.

The selection day

After assessing applications the uni chooses candidates to attend a selection day, so that the admissions team can gain further information on which to base decisions, and distinguish between candidates presenting similar profiles on the UCAS application.

The selection day consists of two assessed elements: a creative workshop (60 minutes) and a seminar (45 minutes). It also includes a tour of the department and the opportunity to meet current students.

In the workshop, assessors look not just for practical skills but for imagination and sensitivity, and the ability to work constructively in a group. In the seminar, candidates are asked to respond to and discuss a brief film clip, television sequence, written text or piece of performance footage, as guided by the seminar leader.

The final decision is based on assessment of the UCAS application and the selection day.

Unis' decisions – FAQs

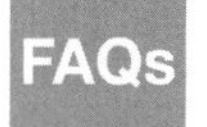

An offer I received direct from a university is not shown on Track. What shall I do?

This means your university has not told us about your offer. As soon as we receive it, you will be able to see it on Track. If two or three weeks have passed since you were given the offer and it is still not shown on Track, you should contact the uni to discuss the matter.

My university says I'm on a waiting list. What does this mean?

Waiting lists are not part of our application procedures, so we cannot advise you on this. You should contact the university to discuss the effect this may have on your application.

My chosen course is not running. What can I do?

The university should offer you another course. If nothing is available that you want, you can apply to another uni in its place. Your university should have sent you a form offering these options. If you have not received this form, contact them immediately for further advice. If you do not receive any advice from the uni, our Customer Contact Centre can help.

A decision on Track is different from what the uni told me. What should I do?
The information we send you is exactly what the university sends to us. If a uni has given you different information, you should contact them direct, not us. They may send changes to us and we'll show them on Track.

I don't understand my offer conditions. What should I do?
You need to ask the uni for an explanation. If they change your offer conditions, we'll show the revised conditions in Track.

Can you tell me why my application was unsuccessful?
If the university has provided a reason, we will show it in Track. If there is no reason in Track or you have already replied to your offers, you will need to ask the uni why you were unsuccessful.

Replying to your offers

Did you know?

You can wait to hear from all your unis before you reply

You don't have to accept any offers until you've heard back from all your universities. All your offers are safe until we've had a decision from each one, so don't worry about losing any of them. But, if you receive the offers you want, you can cancel all your choices with no decisions and reply (as long as you're absolutely sure that you won't change your mind – we can't reverse this later).

If we have received decisions from all of your choices and you have at least one offer, we will email you to let you know there has been a change to your application, and ask you to look at Track. If you didn't provide a valid email address when you applied, we send you a letter which asks you to reply to your offers.

Here's what your Track screen might look like when you need to reply to your offers...

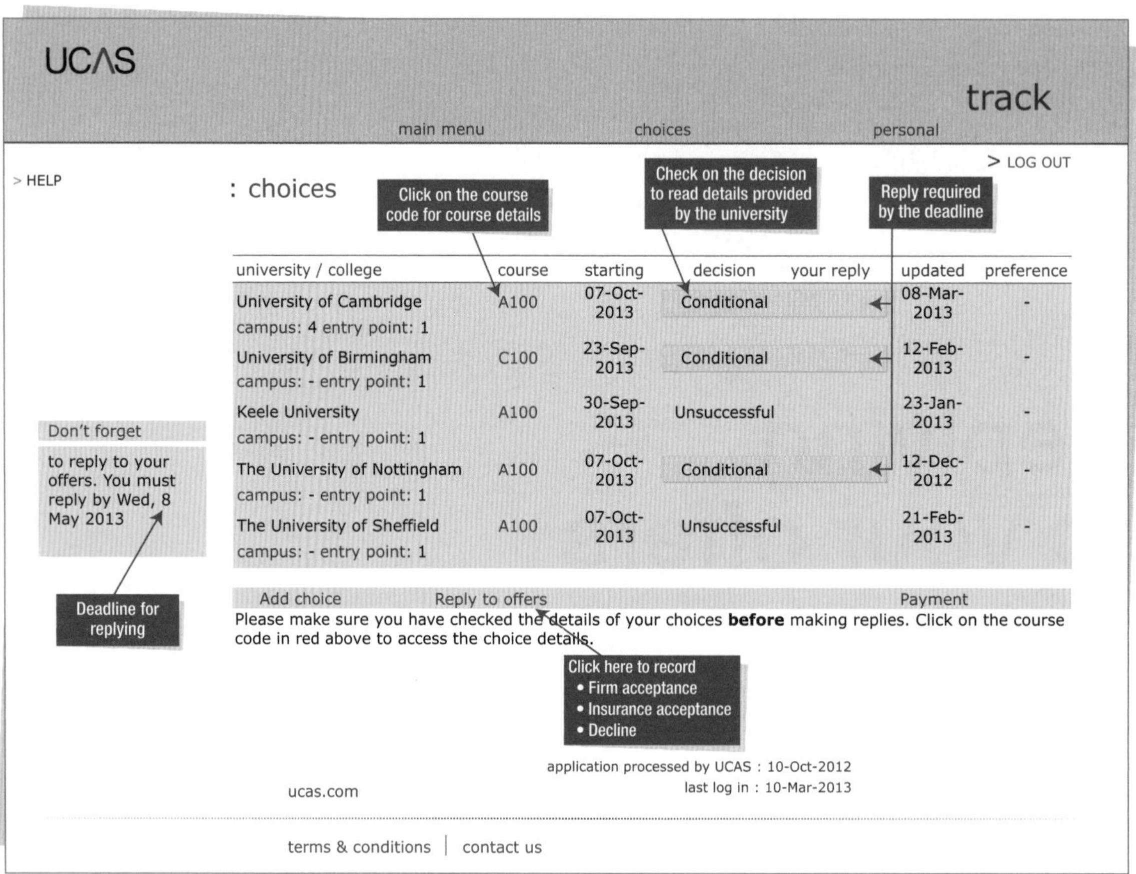
UCAS
track
main menu
choices
personal
> HELP
> LOG OUT
: choices
Click on the course code for course details
Check on the decision to read details provided by the university
Reply required by the deadline
university / college | course | starting | decision | your reply | updated | preference
University of Cambridge campus: 4 entry point: 1 | A100 | 07-Oct-2013 | Conditional | | 08-Mar-2013 | -
University of Birmingham campus: - entry point: 1 | C100 | 23-Sep-2013 | Conditional | | 12-Feb-2013 | -
Keele University campus: - entry point: 1 | A100 | 30-Sep-2013 | Unsuccessful | | 23-Jan-2013 | -
The University of Nottingham campus: - entry point: 1 | A100 | 07-Oct-2013 | Conditional | | 12-Dec-2012 | -
The University of Sheffield campus: - entry point: 1 | A100 | 07-Oct-2013 | Unsuccessful | | 21-Feb-2013 | -
Don't forget
to reply to your offers. You must reply by Wed, 8 May 2013
Deadline for replying
Add choice
Reply to offers
Payment
Please make sure you have checked the details of your choices **before** making replies. Click on the course code in red above to access the choice details.
Click here to record
• Firm acceptance
• Insurance acceptance
• Decline
application processed by UCAS : 10-Oct-2012
last log in : 10-Mar-2013
ucas.com
terms & conditions | contact us

Points to remember when replying to your offers

- Try to attend open days or visits before you decide, but remember to reply by the deadline. See the table on page 252 for the reply deadline dates. If you are visiting a uni after your reply date, please contact the uni for advice.
- Think carefully before you decide which offers to accept because once you accept an offer, including an insurance offer, you are committed to that course (or courses).
- You can reply to offers without waiting to hear back from all your unis. You can cancel any choices that have not made decisions and reply to the offers that you have received using Track. But you must be certain that you want to accept these offers, as once you have made your replies you will not be able to reinstate any cancelled choices.
- If you are replying to a joint conditional offer, eg for a degree and HND, you are replying to the whole joint offer – when your exam results are published, the uni will decide which part of the offer is most suitable for you.

Types of reply

You reply to each of your offers in one of the following ways:

- firm acceptance
- insurance acceptance
- decline.

Myth buster

You don't have to accept an offer as an insurance

The main rule in replying to your offers is to only accept an offer if you'd be happy to study there. When you choose where to accept, decide based on what you want, not what anyone else wants you to do. This is really important – you'd be surprised at how many people accept an offer then change their minds later.

> This is apparent more than ever with insurance choices. If we had a pound for every person who calls us to ask if they can cancel their insurance choice, we'd be rich. We want to help you to make the right decision straight away, and not wish you could go back and change it later.
>
> So – only accept an insurance choice if you really do want it as a back-up to your firm choice. If you're not sure it's right for you, just have a firm choice – there are other options later in the year, such as Clearing, if your firm choice can't offer you the place.

Firm acceptance

Your firm acceptance is your first choice – this is your preferred choice out of all the offers you have received. You can only have one firm acceptance.

If you accept an unconditional offer, you are agreeing that you will attend the course at that uni, so you cannot make an insurance acceptance and you must decline any other offers. We send you a letter which explains whether there is anything else you need to do.

If you accept a conditional offer, you are agreeing that you will attend the course at that university or college if you meet the conditions of the offer. You can accept another offer as an insurance choice.

See the 'Unis' decisions' section on pages 237 to 246 for more information about conditional and unconditional offers.

Insurance acceptance

If your firm choice is a conditional offer, you can accept another offer as an insurance. Your insurance acceptance can be a conditional or unconditional offer and acts as a back-up, so if you don't meet the conditions for your firm choice but meet the conditions for your insurance, you will be committed to the insurance choice. You can only have one insurance choice.

The conditions for your insurance choice should normally be lower than for your firm choice. If they are higher than your firm choice, and if you're not accepted by your firm choice, it's very unlikely that you will be accepted for your insurance choice.

You don't have to accept an offer as an insurance – if you're not sure about any of your other choices once you have accepted a firm choice, you're not obliged to accept one as an insurance option. **Only accept an offer as an insurance if you're definitely happy to take that course and that uni.**

Decline

Once you have decided which offer to accept firmly, and which (if any) to accept as an insurance, you must decline all other offers. If you don't want to accept any of your offers, you can decline them all. You will then be eligible to use Extra or Clearing, depending upon your circumstances. See page 255 for information about Extra and page 299 to find out about Clearing.

There are four combinations of offers and replies:

- **Unconditional firm only** – you've firmly accepted an unconditional offer. You cannot have an insurance choice. You are committed to take up the place on that course at that uni. The choice shows as 'Unconditional Firm' in Track.
- **Conditional firm only** – you've firmly accepted a conditional offer. The choice shows as 'Conditional Firm' in Track.
- **Conditional firm + conditional insurance** – you've firmly accepted one conditional offer and accepted another conditional offer as an insurance. The choices show as 'Conditional Firm' and 'Conditional Insurance' in Track.
- **Conditional firm + unconditional insurance** – you've firmly accepted a conditional offer and accepted an unconditional offer as an insurance. The choices show as 'Conditional Firm' and 'Unconditional Insurance' in Track.

How and when to reply to your offers

You use Track to view the decisions from all your choices and reply to your offers. Your reply date will be shown in Track. Your reply date is based on when we receive the last decision from your choices, so it might be different to other people's dates. If you don't reply by the date given, your offers will be declined. If this happens, you need to call our Customer Contact Centre to find out what you can do.

UCAStv

Watch our video about replying to your offers on UCAStv at www.ucas.tv for more information.

Reply dates are based on when we receive the last decision from your choices:

Last decision received at UCAS by	Your reply date is
End March	Early May
Early May	Early June
Early June	End June
Mid-July	Late July

The exact reply dates may vary slightly in different application years. See the Important dates page on **www.ucas.com** for the current dates.

Here's what your Track choices screen could look like after you've replied to your offers:

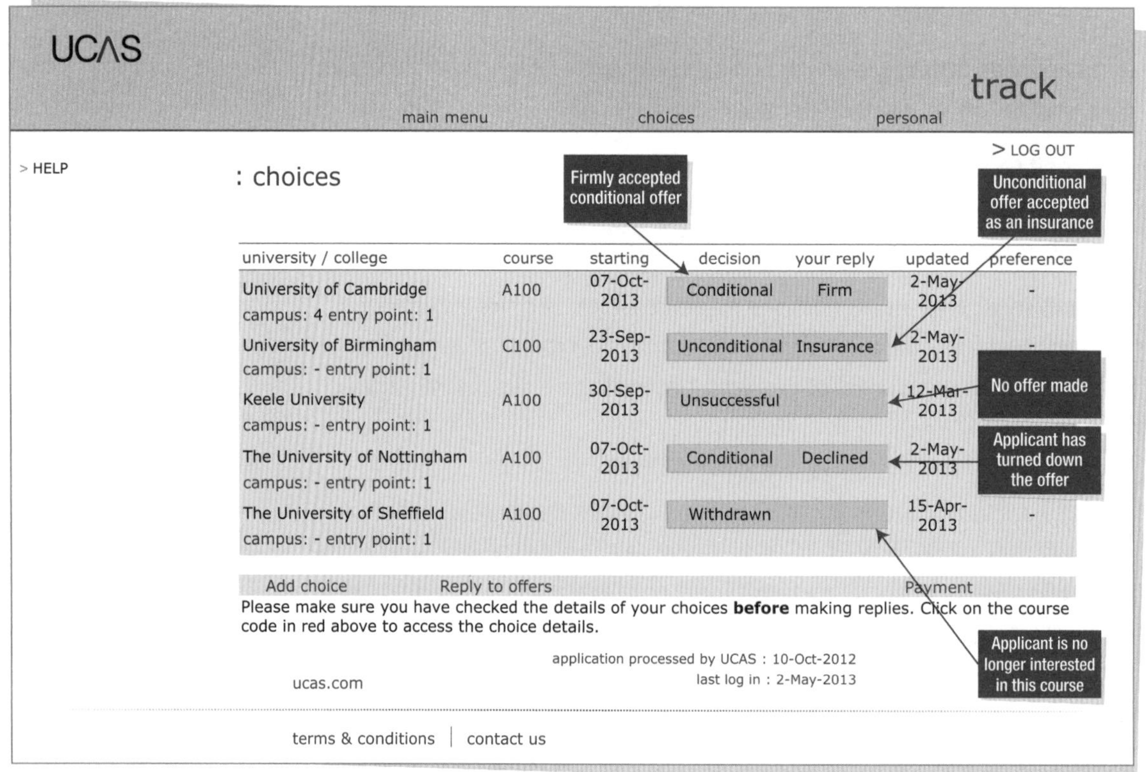

Replying to offers – FAQs

How do I reply to my offers?

You reply to your offers on Track. You do not need to reply to your offers until you have received decisions from all your universities. When they have all sent their decisions to us, we automatically ask you to reply to offers.

If you are no longer interested in receiving offers from the unis that have not made decisions, you can cancel these choices in Track and then reply to the offers you have already received. It may sound obvious, but check you have received the offers you wish to accept from us before doing this.

I want to reply to my offers but there is no reply button on Track. What can I do?

The reply button only appears on Track when you've received decisions from all the universities to which you have applied.

If you want to accept an offer, you can cancel the choices for all unis that have not made decisions on Track. The reply option will then be available. Please check that you have received the offers you wish to accept before cancelling any choices.

If Track shows decisions from all your universities, but there is no reply option, you need to call our Customer Contact Centre.

When do I reply to my offers?

We will ask you to reply when all of your universities have sent us decisions on your application. Your reply deadline will be shown in Track. This date will vary depending on the date that you receive your final decision. Your reply date may be different to your friends' dates. The different reply dates are listed on the Important dates page on **www.ucas.com**.

What will happen if I don't reply to my offers by my deadline?

If you don't reply by your deadline, we'll assume that you don't want any of your offers and will decline them on your behalf. We'll write to you and tell you what has happened. In most cases, we can reinstate and accept offers if you contact us within seven days from when your offers were declined. If you are happy that your offers were declined, we will tell you about Extra or Clearing depending on the stage of the application cycle. See page 255 for information about Extra and page 299 to find out about Clearing.

How many offers can I accept?
If your offers are conditional, you can accept one firmly and another as insurance. Your insurance acceptance acts as a back-up in case you don't meet the conditions for your firm offer.

If your offers are unconditional, you only accept one, as you do not need to hold another. It will be your firm acceptance. At that point, the place will be yours.

If you have a mixture of conditional and unconditional offers, you can hold an unconditional offer as insurance if you firmly accept a conditional offer.

Can I accept an offer as an insurance if it asks for the same grades as my firm choice?
Yes, your insurance acceptance can be whichever offer you prefer. It can even ask for higher grades, but remember that if you do not meet the conditions of your firm offer and your insurance offer asks for the same grades or higher, you may find that you cannot be accepted by either uni. You will then go into Clearing. See page 299 for information about Clearing.

Can I choose between my firm and insurance choices if I get the grades for both?
No. If you meet the grades for your firm acceptance, your insurance acceptance is automatically declined and the place is offered to someone else. If you cannot take up the place at the uni where you have a firm acceptance, you should contact them direct to discuss your options.

Can I change my replies?
You can change your replies within seven days of making them by contacting our Customer Contact Centre.

If you wish to change your replies after seven days, you should contact your chosen universities direct for advice.

Will I get confirmation of my offer replies?
If you provided a verified email address when you applied, we will send you an email asking you to log in to Track and look at the change to your application. In Track you will be able to view a letter that confirms your offer replies.

If you did not provide a verified email address when you applied, we will send you a letter within five working days of making your replies. If you don't receive this letter, you need to call our Customer Contact Centre.

If you've no offers, Extra could be for you

If you've applied through UCAS and you've:

- already made five choices
- received decisions from all these choices, and
- either had no offers or declined any offers you've received

you might be able to apply through Extra for another course. In Extra, you can apply for any course with vacancies. Extra is open between the end of February and the end of June. You apply for one course at a time using Track.

If you decline your offers and add an Extra choice, you will not be able to accept any of your original offers later.

UCAStv

Watch our video about applying through Extra on UCAStv at **www.ucas.tv** for more information.

How does Extra work?

If you are eligible for Extra, a button will appear on your Track screen which you can use to apply for a course in Extra.

Extra

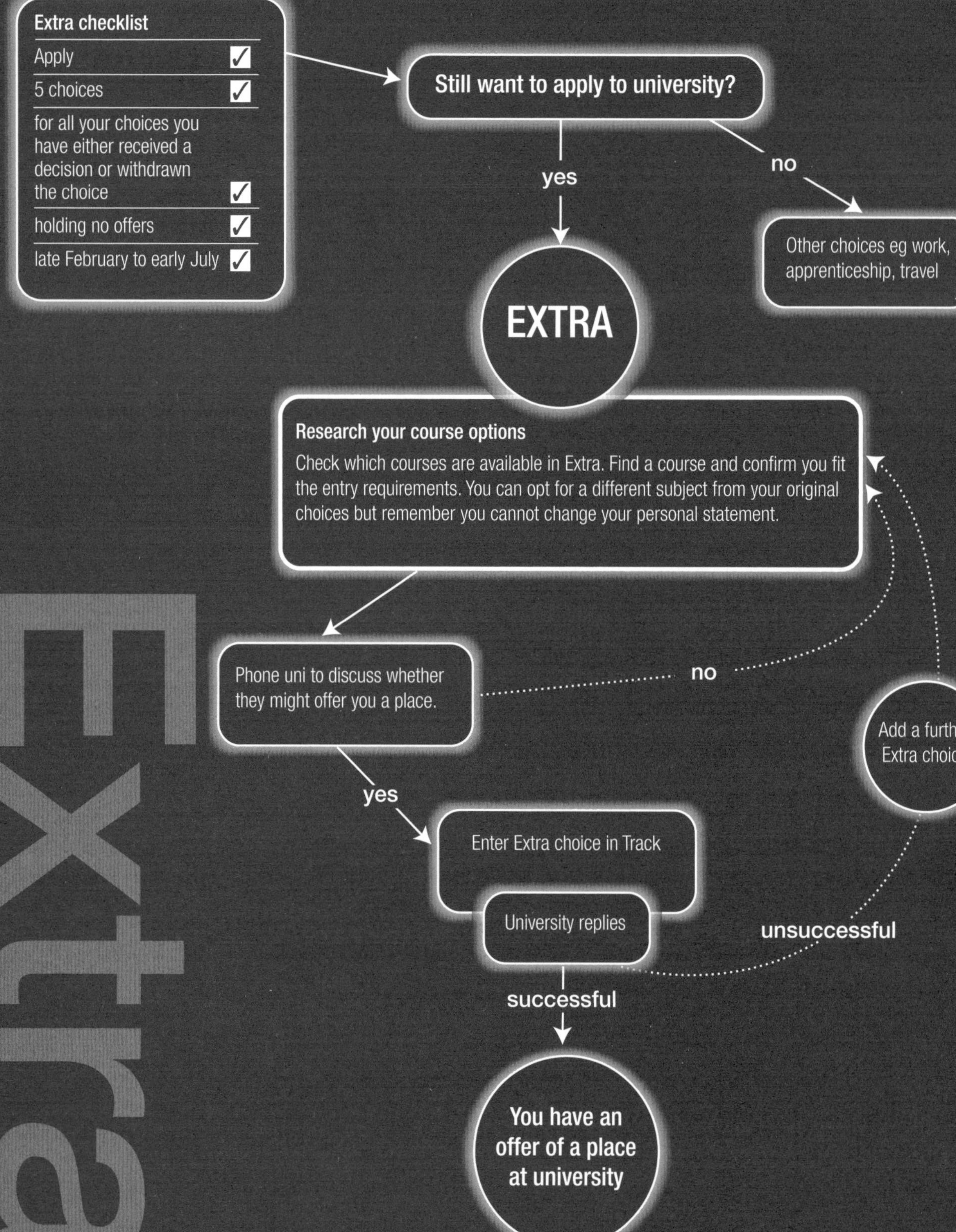

UCAS
Extra checklist
Apply ✓
5 choices ✓
for all your choices you have either received a decision or withdrawn the choice ✓
holding no offers ✓
late February to early July ✓
Still want to apply to university?
yes
no
Other choices eg work, apprenticeship, travel
EXTRA
Research your course options
Check which courses are available in Extra. Find a course and confirm you fit the entry requirements. You can opt for a different subject from your original choices but remember you cannot change your personal statement.
Phone uni to discuss whether they might offer you a place.
no
yes
Enter Extra choice in Track
University replies
successful
unsuccessful
Add a further Extra choice
You have an offer of a place at university
Extra

Before you apply for an Extra choice, you should:

- check if the course has vacancies in Extra on Course Finder at **www.ucas.com**. You need to tick the 'Available in extra' box in the study options section when you do your search.
- look at the Entry requirements and Institution details sections on Course Finder for more information.
- contact the uni to make sure that they can consider you.

When you have decided on your Extra choice, you need to enter the details in Track. We'll then send your application to the uni.

Choosing a course

Research the courses before deciding which to apply for in Extra. If you applied for high-demand courses originally and were unsuccessful, you could consider related or alternative subjects. Your teachers or careers advisers, or the unis themselves, can provide useful guidance.

What happens next?

If you are offered a place, you can choose whether or not to accept it. If you accept an offer, you are committed to it, which means that you cannot apply anywhere else. You will need to reply to your offer by the date shown in Track.

If you decline an offer, or the uni turns you down, you can apply for a different course through Extra (time permitting). Your Extra button in Track will be reactivated.

If a uni has had your application in Extra for more than 21 days and not made a decision, you can choose to let this uni continue to consider you or apply to another uni in Extra. Your Extra button in Track will be reactivated. Before you apply to another uni in Extra, you should tell the uni that currently has your application to stop considering you.

If you don't get an offer in Extra, don't worry! From mid-July you can use our Clearing process which gives you another opportunity to apply for courses with vacancies. See page 299 for information about Clearing.

Here's what two of our applicants said about Extra:

'I now know that going through Extra is nothing to be ashamed of. With the current places versus the amount of people going to uni, it is inevitable that some will not get into their choices, but at least we have Extra and Clearing, so there is still an option for us.'

'Now with UCAS Extra you can 'reapply' if you are not satisfied. That's so good!'

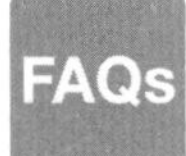

Extra – FAQs

Why can't I apply to a uni in Extra?
To apply for a course in Extra you must have already made five choices, received decisions for all these choices and had no offers or declined any offers received.

When can I apply in Extra?
Extra operates from late February to the end of June.

How do I find out which courses are available in Extra?
You use Course Finder on our website. You need to tick the 'Available in extra' box in the study option section of Course Finder when you do your search.

How many courses can I apply for in Extra?
While Extra is operating you can apply for as many courses as you like in Track, but you may only apply for one course at a time. If you accept an offer through Extra, you cannot apply for any other courses.

How long does the university have to consider my Extra application?
Universities have 21 days from receiving your Extra application to give us their decision. After 21 days if they have not make a decision, you can choose to give them more time or apply to another university in Extra.

I've applied for a course in Extra but I want to change it. What can I do?
You should tell the uni where you've applied that you are no longer interested in a place and ask them to send a withdrawn decision to us. When we receive this decision you will be able to apply for another course in Extra, time permitting.

Case study

Name: Kevin Minors
Kevin started a mathematics degree at the University of Oxford in October 2010.

I had mixed emotions when I received my offer. I was extremely excited because the university decided to give me an offer and not to decline my application, but on the other hand, I was filled with shock because the grades my offer required were better than any grades ever achieved at my high school (I did IB in Bermuda) so I was very nervous. But I did not let that stop me and you cannot let it stop you.

If your university gives you an offer that seems out of your reach, or even if you believe that it is within your reach, continue to give 110% to your studies and you will amaze yourself. Use the offer as a personal goal that you have and create a plan to achieve that goal, whether it is making a review schedule for your exams, forecasting the grades that you will need on certain tests that will allow you to reach the offer conditions in the final exams or things like that. My offer was ridiculous but with hard work, not only did I meet the conditions, I exceeded them. And if I can do it, so can you!

For Oxford's admission process, I had to take a mathematics entrance exam before I would even be considered for an interview. I did it and I'm guessing it was OK because they then offered me an invitation for an interview. While researching Oxford interviews, I heard many rumours like people setting themselves on fire just to get attention from the Selection Committee and crazy things like that but none of them are really true.

While I was in Oxford checking the notice board for when my interview would be, I was extremely nervous. More nervous than when I got my offer, but one of the best things about the whole interview process was that I was able to meet other students who applied to Oxford and were there for interviews as well. It was a great way to make new friends and to meet possible classmates in the year to come. And everyone was nervous together! We could talk to each other for support, which made it that much more bearable.

My interview was not a normal interview. It was academic based. There was no 'Why mathematics?' or 'Why Oxford?' We just went through a few maths problems and that was it. Nothing else. But, bear in mind, this may not be true for all universities. In order to prepare for university, besides doing tons of background information on the university, you need to research yourself. Know what you love and have a passion for and let it show in the interview. That's most important.

Once my exams were finished, the wait started for results day. It seemed that time had stood still. Days were lasting weeks, weeks took months. It was painful both mentally and emotionally. But once school had finished and I started my summer job, my mind was not thinking about the grades. I slowly started to think about summer and all the fun things I could do. I temporarily forgot about UCAS, university, grades and all the other things that were out of my control. If you think about it too much, you will drive yourself crazy. No, I'm serious. You will literally become crazy so don't do it. Keep busy and get your mind off grades and you will be fine.

However, once the results day is only a few days away, you will naturally get nervous and start to worry about everything that could happen. Whether you get the grades and everything is perfect or if you need to reconsider where you want to go. No matter what, just remember that there is nothing more that you can do. Whatever happens will happen. You just have to be mature about it and deal with the situation. I collected my results at 12:30pm and at 10:30am the following day I received an email from Oxford saying that I had met the offer so that was really helpful for me because I was thinking about it all morning. The best advice I can give you is to keep busy during results day until the grades are officially released because you will also go crazy if you continuously check the website or your school office.

Chapter checklist

These are the things you should be doing in Step 3 of your applicant journey:

- [ ] Contact us if you don't receive your Welcome letter and *Your UCAS Welcome Guide* within 14 days of sending your application to us.
- [ ] Check the information on your Welcome letter and tell us if anything is wrong.
- [ ] If your postal address, email address or phone numbers change, enter the new details in Track. If you're at boarding school, don't forget to change your postal address to your home address at the end of the school year.
- [ ] Tell us and your chosen unis about changes to your course or exam arrangements and anything that could affect your exam results.
- [ ] Apply for student finance. If you live in England, Northern Ireland or Wales and you didn't agree to share the personal details and choices information on your application with your student finance organisation when you applied, opt in to sharing this information in Track. It will make applying for student finance quicker and easier.
- [ ] If you have a disability, make sure your chosen unis will be able to meet all your requirements before you start your course.
- [ ] Prepare fully for interviews and auditions.
- [ ] Whenever we tell you your application status has changed, log in to Track to look at your unis' decisions.
- [ ] When all of your unis have made decisions, make sure that you reply to any offers received by the deadline shown in Track.
- [ ] Consider applying for other courses in Extra if you don't receive any offers.

www.ucas.com

Step 4
Results

Now you've taken your exams you can't just relax and forget about university until August. This section provides advice on what you need to do while waiting for your exam results.

In this section you'll find out whether or not you need to send your results to universities where you're holding offers. If you've asked for any exams to be re-marked or your school has not certificated your A level results, we tell you what you need to do. We clearly describe all the possible situations that could apply to you after your unis have received your exam results. You'll find out what you can do if you don't meet all your offer conditions, but a uni makes you a changed offer.

You'll also discover what happens if you don't have any offers or your unis cannot confirm your place.

Step 4 **Results**

You are holding one or two offers and are waiting for your results

↓

Check whether your exam results are sent direct to UCAS (see **www.ucas.com/students/results/examresults)**

listed → UCAS sends your results to the universities and colleges where you hold offers

not listed → Remember to send your results to the universities and colleges where you hold offers

↓

When you receive your results and have forwarded them if necessary, check Track to see if your firm or insurance place is confirmed

Step 4

Preparing for exam results

After you've replied to your offers, there are several things you should do while you're waiting for exam results.

Know your login details for Track

You'll need access to Track to see if you've been accepted, so make sure you know your Personal ID, username and password for logging in. If you can't remember your login details, use the 'Forgotten login details?' service on the Track login page.

Be available

You need to be available when your exam results are published. You might have to make quick and perhaps difficult decisions about your future. You need to be available to contact unis yourself; they'll want to speak to you and not to your friends and relatives.

Check your contact details are up-to-date

You should check that your personal details are correct in Track – we and the unis contact you by email, letter and sometimes by phone, so make sure that we have your up-to-date details.

If you're at boarding school, make sure you change your postal address to your home address when school finishes for the summer.

When you change your postal address, you should arrange for your mail to be redirected in case letters have already been sent.

Making changes

You must contact the uni where you're holding an offer if:

- you're unable to take up a place and you need to withdraw your application
- you want to change the conditions of your offer, such as
    - **the course itself:** you may prefer to take a related course or do an HND course rather than a degree course
    - **the year you start the course:** a uni may have offered you a place for this year's entry, but you now want to take a gap year and start a year later
    - **the point you join the course:** your offer could be to start the course in the first year (year 1), but you've decided that you would rather take a foundation year and start in year 0.

You may need to send your results to your unis

The exam results we currently receive from exam boards and send to the unis are listed on pages 272 to 274. If your qualification is not listed, you need to send your exam results to the unis where you have accepted offers. When the unis have received your results from us or from you, they will decide whether or not to confirm your place.

As soon as one of your unis tells us whether or not you have a place, we will show their decision in Track.

Read the 'What happens after the unis have your exam results' section on page 275 to find out what happens if you do or don't have a confirmed place.

International students

Remember to find out from your school or college how and when your exam results will be given to the universities where you're holding offers. Some exam boards, such as the International Baccalaureate Organisation, may send your results direct to the universities if your school gives them your UCAS Personal ID. If your results are not sent direct to the universities where you're holding offers, you should arrange for a copy of your final results or transcripts to be sent to them.

What applicants have said

Here's what some of our applicants have said about exam results.

'If you think about it [exam results] too much, you will drive yourself crazy… so don't do it. Keep busy and get your mind off grades and you will be fine.'

'Whether you get the grades and everything is perfect or if you need to reconsider where you want to go, no matter what, just remember that there's nothing more that you can do. Whatever happens will happen. You just have to be mature about it and deal with the situation.'

'I did well, but not as well as I wanted… I went to college and boosted my UCAS points up within a year and here I am now. There's always a way to get into uni.'

UCAStv

Watch our video about preparing for exam results on UCAStv at **www.ucas.tv** for more information.

'Fear on results day is rational. Even if you have done superbly, there's still a part of you that thinks 'WHAT IF'… so take it from me, an underachiever; anything is possible if you set your mind to it.'

FINAL EXAM RESULTS

Exam results

You're taking exams for qualifications not listed in this section

We list the qualifications for which we currently receive exam results on pages 272 to 274. If you're taking exams for qualifications not listed, you must send the results to the unis where you're holding offers.

You're taking exams for qualifications listed in this section

If you're taking exams for any qualifications in the list on pages 272 to 274, the exam boards will send us a record of the exams you have entered. We then match this record with the qualifications information on your application.

If there are differences between your exam registration details provided by the exam boards and the information on your application, we will send you a letter in June. You must enter any information requested on the letter and return it to us. This will help us to match your exam results with your application.

If we cannot match the qualification details on your application with the results received, it may take longer for your unis to confirm whether or not you have a place. Applications containing qualifications that cannot be checked against exam results may be considered fraudulent, and may be cancelled.

When the exam boards send us your exam results we match them with your application details. We then send your results automatically to the unis where you are holding offers.

For some of the exam results we receive, we only process the overall result and pass it on to your unis. In some cases if you've taken exams in a modular set of subjects, such as for the BTEC, International Baccalaureate or Irish Leaving Certificate, we pass on the grade for each subject. For A levels we process the unit grades that go towards your overall grade.

If your unis tell you that they've not received your exam results, you must contact your school or college and, if needed, our Customer Contact Centre for advice.

Did you know?

We can't tell you your exam results

We receive some exam results and send them to the universities, but this is managed through a dedicated team who keep the details confidential. Some people contact us to find out what their results are, but we can't provide this information.

We see the same as what's displayed in Track – we can see if you have been offered a place at your chosen uni, not specific results for qualifications, so speak to your school or college to find out when you'll receive your results.

Track during results processing

Track is 'frozen' the week before Scottish Qualifications Authority (SQA) and A level results are published so that universities can give us their decisions. While Track is frozen we don't update your application.

On SQA results day we publish a Clearing vacancy list for universities and colleges in Scotland at **www.ucas.com**. Then on A level results day we also publish Clearing vacancies for the whole UK. Applicants who are already eligible for

Clearing or who become eligible after they receive their results can then contact institutions about vacancies.

We open Track mid-morning on SQA and A level results days, so that you can see if your university has confirmed your place.

Myth buster

Track is not updated at midnight on A level results day

Each year lots of applicants try to log in to Track to view whether they've been accepted. We don't update Track at midnight, and we never have! It's only the Clearing vacancy search which goes live at midnight. So don't lose sleep by trying to log in – it won't be available.

Re-marked exams

If you ask for any of your exams to be re-marked, you must tell the unis where you're holding offers. If a uni cannot confirm your place based on the initial results, you should ask them if they would be able to reconsider their decision after the re-mark. Unis don't have to reconsider their position if your re-mark results in higher grades. Don't forget that re-marks may also result in lower grades.

The exam boards tell us about any re-marks that result in grade changes. We then send the revised grades to the unis where you're holding offers. As soon as you know about grade changes, you should also tell your unis.

'Cashing in' A level results

If you have taken A levels, your school or college must certificate or 'cash in' all your unit scores before the exam board can award final grades. If when you collect your A level results you have to add up your unit scores to find out your final grades, it means your school or college has not 'cashed in' your results.

We only receive 'cashed in' results from the exam boards, so if your results have not been 'cashed in', you must contact your school or college and ask them to send a 'cash in' request to the exam board. You also need to tell the unis where you're holding offers that there'll be a delay in receiving your results and call our Customer Contact Centre to find out when your results have been received.

When we receive your 'cashed in' results from the exam board we'll send them to the unis where you're holding offers straight away.

International students

If you don't achieve the required English language score in your offer conditions, find out if the universities where you're holding offers:

- will accept other online tests or offer their own test as an alternative
- run 'pre-sessional' English courses
- will accept you on to an International Foundation Programme. These are normally one academic year in length and are designed to give international students extra English language tuition and academic skills for successful entry on to a degree course.

Exam results we receive

We currently receive exam results for the following qualifications, match them with application details and send them to the unis where applicants are holding offers.

- AAT NVQ Level 3 in Accounting
- AQA Baccalaureate
- Asset Languages
- BTEC
  - HNC/HND
  - National Award, Certificate and Diploma
  - National Certificate and National Diploma in Early Years – Theory/Practical
  - National Extended Diploma, Diploma, 90 Credit Diploma, Subsidiary Diploma, Certificate
  - Specialist (Award, Certificate and Diploma)
- CACHE Diploma in Childcare and Education, Extended Diploma for Children's and Young People's Workforce

- Cambridge ESOL
  - Certificate of Proficiency in English (CPE)
  - Certificate of Advanced English (CAE)
- Cambridge International Examinations (CIE)
  - Advanced Level, Advanced Subsidiary
  - Advanced International Certificate of Education (AICE) Diploma
  - Higher 1, Higher 2 and Higher 3
  - Pre-U Diploma, Pre-U Certificate, Pre-U Short Course, GPR (Global Perspectives and Independent Research)
  - Special Papers (overseas applicants only, winter results only)
- Certificate of Personal Effectiveness CoPE awards (ASDAN)
- Community Volunteering Award (AQA, Edexcel OCR) and Certificate (ASDAN)
- Diplomas (Advanced, Progression)
- Diploma in Fashion Retail (ABC)
- Diploma in Foundation Studies (Art and Design) (ABC, Edexcel, WJEC)
- EDI Level 3 Certificates in Accounting and Accounting (IAS)
- Essential Skills (CCEA, City & Guilds)
- Essential Skills Wales (WJEC, City & Guilds, Edexcel)
- Wider Essential Skills Wales (WJEC)
- Extended Project
- Free Standing Mathematics (AQA and OCR Level 3)
- Functional Skills
- GCE Advanced and Advanced Subsidiary (Single and Double Awards), 9 Unit Awards and Advanced Extension Award
- *ifs* School of Finance Certificate and Diploma in Financial Studies (DipFS)
- International Baccalaureate (Diploma and Certificate) (if you have agreed)

- Irish Leaving Certificate
- Key Skills (Levels 2, 3 and 4)
- Music examinations grades 6-8 (ABRSM, LCM, Trinity)
- OCR
  - iMedia Certificate and Diploma
  - iPRO Certificate and Diploma
  - Mathematics STEP Papers I, II and III
  - National Certificates, Diplomas and Extended Diplomas (all at National Qualifications Framework level 3 only)
  - Principal Learning
  - Certificate in Mathematics for Engineers
  - Certificate for Young Enterprise
- Speech and Drama – grades 6, 7 and 8 (ESB, LAMDA, LCM and Trinity Guildhall)
- SQA
  - Baccalaureate
  - Core Skills
  - Highers, Advanced Highers
  - HNC/HND
  - Interdisciplinary Project
  - Intermediate 2
  - National Certificates
  - PC Passport
  - Skills for Work
- Welsh Baccalaureate

The above list was accurate at the time this book was published, but further qualifications may have been added since publication. The latest list can be found at **www.ucas.com/students/results/examresults**.

What happens after the unis have your exam results

After we've sent your exam results to the uni or unis where you're holding an offer, they tell us whether or not they can accept you and we show their decisions in Track. This process is called 'Confirmation'. If you meet all the conditions of your offer, the uni will confirm your place. Even if you've not quite met all the offer conditions, the uni may still be able to accept you. You need to look at Track to find out if you have a confirmed place.

We update information on the Track 'choices' screen exactly as it is provided by the unis. If you have any queries about changes to choice details, you need to contact the unis and not us.

The sections below describe the different scenarios that could apply to you after the unis have given us their final decisions and what happens next.

You're accepted by your firm choice

If you're accepted by your firm choice, we send you a Confirmation letter in the post. This letter confirms that you have a definite place at the uni and lets you know if there is anything you need to do. You may still need to tell the uni whether or not you will be taking up your place. When you receive this letter, you have officially gained a place. The uni will contact you with any further information.

You're accepted by your firm choice and you meet and exceed the conditions of the offer

If you meet and exceed the conditions of the offer from your firm choice, you can apply through Adjustment. In Adjustment you can apply to other unis with vacancies for a limited period while still keeping your place at your firm choice. See page 292 for more information about Adjustment.

You receive a 'changed course' offer

If you receive a 'changed course' offer, it means that the uni is unable to confirm your place on the course you accepted because you have not met the original offer conditions. They have, however, been able to offer you a place on a different course. For example, you may have applied for a degree course, but the uni now offers you a place on an HND course in the same or a similar subject. You could have applied for medicine and the uni now offers you a place on a related course such as biomedical sciences.

A 'changed course' offer may also cover a change of:

- **start date** – you may have applied to start a course in one year but the uni offers you a place to start in the following year
- **the point you join the course** – you may have applied to start the course in the first year (year 1), but the uni wants you to take a foundation year and start in year 0.

The procedure for replying to 'changed course' offers depends on the status of your application. Here are the different scenarios.

You've only applied for one course

You must accept or decline a 'changed course' offer in Track within five days of the offer being made. If you don't make your reply within five days, the offer will automatically be declined.

If you decline the offer and you've paid the reduced fee for a single choice, you must pay an additional amount in Track if you want to apply for courses with vacancies in Clearing. See page 299 for information about Clearing.

When you've made your additional payment, your Clearing Number will be shown in Track.

You've applied for more than one course, but you've only accepted one offer

You must accept or decline the 'changed course' offer in Track within five days of the offer being made. If you decline the offer you will automatically go into Clearing. See page 300 for information about applying for courses with vacancies in Clearing.

You've applied for more than one course and you've accepted firm and insurance choice offers

There are three possible scenarios.

- **Your firm choice makes a 'changed course' offer** – you must accept or decline the revised firm offer in Track. If you decline it, you will either be accepted by your insurance choice or, if they cannot confirm your place, you will automatically go into Clearing.
- **Your insurance choice makes you a 'changed course' offer** – you will only be able to accept this revised insurance offer in Track if your firm choice does not accept you. It is possible to decline a changed insurance offer immediately. If you are then not accepted by your firm choice, you will be automatically entered into Clearing.
- **Both your firm and insurance choices make 'changed course' offers** – you may accept either revised offer in Track, or decline both and move automatically into Clearing.

Your exam results don't meet the conditions of your firm choice offer, but they meet the conditions of your insurance choice offer

If you don't meet the conditions of your firm choice offer and the uni doesn't confirm your place, but you do meet the conditions of your insurance choice offer, your place at your insurance choice will be confirmed. When the uni confirms your place, the choice will show as 'Unconditional Firm' in Track. We will send you a Confirmation letter by post. This letter confirms that you have a definite place at the uni and lets you know if there is anything you need to do. You may still need to tell the uni whether or not you'll be taking up your place. When you receive your Confirmation letter you've officially gained a place. The uni will contact you with any further information.

Your exam results don't meet the conditions of your firm or insurance choice offers

If you don't meet the conditions for the offers you've accepted and the unis can't offer you a place, you'll be automatically entered into Clearing. Your Clearing Number will be shown in Track. See page 300 for information about applying for courses with vacancies in Clearing.

What if you're not holding any offers?

You may not have any offers because:

- none of your choices was able to offer you a place
- you declined any offers received, or
- you applied after 30 June.

If you're not holding any offers and you have paid the full application fee, you'll be entered into Clearing automatically. Your Clearing Number will be shown in Track. See page 300 for information about applying for courses with vacancies in Clearing.

Applicants with disabilities

If the uni where you have a confirmed place has agreed to adapt buildings or the course provision to meet your requirements, check with them that work is under way and that everything will be in place before you start the course. You may want to visit the uni to make sure the changes will meet your needs.

Case study

A level results day at The Grammar School at Leeds, West Yorkshire

You will probably have seen exam results day in the media or may have experienced it second hand either through a sibling or other family member. So what is your impression of the day? Chaos, excitement, terror? If you are applying to university from school, you are inevitably going to experience results day yourself.

All schools offer advice and support in different ways on the 'big day', but Jane Pratt, UCAS Co-ordinator, describes what happens at The Grammar School at Leeds.

We give advice and assistance to students from the moment they register on UCAS Apply in the June of Year 12 through to results day and beyond. There are students who make a late decision to apply just ahead of the June deadline having researched courses at the last moment on UCAS Course Finder and those who apply after 30 June knowing they will automatically be in Clearing. Others have completed a first year at university but have decided that they want to change institutions and need to reapply; they too use UCAS Course Finder and information from individual universities.

The day before A level results day is one of the most nerve-wracking for staff as the Higher Education Team at The Grammar School at Leeds (GSAL) assesses results against the UCAS Applicant Status Report and our own database, which contains the idiosyncratic aspects of offers such as 'must have a B in Chemistry' or '260 points from three A2 subjects'. This helps us to identify those students who are the most likely to require guidance and help over the following days.

GSAL students are able to access their results online from 6am using the school's network and later in the morning they can log into the UCAS Track system to find out whether or not they have been accepted by their firm or insurance choices. Students begin to arrive at 7am and, although many already know their results, virtually all students come into school to celebrate (or commiserate), see tutors and other members of staff and participate in the extensive breakfast laid on by the catering staff. At 7am staff have access to UCAS Track, which confirms our work of the previous day and often gives us a pleasant surprise when a student who we thought had 'missed' an offer has actually been accepted. We have an hour window before students can access this information, which gives us time to reappraise our lists and focus on those who will need one-to-one support.

AS students are also able to access their results and separate provision is made for those who wish to reconsider their A2 subject choices or who want information about re-marks.

The atmosphere is very emotional with tears and laughter in equal measure. Often the tears are from those who have done well, and from parents who are relieved. The volume of shrieking seems to grow minute by minute.

For those students who require advice, the Sixth Form Centre computers are available and mobile phones are essential. Members of staff also keep a record of students' problems. Students are advised to be prepared to travel to meet admissions tutors, often at short notice. As Clearing opens later in the day there is still time to think things through and really consider the appropriateness of courses and places.

Results day continues into the following weeks as some students discuss options and others start the applicant journey again by logging into UCAS Apply for entry the following academic year. The process starts all over again on the return to school: a new round; a high level of encouragement and UCAS support staff available to answer new queries.

A level results day is always one of the highlights of a teacher's life as students begin their bright and promising future.

Top tip

If you do want to speak to sixth form staff for support and guidance, arrive fairly early in the day. Many students arrive late morning, sometimes at the same time and then have to wait to speak to someone. The 'early bird' will often walk straight in!

HELOA members in several higher education institutions have put together this timetable and top tips for a typical A level results day in a uni or college.

The Higher Education Liaison Officers Association (HELOA) is the professional association for staff in higher education who work in the fields of education liaison, student recruitment, widening participation and marketing. Its members provide guidance and information to prospective higher education students, their families and advisers at both a regional and national level.

For more information about HELOA, please visit **www.heloa.ac.uk**.

07:30 – Phones at many universities and colleges 'go live' allowing potential students to ring up and ask about courses that interest them. Clearing hotlines vary greatly from uni to uni, but they are by far the most popular way for students to contact institutions about vacancies. The number of calls received in the first few hours can range from a few hundred to over 10,000, depending upon the number of places a uni or college has available.

Top tip

Be prepared to wait in a queue, but make sure that it is you who is on the end of the phone and not a parent, carer or school teacher. Unis want to speak to you and know why you want a place on one of their courses! Try not to be away on holiday during this period, especially out of the country. Have the phone numbers of your firm and insurance choice universities stored in your phone, so you're not wasting time on results day!

09:12 – With many students now having received their exam results from their school or college, it can be a time when they need expert advice on what to do next. Some universities send out advisers and school liaison officers to local colleges and sixth forms to offer information, advice and guidance. Some of these advisers are also able to make offers on the spot to students who meet their institution's entry requirements.

Top tip

Don't panic and start making applications for courses you don't have any interest in. Look through the newspapers to see what is available and keep checking the UCAS and unis' websites for live information about which courses still have vacancies.

11:45 – Lots of students will have had their call dealt with by one of the Clearing advisers working in the hubs. In some cases, after students have confirmed their grades and personal details they are verbally offered a place on a course, only needing to go onto **www.ucas.com** to confirm it. However, for some courses students will need to speak to an academic member of staff who will ask them about why they want a place on the course and at that particular university.

Top tip

When you are applying through Clearing, it is unlikely the university will have a copy of your personal statement, so be prepared to tell them why you think you would be suitable for a place on the course and any experience that you have had in your chosen subject area.

14:52 – When students are offered a place on a course they are also usually invited to attend a Clearing open day. This is an opportunity for them to visit the uni, speak to academic staff about the course they will be studying and to find out about accommodation, finance and student support. These open days can start as early as the afternoon of A level results day with some running every day for the whole of the following week. Some academic staff also use Clearing open days to interview students for a place on their course.

Top tip

Universities often don't have the capacity to deal with students who turn up on results day without having previously made an appointment or having been invited to a Clearing open day. Check the website or wait to speak to a Clearing adviser, before travelling to a university where you want to apply.

17:30 – Universities often report a surge of calls around this time as parents and carers return home from work. Students will call again, trying to secure a place.

Top tip

Local press and websites will be reporting on the first day of Clearing and what places local universities have left. Always make sure you check on the university's own website or ring the Clearing phone line to get the most up-to-date information.

19:00 – By now some universities will have filled their Clearing vacancies and will close their phone lines. Many unis will still have places available on the Friday after A level results day and will accept applications from students right up until the middle of September.

Top tip

Keep checking the UCAS and unis' websites during the week following results day, some courses go back into Clearing when students don't confirm their place with the university. There is also plenty of support and advice available for those students who don't get a place on a course of their choice, so don't worry!

Here's what a few HELOA members in unis or colleges have to say about A level results day.

Nottingham University

'At Nottingham we run a Clearing and Adjustment hotline and also offer applicants the opportunity to visit the university on the Friday after results day. In 2012 we had a small number of course places available, for which we received a large number of calls'

Myerscough College

'For us, Clearing is becoming less important each year as we've not really had that many spare places to fill. Increasingly we are recruiting more of our own FE students to stay on with us to our HE programmes, obviously a luxury that other HEIs tend not to have.'

Liverpool John Moores University

'At Liverpool John Moores in 2012, a team of over sixty members of staff dealt with Clearing course enquiries as well as confirming places with students who were holding firm or insurance choice offers. In total on the first day alone, we handled over 6,000 calls to the university. We were delighted to be able to make a number of offers to students who met our entry requirements and wanted to study at Liverpool John Moores.'

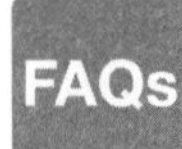

FAQs

I've met the offer conditions, but my uni has not confirmed my place. What should I do?

Don't worry – if you have met all the offer conditions the uni will confirm your place in due course. As soon as we receive confirmation the choice will show as 'Unconditional Firm' in Track.

If you are really concerned, you can contact the university, but don't forget that phone lines will be very busy.

I haven't heard from my uni. What should I do?

If you haven't heard from your firm choice uni, read through the conditions of the offer to check that they are not waiting for further details from you, such as exam certificates or the results of health or criminal record checks.

If you haven't met the offer conditions, the uni may still be considering your application. They may still be able to confirm your place if other applicants have not met their offer conditions. Not all applicants receive their exam results at the same time as you so the uni may have to wait a few days to see if they have available places.

If you have met the conditions and the university has received everything they need, you can contact them direct to find out what's happening.

I've met the grades for my firm offer but I now want to go to my insurance choice. What should I do?

When you firmly accept a conditional offer you are making a commitment to go to that uni if they confirm your place. If you no longer want to take up your place, you should contact the university to discuss your situation.

As soon as you were accepted at your firm choice uni, we would have told your insurance choice uni. This means that they will no longer be holding a place for you, even if you have met the offer conditions, so you'll need to contact them to see if they can still offer you the place. If your firm choice agrees to withdraw your offer, you will be entered into Clearing. If your insurance choice can still offer you a place, they can make you an offer in Clearing. See page 299 for information about Clearing.

My firm choice cannot give me a place, but I don't want to go to my insurance choice – can I apply elsewhere?

When you accept an insurance offer you are making a commitment to go to that uni if they confirm your place. If you no longer want to take up your place, you should contact the uni to discuss your position. If they agree to you not taking up your place and tell us, you will then be able to apply for another course in Clearing. See page 299 for information about Clearing.

What is my AS12 letter? My local authority and bank have asked for a copy.

We send you an AS12 Confirmation letter when a uni confirms your place. If you have not received this letter within five days of seeing 'Unconditional Firm' next to a choice in Track, call our Customer Contact Centre to ask for a copy.

Chapter checklist

These are the things you should be doing in Step 4 of your applicant journey:

- [ ] Make sure we and the unis can contact you. Check all your contact details in Track are up-to-date.
- [ ] Be available to manage things when your exam results are published.
- [ ] Tell the uni if you cannot take up a place or you need to change your offer conditions.
- [ ] Find out if you need to send your exam results to the unis where you're holding offers at **www.ucas.com/students/results/examresults**.
- [ ] After you've received your exam results, log in to Track regularly to find out if your place has been confirmed.
- [ ] If you've met and exceeded all the conditions for your firm offer and the uni has confirmed your place, you could consider applying for other courses through Adjustment. See page 295 for information about Adjustment.
- [ ] Make sure you accept or decline 'changed course' offers in Track. There may be a deadline shown in Track depending on the status of your application.
- [ ] Tell your unis if any of your exams are being re-marked. If they cannot confirm your place based on your initial results, ask them if they will be able to reconsider their decision after the re-mark.
- [ ] If your school or college has not certificated your A level results, ask them to send a 'cash in' request to the exam board and tell the universities where you're holding offers that there'll be a delay in receiving your results.
- [ ] If you do not receive a Confirmation letter within five days of your place being confirmed in Track, ask our Customer Contact Centre to send you a copy.
- [ ] If you don't have a confirmed place, consider applying for other courses in Clearing. See page 299 for information about Clearing.

Step 5
Next steps

The waiting is over and your results are through. It is time to act on the plans you have made, adapting them to the known circumstances you now face. You might be right on course to carry out your plans to the letter, or you might find yourself almost back at square one, or anywhere in between… The video *Next steps after results* on **UCAStv** gives you a flavour of what this step can entail.

Next steps

Step 5 **Next steps**

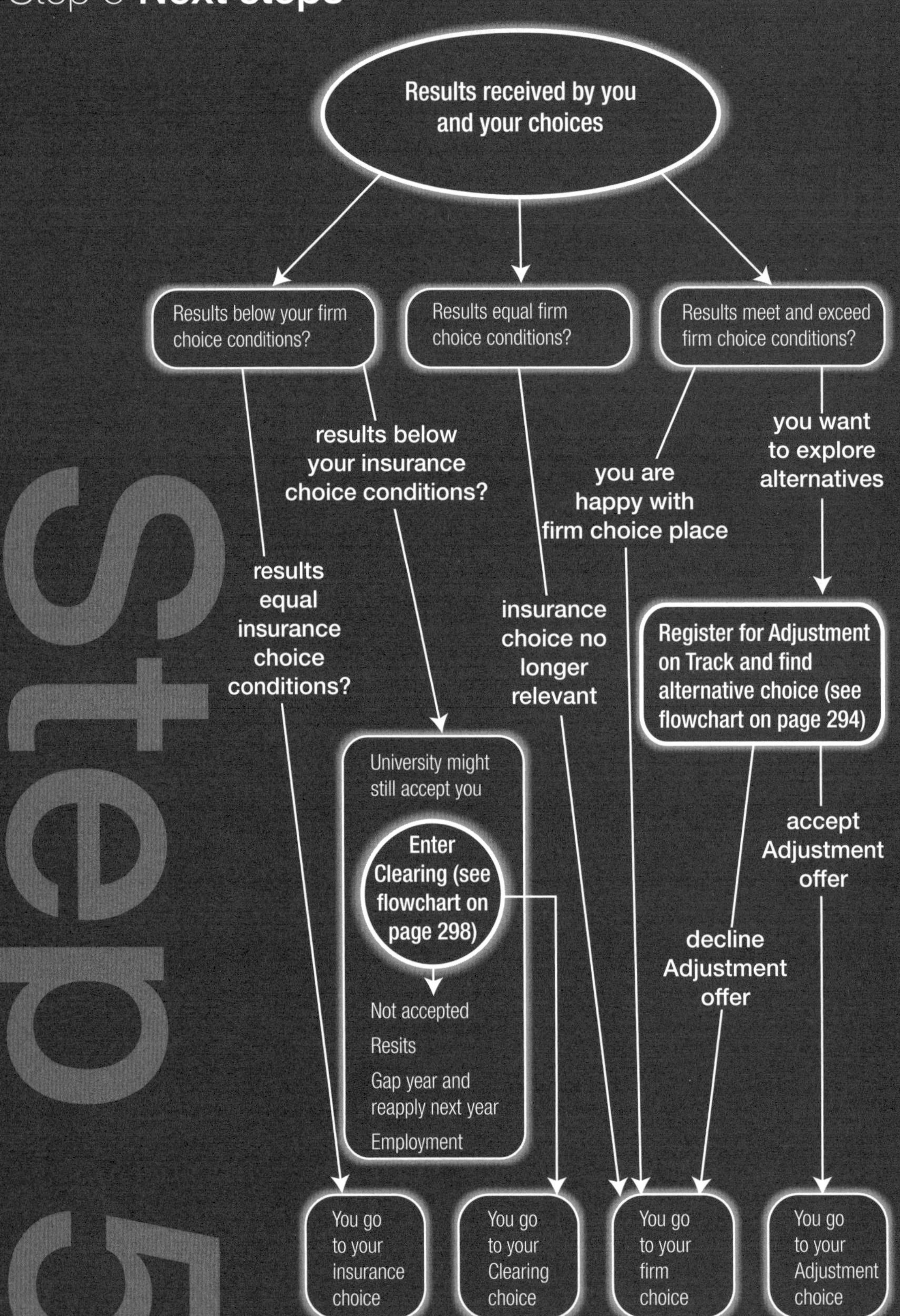

Results received by you and your choices
Results below your firm choice conditions?
Results equal firm choice conditions?
Results meet and exceed firm choice conditions?
results below your insurance choice conditions?
results equal insurance choice conditions?
insurance choice no longer relevant
you are happy with firm choice place
you want to explore alternatives
Register for Adjustment on Track and find alternative choice (see flowchart on page 294)
University might still accept you
Enter Clearing (see flowchart on page 298)
Not accepted
Resits
Gap year and reapply next year
Employment
accept Adjustment offer
decline Adjustment offer
You go to your insurance choice
You go to your Clearing choice
You go to your firm choice
You go to your Adjustment choice
Step 5

What next?

What you do next after getting your results depends on both how you got on and what you want. You'll always have options, and sometimes your choice will be obvious and at other times the choice will be agonising. Preparation and thinking in advance can only help, and this chapter introduces you to the possibilities and challenges of Step 5.

If you met the conditions of your firm choice, you have a commitment to go to the university that made you the offer, so you can start planning your freshers' fair activities and get on social media to get to know other people on your course. If however you think you might like to change your mind, remember that when you accepted your offer you took a place that would have been offered to someone else if it hadn't been you. No-one wants you to be unhappy but you have to take your commitment seriously and see it from the university's point of view too. One way to back out of the situation is to withdraw from the UCAS scheme completely, which leaves you free to reapply next year if you wish. If you do want to change your mind, the first step is always to contact the university which is expecting you to turn up to their course and discuss your options with them.

If you have met and exceeded the conditions of your firm choice, you may want to consider Adjustment (see page 295) to a course with higher entry requirements. But remember that there was a lot more than entry requirements in your mind when making your original choices and you may have to rearrange such matters as accommodation and financial support if you change institutions at this late stage.

If your results mean that you will have to go through Clearing in order to enter higher education this year, then you should start researching courses as soon as possible. The list of courses with vacancies is available in newspapers and on **www.ucas.com**. Bear in mind that the list continually changes as places are taken up or released, so be prepared to keep checking and act speedily once you see a course that you like the sound of and have the entry qualifications for. (Read more about Clearing on page 299). Alternative approaches are to reapply next year (having re-sat your exams or not), or after taking a gap year, which incidentally can be a great experience in its own right over and above giving you relevant experience or a better bank balance or both, or even studying abroad. (Read more about gap years on page 311, and studying abroad on page 305).

Disappointing results are really not the end of the world, although they can definitely feel like it. You could consider a foundation degree – have a look at **www.ucas.com** to find out more. Another good option is part-time study. UCAS offers a part-time course search from July until September but you can also search in the websites of universities and colleges to see what they have on offer. Other ways of studying include distance learning or online learning – have a look at the website of the Open University to get some ideas of the range of subjects and ways of learning.

Another option is employment, or maybe an apprenticeship. Find out more at the end of this chapter.

Disability – start talking to your university now

If you are disabled and need the university to prepare facilities to suit you, it can be advantageous if you contact them as early as you can. Tutors can discuss with you different course options and the number of assignments, lectures and seminars. Speak with them about how your individual needs can be met; after all, you know more about your condition than they do. Ask what kinds of adjustments the university or college will make so you can access the course. If you will need flexible exam arrangements, it will be useful to talk about these as well.

The disability coordinator should be able to tell you about the institution's services for disabled students, including accommodation and support arrangements. If the institution agrees to adapt buildings and elements of your course, ask them to put this in writing. Once your place is confirmed, check that preparation and activity is under way and, if necessary, visit again to make sure the changes meet your needs and are as you expect. Disabled students who are already at the institution can tell you how good they find the support arrangements and what life is like there. Students who are already on the course will also be able to tell you about the level of work expected and any difficulties they have had. If the people you meet are not able to answer your questions, ask to speak with someone who can or ask for information to be sent to you. If you have further questions after your visit, do not be afraid to ask.

Adjustment flowchart

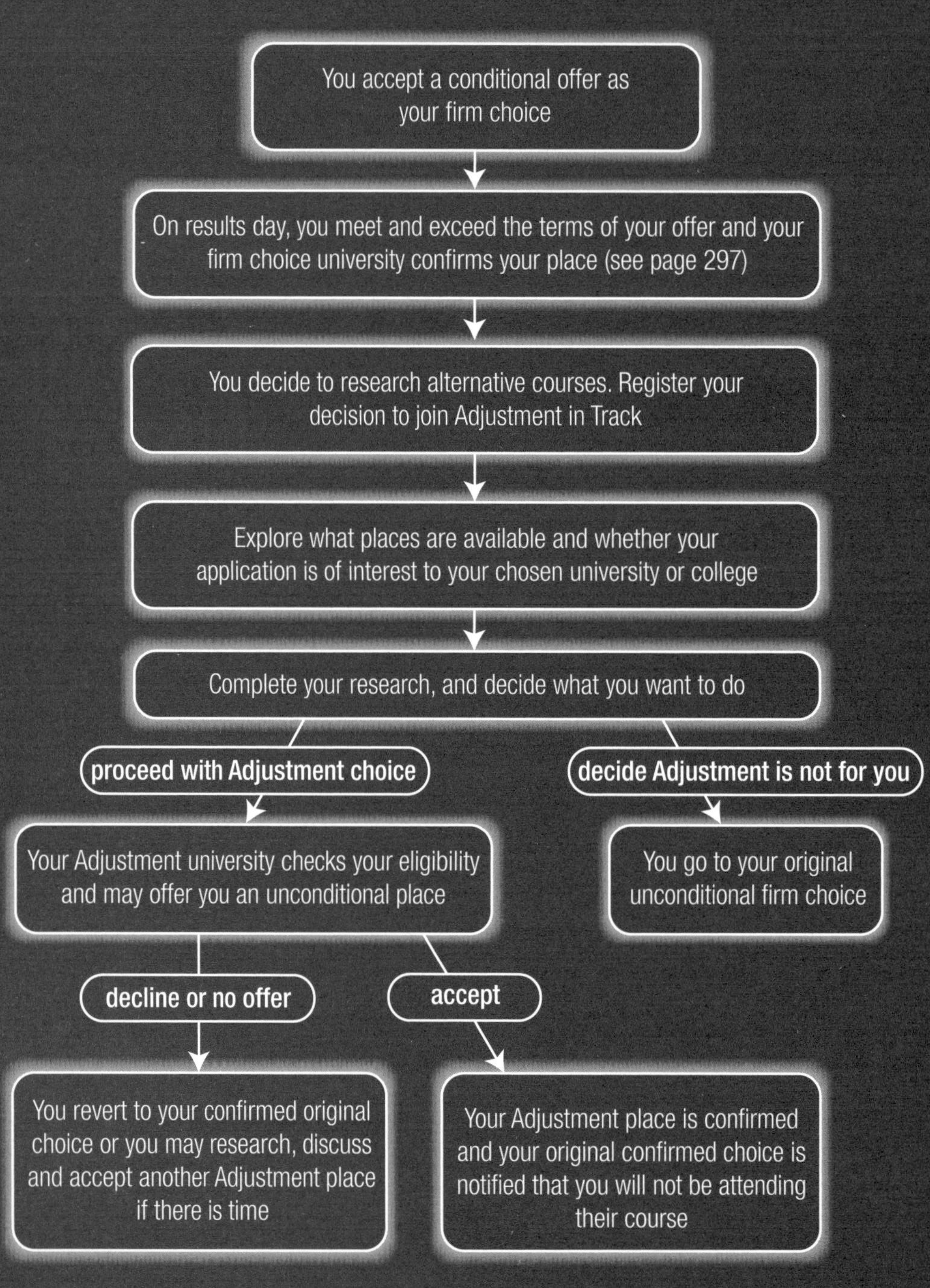

Adjustment

Some people get such a pleasant surprise when they receive their exam results that it seems to open up undreamt-of possibilities and propel them onto a new path before they can take breath. If this is the case with you, then you do in fact have a few days in which to consider what to do for the best.

Don't forget to look at Adjustment on UCAStv *how-to* guides

It might be that such applicants:

- played safe and applied for courses below their real capabilities
- discovered their real passion rather late and their choices now seem as if they were made in a former life or by another person
- were extremely lucky in their exams and now find a whole new world at their feet potentially.

In any event, if your grades meet and exceed all the conditions of your conditional firm offer, you can register for Adjustment and spend up to five days researching alternative courses more commensurate with your exam performance. But only if you want to – there is absolutely no necessity to throw out all your well-laid plans.

You have up to five days to do this research and commit yourself to an alternative place, and the Adjustment period ends on 31 August in any event.

In 2012 1,329 applicants took the opportunity to secure a different place during the Adjustment period. It enabled them to raise their aspirations while keeping the security of their confirmed place at their firm choice. For a quick guide, have a look at the short video about Adjustment on **UCAStv**.

If you find yourself in the happy position of having your results meet and exceed your needs and expectations, you should start by talking to your careers or HE adviser. You need to check that you really are eligible for Adjustment, and then start checking on Course Finder what courses are available that match your interests and results. Universities and colleges might have places available for Adjustment applicants that they will not offer to Clearing applicants, so make sure you look in the correct list and you make it clear to any admissions tutors that you are applying through Adjustment not Clearing.

If you register for Adjustment, the university where you hold a firm place will keep that place for you, and they will be able to see that you are researching your options elsewhere. If you do not find or do not accept an Adjustment place you will still hold your original confirmed place. If you decline an Adjustment place you can research an alternative, but your Adjustment period is still the original five days – it will not be extended for a subsequent search.

Applicants who use Adjustment have a lot of extra work to do, which might include rearranging their student finance, their accommodation, their travel arrangements, and even their career plans. You need to be quite sure that this is what you want to do before throwing overboard all the planning you have been committed to all year so far. But sometimes, using Adjustment can enable applicants to make an off-the-wall switch that makes total sense to them, such as changing from a course in Neuroscience to one in Philosophy and Music, or vice versa.

Examples of meeting and exceeding offer conditions – you are eligible for Adjustment

Offer	Actual grades achieved
You must get A level grades of AAB	You get A level grades AAA
You need A level grades of CCD (with grade C in chemistry)	You get A level grades of ACD (including grade A in chemistry)
You must get a minimum of 280 UCAS Tariff points including grade B in A level French	You achieve 280 UCAS Tariff points with grade A in A level French
You must get SQA Higher grades BBC (with grade C in geography)	You get SQA Higher grades ABC (with grade B in geography)
Your uni wants you to get International Baccalaureate results of 30 points in total to include at least 5 in English and 5 in physics	Your result in IB is 30 points including a 6 in English and a 5 in physics
You must get Irish Leaving Certificate (Higher level) grade B in mathematics and grades BCC overall	You achieve Irish Leaving Certificate (Higher level) grade B in mathematics and grades ABC overall

Examples of NOT meeting and exceeding offer conditions – you are NOT eligible for Adjustment

Offer	Actual grades achieved
Your conditional offer stipulates A level grades CCD (grade C in psychology)	You get A level grades ACD (with grade D in psychology)
You must get A level grades ABB (with grade A in history)	Your results are A level grades A*ABB (including grade B in history)
Your offer requires a minimum of 280 UCAS Tariff points including grade B in A level French	You achieve 290 UCAS Tariff points overall but with grade C in A level French
You must get SQA Higher grades BBC (with grade B in chemistry)	You get SQA Higher grades ABC (including grade C in chemistry)
Your uni wants your International Baccalaureate results to total 30 points and include a 5 in mathematics and a 5 in chemistry	Your IB results turn out to be a total of 32 points with a 4 in mathematics and a 5 in chemistry
You need Irish Leaving Certificate (Higher level) grade B in art and grades BBC overall	You achieve Irish Leaving Certificate (Higher level) grade A in art and grades ACC overall

Clearing flowchart

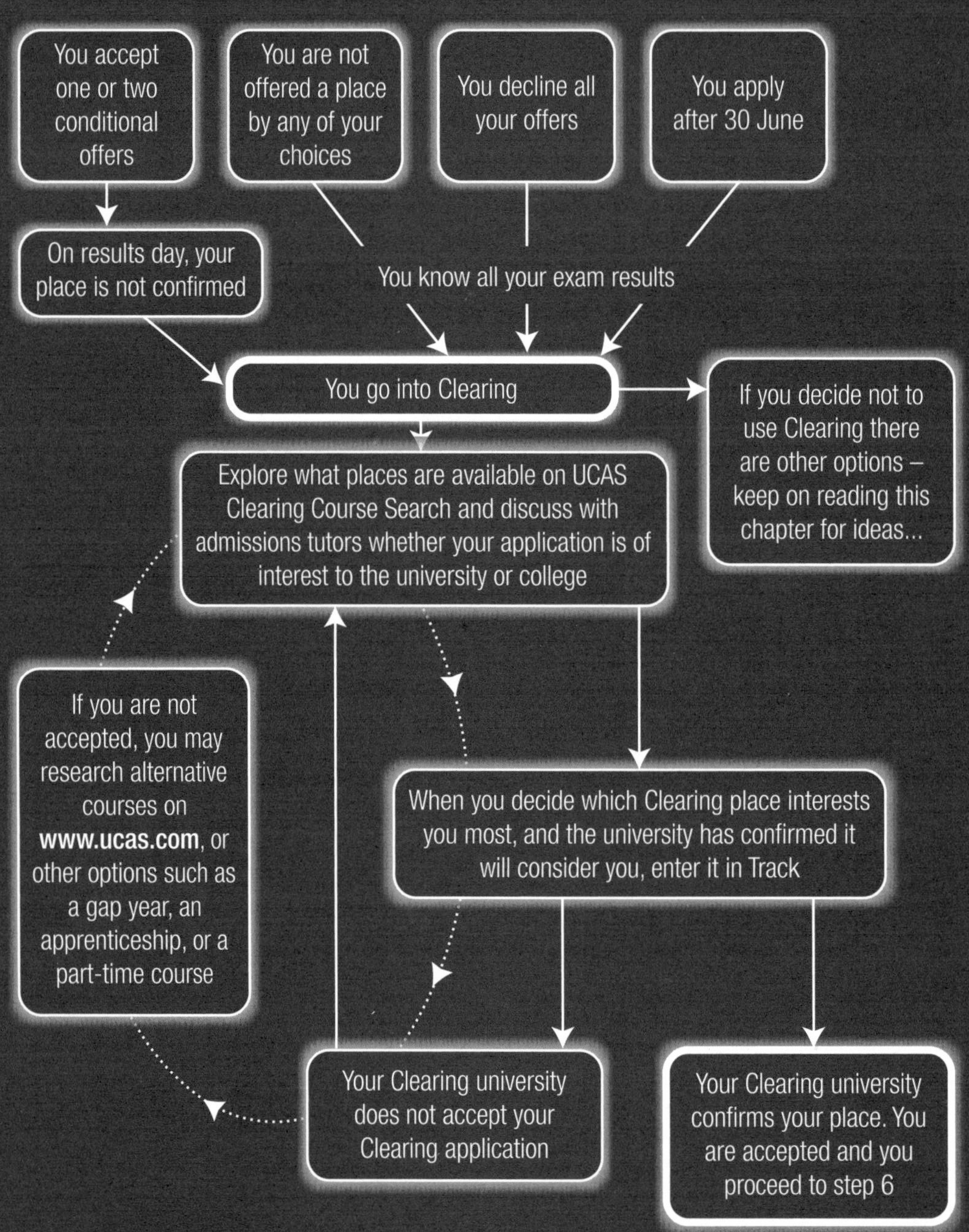

You accept one or two conditional offers
You are not offered a place by any of your choices
You decline all your offers
You apply after 30 June
On results day, your place is not confirmed
You know all your exam results
You go into Clearing
If you decide not to use Clearing there are other options – keep on reading this chapter for ideas...
Explore what places are available on UCAS Clearing Course Search and discuss with admissions tutors whether your application is of interest to the university or college
If you are not accepted, you may research alternative courses on **www.ucas.com**, or other options such as a gap year, an apprenticeship, or a part-time course
When you decide which Clearing place interests you most, and the university has confirmed it will consider you, enter it in Track
Your Clearing university does not accept your Clearing application
Your Clearing university confirms your place. You are accepted and you proceed to step 6

Clearing

Myth buster

Clearing is not just for people with lower exam results

It's a big myth that Clearing's used only by people who didn't get the results needed for their uni choices. In fact, Clearing is for anyone who finds themself without a place at university or college after their exam results have been received, for whatever reason. It could be because they found a new course in Clearing which didn't have vacancies when they applied, or it was only after 30 June that they decided they wanted to apply for university or college.

Who is Clearing for?

You might not expect to find yourself unplaced on results day, but this is what happened to over 150,000 applicants in 2012.

- Some did not hold any offers (either because they were not made any or because they declined them, including changed course offers) and so entered Clearing automatically.

Don't forget to look at Clearing on UCAStv *how-to* guides

- Some entered Clearing because they did not meet the terms of their conditional offers. Perhaps they did not meet the required grades or Tariff points.
- Some were late in filling in Apply. If you apply after 30 June you will be advised that you are automatically entered into Clearing, and you should fill in all the sections of Apply except for choices. You then approach the universities and colleges direct, after receiving the results of any exams you have taken, and they look at your application online.

In 2011, just under 500,000 applicants were accepted onto HE courses in the UK. Approximately 10% of these applicants were successful in finding their course at university or college through Clearing. If you are hoping to join them, have a look at the Clearing video on **UCAStv** and the Clearing flowchart on page 298 which will help you navigate your way through.

How do I get a Clearing place?

First, if you think you may need to use Clearing, it is a good idea to talk again to the people who have been advising you so far. They know you and they know your priorities and wishes, and they know what people like you have done in the past. You should discuss with them what you feel about your situation and what you want to achieve, and they will help you to get there if they can.

You cannot approach a university for a Clearing place until you have received your exam results, but you can and should meanwhile start thinking about what courses you would like to consider and how you want to present yourself when you discuss the matter with admissions staff. Prepare for that phone call as if it were a kind of mini-interview.

As soon as you become eligible for Clearing, Track will give you your Clearing Number, which you will need to quote to the universities that you contact so that they can see your UCAS application online.

Course vacancies in Clearing are a moving target as people think over offers and universities fill places, so keep looking at the list of vacancies on our website **www.ucas.com** and in newspapers. When you have found a course that looks interesting and after checking you fit the entry requirements, you should contact the admissions office to confirm that places are still available and ask any further questions, and to try and persuade them to offer you a place.

Remember you can contact universities and colleges direct as soon as your results come through.

Your list of questions will be similar to any such list you made if you applied earlier on in the cycle (see pages 72 to 74), and may include for instance:

- How is the course taught – through lectures, tutorials, seminars, laboratory work, field work, other? (see pages 328 to 329)
- What is the assessment model – final year exams, interim exams, continual assessment?
- What materials or equipment will I be expected to supply?
- What support is available to disabled students?
- What are the accommodation options, and how do I apply for accommodation?
- What are the computing and library facilities like?

Some questions will be very course-specific, perhaps enquiring about access to hi-tech equipment for sports or science courses, while others may be generic and tied to the fact that you are not going to be front of the queue for accommodation for instance, or may have material to identify or purchase before the start of the course.

If the admissions tutor provisionally offers you a place, you need to think about whether you want to accept it. If you're sure you want to accept it, enter the course details in Track. The university will normally confirm your place and you will receive a Confirmation letter from UCAS. If you're not accepted you can apply to another choice in Clearing.

There's help all the way along although the final decision must be yours – after all it is you who will be studying for the next three or so years! If your results look like they're leading you into uncharted waters, you might find it helpful to talk things through with the professional careers advisers on the Exam Results Helpline, who are used to helping applicants to explore and evaluate their options at this stage. The number will be available on **www.ucas.com**.

www.ucas.com

Case study

Name: Danielle de Massimi
Studied: Religion, Philosophy and Ethics
at: University of Gloucestershire

I was at college studying to get an ABC Diploma in Media Make-up when I went through the Clearing process. I had to find out how many UCAS points I needed to apply to university which meant phoning UCAS and explaining what my qualification at college counted for; I had 4 AS levels too so when I spoke to UCAS they explained to me that I did have enough points to get on to the course that I wanted, but that I would have to go through Clearing as I was applying after the deadline.

Once I decided I wanted to go to uni I had to rely on help from my family to help me think about the practicalities of finding somewhere to live and thinking about what I would need to take with me and how I would be able to cope financially. I think one benefit of going through Clearing was that I wasn't overwhelmed by options of which university to choose; I never had a particular one in mind so when I picked the Uni of Glos, I just went for it and had no time to worry about whether I had made the right choice. That might sound stupid but I was glad I didn't over-think my choice.

I found that universities responded well when I phoned them although my college qualification did cause a bit of confusion, as they are obviously used to speaking to people with A levels. The main things they wanted to know about were my AS levels and my college course – because the course I had studied at college was in no way related to the degree I was applying for, I think they were intrigued to know why I had picked that course.

I don't think universities treated me any different because I applied through Clearing, although it did take a bit longer for me to register on the first day (and I did lose the rest of the group but that was probably my own fault).

I wish I had known that it doesn't matter what qualifications you arrive at uni with because everyone is in the same boat and nobody knows everything. Before I arrived at uni I felt like my qualification wasn't worth as much as A levels. I'm really glad that I went through Clearing because I had an amazing time at uni and if I hadn't ended up at the Uni of Glos on the RPE course then who knows what I would have ended up doing!

Studying in another country

This section gives you information about studying abroad. Studying abroad is not a minority occupation: some three million students worldwide were involved in higher education outside their own countries in 2009, though relatively few leave the UK to study for a whole qualification (22,400 in 2005). Continuing your education in this way can happen in two ways – you can either take a whole degree at a foreign university or you can include a year abroad as part of your UK degree. Many of the considerations are common to both situations, but at the end of the section we give a little more information which is applicable to each independently.

Though international study is the norm for language students, it can be a real benefit for almost any student, particularly if you are thinking of a career which has international dimensions. Your personal growth may well be accelerated by studying abroad with its extra demands of cultural and educational adaptation. If you want a head start in learning about people from other cultures, studying abroad is a good way to go about it because as a student you are expected to be inquisitive! And that's besides developing a more objective view of your own society and the possible bonus of increased language skills, including, paradoxically, better precision in your own language.

You might have planned this all along, or you may be considering it unexpectedly. Sometimes your plans don't work out as expected and then you somehow start thinking very radically. Some people in this situation do extend their horizons by considering and researching applying to study in other parts of the world. But whether planned or unplanned, when you go you'll be joining a wide variety of students whose choice to learn overseas might be prompted by many situations and aspirations. For some, the prestige of an internationally respected and renowned centre is irresistible – and by considering going abroad you'll increase the number of top institutions you put within your sights – and sometimes the opportunity to experience a different system is too attractive to forego, even when your own country has so far served you very well. Alternatively, the precise course or element you seek might be unavailable at home, either in content or in terms of methodology, and so you might be moved to widen your search to fill that gap.

Practical points that you need to consider are very like those applicable to studying in the UK, though with some extras:

- Visit – if you are thinking of going very far away from home then it makes even more sense to check it out before you finally commit yourself to a long period away. Try and meet current students as well as the tutors and other staff (try and find out who is responsible for international students, for instance).
- Research what courses are available and how they are taught and assessed. This might take extra care as some terms might not mean the same things in an international context. For instance, you might want to check whether exams are written or oral, though they would normally be written in the UK. You need to know if you are letting yourself in for the unexpected! You might like to check the ranking tables at **www.timeshighereducation.co.uk/world-university-rankings/** or **www.shanghairanking.com/** (the latter is a bit of a work in progress but offers an alternative perspective with weighting given for example to numbers of Nobel prizewinners among the alumni).

- If you are disabled and receive benefits such as Disability Living Allowance (or its successor PIPs or Personal Independence Payments which replace DLA from April 2013) you should investigate how this will be affected by going abroad to study. You should also enquire whether you are eligible for funding to help with extra expenses. These may be in the form of Disabled Students' Allowances, Access to Learning Fund, Employment and Support Allowance and Incapacity Benefit. Keep up-to-date with changes in what's available by visiting **www.gov.uk**.
- Disabled students will also have to be extra-rigorous in checking that their needs can be catered for. The law and culture in your chosen country might be different and complicated. (Anecdotally, some international agents say they are amazed at the amount of support disabled UK students can access at a home university.) Remember that studying at a higher level might bring extra challenges and the earlier you think about this the earlier you can start arranging your support. That means you'll have a better chance of being able to engage fully from day one, and the more likely it will be that your experience will be on the same level as that of the other students around you. Contact the universities you are considering applying for, as well as the embassy here of the country concerned and the British Embassy there. UKCISA (UK Council for International Student Affairs) at **www.ukcisa.org.uk** also lists useful information and further contact information.

And there are some points to consider that might apply only to international study:

- You'll definitely need to understand procedural matters such as immigration and visas.
- You'll need to check the status of any qualification you are planning to achieve – you might still want to take the course even if the resulting qualification is not recognised here in the UK, but it is better to make an informed choice on such matters rather than find out too late that you'll need, for instance, to undertake further study before your degree is recognised at home. If you are studying within the EU, you can take a look at the European Credit Transfer and Accumulation System (ECTS) on the EU website **http://ec.europa.eu/education/lifelong-learning-policy/ects_en.htm**. It might be a good idea to check the status of the institution in its home country, too; visit the Enic-naric

network (**www.enic-naric.net**) for information about the education systems in over 50 countries.

- There may be cultural differences, often a foreign language, and you may miss some of the things you take for granted at home. You'll almost certainly return home with changed views on your country of origin: you'll have new insights into things you'd never questioned before and you'll appreciate some things you'd taken for granted but now realise are anything but universal. Even where language is not an issue – for instance English may be the local language or the course may be taught in English even when it is not a local language, or you may already be competent in the language of your studies – you'll still be doing some cultural acclimatising. You may get help with this through cultural liaison organisations; contact the British Council for ideas (**www.britishcouncil.org**) or research whether there are friendship societies between the country or region and the UK.

But the benefits can be huge:

- Many employers consider that international students develop a greater maturity and breadth of experience than domestic students.
- Employers with a global profile will be particularly interested in students with more varied affiliations.
- You will already have proved you're flexible and culturally mobile, and employers will recognise that you will probably have the means to adapt to new circumstances. After all, you'll have built up your confidence in your abilities to rise to the challenge and cross boundaries successfully, and that will come across.
- Provided you can explain how the experience of studying abroad gives you added value, you will have an important extra dimension that could make the difference for employers choosing between two otherwise similar candidates, particularly if there is an international or diplomatic dimension to the role.

Studying for a degree abroad

You do not apply to an overseas university through UCAS. Contact the university or universities where you are thinking of applying and ask for details of the application procedure. There will usually be some information on their website to start you off. Application may involve a mixture of factual information about yourself and your educational background (with certificates in support), references, a statement about yourself and your reason for applying, and possibly an interview, either in the UK or in the country where you intend to study. You might well also have to provide a portfolio of some sort, or send in some work (say an essay) on a subject relevant to the course you are applying for. Broadly, universities make their decisions on a fairly standard set of facts, but detail here is important and you should make sure you understand their requirements fully before submitting your application.

Funding your studies abroad will need to be thought about at an early stage – your first source of information will be the institution you are hoping to attend.

- For study in the EU, you need to explore EU-wide funding programmes as well as those particular to the state you are planning to visit. Some information about the former can be found at **http://europa.eu/youreurope/citizens/education/university/financial/index_en.htm** and **www.eu-student.eu/category/study-abroad/**.
- For study in the US, **www.salliemae.com**, **www.FedMoney.org** and **www.fulbright.co.uk** give general information.
- For study in Australia, have a look at **www.deewr.gov.au**.
- For study in Asia, look at **www.moe.gov.sg** for Singapore; at **www.malaysia-scholarship.com** for Malaysia; at **www.kafsa.or.kr** for Korea; at **www.japan-guide.com/e/e2232.html** for Japan and for China at **http://en.csc.edu.cn**. Information about Thailand may be found at **http://studyinthailand.org** and about India at **www.highereducationinindia.com**.

- Some general hints may be found at **www.studyoverseas.com**, **www.thirdyearabroad.com, www.thestudentworld.com, www.intstudy.com/**, **www.topuniversities.com/studying-abroad**, **www.goabroad.com/study-abroad**, **www.acu.ac.uk** (website of the Association of Commonwealth Universities), **www.ukcisa.org.uk** (the UK Council for International Student Affairs) and **www.unesco.org/education/studyingabroad**, the website of the United Nationals Educational, Scientific and Cultural Organization.

Please note that this is not an exhaustive or authoritative guide to helpful websites, but just a few leads to get your research started.

A year abroad as part of your UK degree

In some institutions fewer than two thirds of students spending a year abroad are taking a language degree, so don't feel it is an option restricted to those on language courses.

Much of what is written above applies equally to those taking a year abroad as part of their degree at a UK university or college. The main difference is obviously that you are likely to be part of an established exchange or at least receive practical support from your UK department. Sometimes for instance get-togethers are arranged between previous successful Erasmus students to pass on good practice and helpful tips. Further information about Erasmus is available on your university's website, and on the British Council's website at **www.britishcouncil.org/erasmus**. You can read case studies at **www.britishcouncil.org/erasmus-britishcouncil-casestudy-4.htm** and on some university websites.

Don't forget too that if you are thinking you might go on to postgraduate study in Europe, having an Erasmus year behind you can give you a head start.

The information about taking a gap year in this chapter has been contributed by *STA Travel.*

STA Travel is the world's leading student and youth travel specialist, with over 30 years' experience advising young people on holidays and adventures abroad. From New Zealand to New York, they assist students with everything from flights and tours to gap years and accommodation.

STA Travel offers support to all travellers specific to their needs and destinations, and is a member of ABTA, IATA and ATOL for total peace of mind. See www.statravel.co.uk for inspiration and ideas, to contact STA Travel or to book an appointment, a flight or the gap year of a lifetime.

Plus with STA Travel's 'Price Beat Guarantee', students will have more money for their travels.

Taking a gap year

'Employers report huge variability in the nature of students' gap years – most say that they value these experiences when a student has actively managed the experience, set themselves goals, operated outside their comfort zone and stretched themselves. Simply sitting on a beach or ticking off the tourist sites doesn't really cut it.' **(Edinburgh University admissions officer)**

Why a gap year can be great for your CV...

A gap year can be an attractive idea for a change of scene after 14 or so years of school education and before going on to study further and even more intensively at university. But the good news is that it can also be great for your CV, and that is not a benefit to ignore while unemployment is high and applying for jobs still extremely competitive.

A gap year can be attractive to admissions tutors who know that though some may take a little time to readjust back to academic life, most former gappers are generally more focused and responsible. Having students around who take a more mature outlook on their studies lifts the whole student population – this is one reason why mature students who have experience of living independently out in the real world are usually welcomed so warmly, after all. Gappers, like mature students, are often reckoned to be less likely to drop out half way through their course. Gap years can be a telescoped course in life experience, and the value of such wisdom is widely recognised, so much so that some universities are offering similar opportunities within their courses:

> *'By 2013 all undergraduate students will be offered the opportunity to take a placement year and work in an industry area of their choice (linked to their course). This demonstrates the value of having professional work-based learning as part of the curriculum. A gap year can also have the added benefits of widening the students' experiences in readiness.'*
> **(Bournemouth University admissions officer)**

And when you graduate your CV will grab the attention of employers, who appreciate that those with gap year experience are quicker at fitting in and take less time to become productive employees.

It might take some effort to readapt to study however.

> *'Having a year out at the moment so not looking forward to having all the coursework again!'* **(Student tweet)**

What you can do

Gap years in the past were often seen as a rare chance to travel and experience other cultures. Now that far-flung travel is almost commonplace the emphasis has changed slightly and gap years or partial gap years in Britain and Europe are now firmly on the agenda.

> *'I worked in a call centre for 8 months before spending two months mountain-biking in France with a group of friends. The working helped me build funds and it was incredible work experience being part of a team but also part of a wider organisation. I got plenty of opportunity to see how different parts of the organisation worked and I hope I will be able to temp there during the summer holidays. The biking took a lot of organising but was a fantastic work-out and I came back refreshed and ready to go to uni.'* **(First year physiotherapy student)**

Gap years today can take almost any form, and it is up to you to set up your year to answer your personal ambitions and reflect or discover your own strengths and interests. Think about why you are delaying your further study and how you can get the balance right between time spent and benefits gained. Maybe you want to test yourself or explore in some way and be as independent as possible; or maybe you want to get stuck in to helping the environment and be part of a well-established scheme. Perhaps you feel privileged and want to help those less fortunate than yourself by passing on your existing skills – volunteer teaching placements are increasingly popular as a gap year activity. It is your life, and your gap year can reflect and develop any number of your passions.

It is also important that you are aware of your responsibilities. Dropping out of a placement or programme before it has finished can be disruptive not only to you but also to others directly and indirectly involved.

Going abroad is still very popular. There has been a rise in the number of students heading overseas to work, study and take part in projects, as young people look to alternative means of bolstering their CV and skill-set in a bid to appeal to future employers or university admissions or interview panels. Recent research estimates that 2.5 million young people in the UK planned a gap year trip in 2012 (however youth travel specialists put this figure at nearer three million). Young people have used travel to broaden their horizons for years, however this avenue has become more formalised with many young people incorporating some sort of skill and CV-boosting activity while they're away.

Traditionally gap trips were a full 12 months, however last year the average trip length was about 54 days, which indicates, as noted above, a shift towards a series of shorter stints of travel – or 'snap gaps'. Usually these mini-gap trips are for a specific reason, such as to take part in a volunteer project, go to a festival or go on a language or skill course overseas. Examples of popular projects are spending two weeks working with elephants at a rescue centre in Thailand, which includes local conservation projects too; three weeks volunteering with underprivileged children in the favelas of Rio de Janeiro; or two weeks working alongside an experienced orang-utan conservation team in Borneo.

For example, you could investigate options to work in Australia or New Zealand under working holiday visa schemes, or to take part in work programmes in the USA and Canada, and these are proving popular with young people looking to earn while they travel. Asia and North America are the most popular destinations among those opting for a 'mini gap' with numbers up considerably thanks to the wide availability of direct flights.

Last year Asia was an increasingly popular area thanks to the myriad of travel options to cities such as Bangkok, which is a great starting place for a trip. However others such as Beijing, Singapore, Delhi and Hong Kong are seeing high growth as secondary hub cities from which to explore countries including China, Vietnam, Laos, Cambodia, India and Thailand.

In terms of the USA, New York is consistently one of the most popular destinations; however there is also increased interest from the youth travel sector in the West Coast too with San Francisco, Los Angeles and San Diego all seeing significant growth. Plus party cities Miami and Las Vegas are doing well as students want to go and let off steam post-exams, besides being an excellent gateway to South America, one of the most popular destinations for gappers.

There are expert advisers who can offer advice with everything to do with a gap trip from working holiday visas in Australia, to jobs while travelling, to tax rebates on return to the UK, to Multiflex passes which allow changes to planned itinerary mid-trip. Taking time to get a job during a gap year can be daunting, however help is at hand. Working holiday visas are available in Australia, New Zealand, USA and Canada through specialist companies.

For those interested in Australia specifically, STA Travel offers advice on working holiday visas and they are also offering exclusive Aussie starter packs which includes bank account set-up in Australia, tax packs, and login details to a members-only job website. There's a perception that Australia is an expensive destination for young people, however while earning Aussie dollars currency fluctuations will have a smaller effect. Plus don't forget that you can claim tax back on work you do in Australia on return to the UK – if you work for a year in Australia the average tax refund back in the UK is around £1,500 which more than offsets the cost of your flight at the very least.

In a bid to help young people make the most relevant choices for them, STA Travel has launched its first 'Volunteer, Work and Learn' programme. Options range from learning a language; working holiday visas in America, Australia or Canada; or learning a new skill such as cooking, dancing or sailing.

Never before has gap travel been so meticulously planned – too many people have learnt the hard way that a gap year that is unplanned can all too easily deteriorate into a wasted year. With the information available through the internet and through specialist services, it is not such a step into the unknown as it once was to take a gap year, but it is still a serious and exciting time which could, and probably will, change your outlook on life forever.

Staying safe

Be sure to look at **www.mindthegapyear.com** and **www.carolinesrainbowfoundation.org** for important information which will help you stay safe in any unfamiliar and unwelcome situations which may arise.

Nothing worthwhile is risk-free but there are some commonsense precautions you can take. Just a snapshot of the sorts of things you should be considering might include:

- taking photocopies or scanned copies of all your passport and identity documents and keeping them separate from the originals
- making sure your inoculations are correct and up-to-date for all your destinations and that you have certificates to prove this
- working out how you will access phone credit when you are away (are local cards available and will your phone take them?)
- if you are on medication, take plenty of supplies and try and prepare the necessary vocabulary if you might need to talk to a local doctor about your condition; and if you wear glasses, take a spare pair and perhaps even a copy of your prescription

- take the advice of the Hitchhiker's Guide to the Galaxy and take a towel – microfibre are effective and pack down small but can still double as a pillow, a bandage or sling or a headscarf or a parasol
- when crossing the road, don't forget that in many countries they drive on the other side of the road and you must look both ways!

Remember, if a situation feels wrong, even if it is for reasons that you can't identify or explain, you can decide to leave it. Remembering this frees you from feeling unable to take action and lets you trust your gut feeling.

Remember also however that the overwhelming majority of young people complete their gap year without any problem at all.

STA Travel customer case study

Name: Lucy Fenwick, 20

Lucy took a gap year working and travelling in Australia

I spent a year, before heading to uni, working in Australia on the Working Holiday Visa Scheme as a means to fund my travels around the country. I've always wanted to explore Australia and this was a brilliant way of doing it - without running up huge credit card bills.

I started in Sydney and worked in a restaurant as a waitress for a few months, which gave me the chance to see the city through the eyes of a local! I moved from Sydney and worked behind a bar in Melbourne and in a clothes shop in Brisbane.

The team at STA Travel couldn't have been more helpful in putting together my Working Holiday Visa, flights and accommodation for the first couple of weeks in Sydney. They also set me up a bank account in Oz and gave me advice on job sites to use, it made a huge difference to have this expertise and support as I headed to the other side of the world. Plus knowing that I could pop into their branches while in Australia for extra advice was brilliant too.

I got to know some great people on my travels and through them went to lots of different restaurants and shops that I might never have found on my own as a backpacker. Plus a few of my new mates came on short trips with me too, we hit the Barrier Reef and also checked out Uluru and Tasmania too.

I loved feeling part of the community rather than just another young Brit girl passing through on her travels, and the experience has totally boosted my confidence and made me realise that if I set my mind to things I can get loads done!

After returning to take up my place at uni I've got a far broader outlook on life, thanks to all the things I've done on my gap year and all the people I met, worked and partied with. And, I reckon that when it comes to finding a placement or a summer job the experience will look great on my CV, hopefully it'll make me stand out a bit from the other thousands of graduates.

I can't thank the team at STA Travel enough for all their help and advice, my gap year has made a massive difference to my confidence and outlook on life.

More options...

Did you know?

You can also study part-time

It's not just about full-time degree courses – there are part-time courses, foundation degrees, distance learning options, and plenty more. Although UCAS doesn't process applications for most of these options, we have some information about them in the 'Next steps' section of our website – take a look at what's available and how to find out more.

Part-time study

Another alternative to consider if for any reason your plans change at this stage is part-time study. The benefits are obvious: you can undertake your study at the same time as being employed. Often your employer will contribute study time or even help towards your fees if your study will enhance your relevant skills and understanding; you spread the costs in terms of both hard cash and your time. Part-time study tends to attract a higher proportion of mature students, so you'll be meeting a huge range of people who have taken different career paths which will perhaps widen your ideas about your own future and give you some useful insights into how career development works.

You apply direct to institutions offering part-time courses so look on university and college websites to find out what is on offer and how to apply. A visit to a local provider is just as important as to a place you're moving away from home to join – after all you're likely to be involved with the facilities and teachers for even longer than for a full-time course. Check the dates of open days on websites and if none of them suits you, still contact the part-time admissions office to check whether you can arrange a visit at a different time.

One of the main benefits of part-time study is the flexibility it gives you. You're not going for total immersion in the way that full-time study demands, so the rest of your life gets more of a look-in. But part-time students are an integral part of the student community and tutors will still give you the back-up you need academically and you will normally have access to the same range of pastoral support.

Part-time degrees tend to be modular in structure, which means they are made up of smaller parts each of which stands alone to some extent. The size of each module is measured in credits which tend to equate to a certain number of hours of study time. This gives you some measure of the practical commitments you would be entering into and the importance of each section of the course to the final result.

Make sure you check entry requirements not only on websites but also in direct communication with admissions tutors, as arrangements can often be tweaked and advice given which can show you what the university needs to see in applications. Many institutions offer informal interviews for part-time courses where you can discuss the best route forward from the range on offer.

Distance learning

Distance learning might also be an option worth considering, particularly if your situation is unusual or fluid. In distance learning, you study in your own time with materials that are delivered to you or which you research yourself. You arrange your study to suit your own timetables and domestic demands. Because it is ultra-flexible it can suit students in a wide range of circumstances.

For instance, over 12,000 students with a disability, health condition, mental health difficulty or specific learning difficulty (such as dyslexia) are currently undertaking distance learning with the Open University. The OU offers a wide range of support services and facilities to enable students to succeed in their studies, including advice about funding, support with arrangements for tutorials, examinations and residential schools, and the provision of equipment. Help with careers advice is also offered not only with assembling a coherent package of courses, but also with such practical matters as completing forms, CVs and letters, interview preparation, finding voluntary work, and the options for further study or professional training. As there are generally no entry requirements for undergraduate OU courses, the tutors are also very helpful in suggesting preparatory work in order to be sure you have a suitable level of study skills.

Don't worry that distance learning is isolating – you might study in your own time but you have tutor support and students form their own support networks very readily. There's always someone else with similar problems or enlightening suggestions on hand and online student communities are particularly active when it comes to distance learning.

Also don't fall into the trap of assuming that distance learning is second class learning. The OU states that three quarters of traditional universities and colleges use their learning materials, which suggests that what they offer is not just as good as traditional universities, but in many cases better!

Apprenticeships

If part-time study appeals to you but you want even more emphasis on the employment side of combining study and working, you could think about starting an apprenticeship. The first websites to visit if this is something you would like to consider are **www.apprenticeships.org.uk** (which offers a vacancy matching service) and **www.gov.uk/apprenticeships-guide**, both of which give you lots of background information, case studies, and pages of information for parents too. At those sites you can learn about how apprenticeships work and how they fit into the government's vision of opportunities and training for young people, and you can also find lists of vacancies and explore the online support available to apprentices.

Apprenticeships are schemes whereby young people take on employment and gain qualifications at the same time. (The qualifications gained by apprentices range from GCSE equivalents to NVQ level 4 or a foundation degree.) Your skills and knowledge are put into practice as you develop them and you learn about the reality of applying your ideas in the workplace. You also get paid for your work as you progress towards your qualification. Some companies offering apprenticeships have dedicated website pages (eg **www.baa.com/jobs-at-baa/apprenticeships**). Also, employers' organisations can be a useful source of information, for example the Manufacturers' Organisation website **www.apprentices.co.uk** or the Institute of Engineering and Technology website **www.theiet.org/apprentices/**.

Chapter checklist

These are the things you should be doing in Step 5 of your applicant journey:

- [ ] Check Track to see whether your choices have accepted you.
- [ ] If your results are below your firm and insurance offers, look for a place in Clearing on **www.ucas.com**

  - ring the unis to find out if they'll accept you

  - if a uni wants you and you're sure you want to go there, enter it in Track.
- [ ] If your results are better than expected and meet and exceed your firm offer, read the section on Adjustment to see if it's something you want to consider, but remember, there's a five day limit.
- [ ] If you have a disability talk about your needs with the university disability coordinator.
- [ ] Consider taking a gap year. If your place is confirmed, ask your university if you can defer your entry.
- [ ] If things haven't worked out as planned, consider:

  - resits

  - reapplying next year

  - studying in another country

  - finding employment

  - part-time study, distance learning or apprenticeship.

www.ucas.com

Step 6
Starting university and college

You've researched, chosen, applied, responded and waited. You've worked and studied until you almost feel you can work and study no more. And at last you're off to start your higher education career!

Scary! But thousands if not millions have succeeded in having a great time at university with rewarding study, fascinating opportunities and a terrific flowering of their minds and aspirations – and the same can be true for you too. Have a quick look at the 'Starting university' video on UCAStv, which will give you some pointers about what you'll have to deal with and what help is available.

Step 6 **Starting at university or college**

Congratulations!
Your place at university or college is confirmed
Make detailed arrangements based on previous planning
Accommodation
Hall
University flat
Independent flat
Family home
Deposit
Insurance
Equipment
TV licence
Student union
You can find details of the union on your university or college website
yougo on Facebook
Meet people on your course before you go
Finance
Final checks to confirm your:
Loans
Grants
Bursaries
Scholarships
Allowances
(including Disabled Students' Allowances)
Bank account
Part-time employment
Budgeting

Preparing to study and getting support

One of the first things you'll notice once your course starts is that you will have lots to do and won't be told how to do it – you'll be much more on your own and will probably need to ask for direction and help at first. You will have a course director and tutors and the university or college will also have counsellors available to give you support as you get used to this new mode of self-directed learning. The courses at uni are more in-depth than at school and you'll soon learn that you have to set some of the boundaries yourself. The change can be quite difficult as you won't get any spoon-feeding now. Re-read the description on p21 to remind yourself about the differences between school and university.

Student tip:

'Uni is great but it usually takes a little while to settle in.'

The thing to remember is that you are not alone. Everybody is experiencing the same as you (or they did last year or the year before) and there is plenty of help if you go and look for it.

Your tutors are crucial in helping you to make the change but it is down to you to think about what you are learning and what it all means. The bonus is that you get a sense of independence and credit about your work right from the start.

First-year students are often known as 'freshers', especially in their first term at university.

There are also likely to be some second-year students who will have volunteered to act as mentors to freshers like you. Your tutors may be able to direct you to a central panel or put you in touch with someone in the same faculty but a bit further on than you.

Student tips

Here are some things students say to freshers on student forums:

I'm a Final Year in Business IT. It's a good course – if the current course director stays then you'll have a right laugh! It is quite easy and chilling in the beginning but around 2nd year you'll wish you paid attention during the first year. Trust me I've been there!'

'Just finished first year, anyone need advice add me on Facebook x'

'I would HIGHLY rate the students union and its events and societies. They make sure you're sorted for stuff to do no matter what campus you're at. Also the tutors are fantastic. They are always available and are always down to earth and honest with you.'

'I'm sure you'll be fine; everyone is nervous when they first start because you don't know anyone.'

You'll learn in a mixture of ways which might include:

- lectures (large groups, listening and note-taking; there might be question and answer sections, electronic response technology or quizzes)
- seminars (small groups, active discussion led by assigned individuals who may be staff or students)
- tutorials (may be groups of two or more or may – rarely – be individual, when you discuss your own work)
- individual lessons (if you are studying a musical instrument for example)
- crits (when you and others each take turns to present your finished or unfinished work within a group of students and tutors and sometimes visiting critics, who all question you and discuss it)

- show and tell (similar to crits but more informal, more of a feedback-gathering exercise)
- laboratory sessions (which are usually practical and hands-on, but may be demonstrations)
- computer-based learning. Many courses include content that is accessed online in formats such as:
  - podcasts – where the student listens to a pre-recorded lecture
  - webinars – where students and tutor meet online for a virtual seminar
  - weblogs – where students keep a record of their learning
  - interactive online exercises – which offer information and then test understanding
- peer-assisted learning (where senior students hold face-to-face sessions with a group of junior students: a sort of mentoring)
- fieldwork (practical and experiential learning under guidance)
- work placement (simulated or real work environments where you apply and refine your more theoretical learning).

Exactly how teaching happens depends on many things, such as whether you're on a course with many other students or you are one of just a very few students in your subject, and the traditions and policies of your particular university and course. It also depends partly on your subject, for example crits tend to be used in architecture courses and peer-assisted learning in nursing courses. The lower level of direct contact can be unnerving at first and you will almost certainly need to exercise some rigorous time management to get those first assignments done in time. University study can seem very unstructured after the set school timetable you may be used to. Make use of the opportunities you have to get to know staff in tutorials and seminars and fieldwork sessions, and remember that discussing your ideas can elevate them to a new level besides helping you identify and resolve any misconceptions you may have.

Student tip:

'You feel much smaller than at school. You have to organise yourself and make your own decisions.'

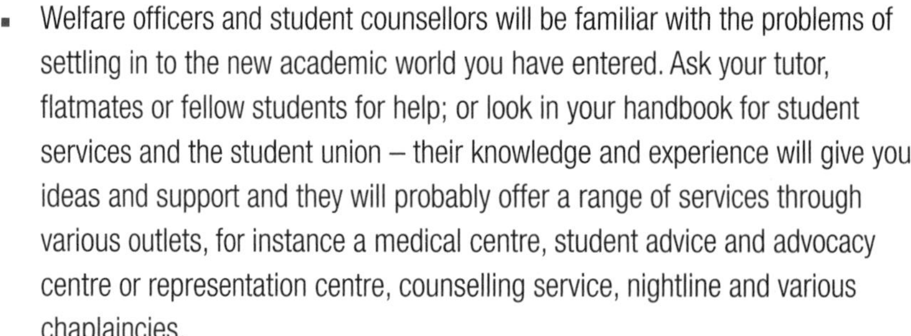

- Welfare officers and student counsellors will be familiar with the problems of settling in to the new academic world you have entered. Ask your tutor, flatmates or fellow students for help; or look in your handbook for student services and the student union – their knowledge and experience will give you ideas and support and they will probably offer a range of services through various outlets, for instance a medical centre, student advice and advocacy centre or representation centre, counselling service, nightline and various chaplaincies.

- Make sure you know which way your Disabled Students' Allowances are going to be paid – it might be paid direct to your institution to administer on your behalf; or direct to the supplier of your support; or it may be paid to you so that you can pay your expenses as they arise. If this is the case you may have to show receipts (for instance for taxi fares) for the amounts you have claimed so make sure you keep these carefully. Also check to see that your home Social Services Department or equivalent is liaising with the equivalent body where you are going to study and with the university or college itself. The university's disability coordinator should be able to help you keep all the right people informed. A 20-page PDF called *Funding from Charitable Trusts* is downloadable from **www.disabilityrightsuk.org/skillpubct.pdf**. This gives general advice about how to apply to charitable trusts and also gives contact and criteria details of trusts which may be able to offer support.

International students should familiarise themselves with **www.ukcisa.org.uk**, the website of the UK Council for International Student Affairs, and make contact with the international office at their own uni.

- The new approach to your subject may well contain surprises, and realistically you have to recognise that for just a few students this will not be all good news. If you're finding the course is too different from what you expected, then it is really important that you check things out with your tutor. Things might be about to change, or you might be just in time to switch to a course more like you wanted – so don't be shy about discussing how you're finding it with people who are there to help.
- Your motivation will grow and develop as you understand more of what is expected of you. Your initial enthusiasm will take you through the first stage, but will need to be refreshed gradually as your awareness grows. Don't get so immersed in the day-to-day that you forget either to enjoy yourself or what you're ultimately there for.

You may be sent an enrolment pack when your place is confirmed. This will include full joining instructions and various other information, such as any reading list you need to start looking at before you start college. If this is very long it may be best to wait before spending huge amounts of money. Or even if the reading list is short, the following points may also apply to you.

- It may be a generic reading list which is only partially relevant to you. Or it may relate to one module only so you need to pace your purchasing and reading.
- It may cover the whole year and some texts may not be needed for months yet.
- Don't forget many if not all of the titles will be available in the university library. Be aware though that many university libraries charge hefty fines for late returns, especially on short-term loan items or those in greatest demand.
- Second-hand books may be on sale from second and third year students.

When you start your course, you may be introduced to new ways of doing familiar things as well as many new things. It won't stay like this forever! You'll be learning many things concurrently – and this will be even more the case if you are relying on the support of interpreters or note-takers as you'll have to get used to each other's ways of working – but you will gradually get the hang of it.

University tip

University of Nottingham says:

There is a wide range of support available to assist with the transition from school or college, or indeed employment, to university.

Students are sent a pre-arrival welcome guide detailing all of the support available and they will also have an induction meeting with their academic personal tutor, usually in the first week, to introduce them to their studies.

The University of Nottingham runs a welcome week programme to ensure that students are well prepared for their degree programme; this includes introductory sessions held within academic departments.

Case study

Name: Rochelle Weir
Course: Paediatric Nursing
At: University of the West of England

The first day at university was very scary, nerve-wracking but exciting. It is important to remember that everyone who is starting the same day feels exactly the same as you. It felt very relaxed and calm and the course staff were fantastic, as they were more than happy to help students feel more at ease.

On the first day relating to my course, which is paediatric nursing, the morning consisted of students having the opportunity to do some team building and to get to know one another. The afternoon consisted of more information about the course, and what was their expectation of us.

My experience from UWE has been fantastic. I believe and know that the majority of the university staff is very supportive and always willing to help students. Their level of explanation is very clear and precise. If the student is in doubt, the staff are more than happy to assist them further when required. If the students are dealing with the incorrect person, the lecturer or staff member will signpost the student to the appropriate person.

Students that are beginning university are required to remember that they are adult learners. They do not have the same support as when doing A levels at school, because teachers would ensure that they have done their work. University is independent study and working.

Freshers' Week involved:

- paper work which was advised to have been completed by the module leader including occupational health form prior to starting

- signing up to the students' union (if students wished to do so, depending on their course)
- buying books at the students' union with a percentage off because of starting university
- signing up to sport clubs
- being fitted for nurses' uniform – that was very exciting and made the situation more real
- meeting staff from the course which the student will study.

Finally, it is important to be yourself and enjoy most things about the course. It is very important to prioritise your workload, do not leave work till the last minute. If you require help ask from the module leader. The staff at UWE are more than happy to support students when they recognise that they are struggling rather than have the student going along and struggling alone.

Three years may feel like a long time but it will fly by so enjoy!!!

Making friends

There are many ways of getting to know people at university. We have a look at the main ones below, but don't forget you've also got your family and friends from school or work, as well as the specialist and general advisers at your university. Your friends at home know you well but won't necessarily have much idea about what you're dealing with and what your options are, and you may feel that the university advisers don't know you yet but don't forget that they will have vast experience of helping new arrivals settle in.

Meeting people before you go

University tip

Kingston University says:

Freshers' Week is designed to enable students to form friendship groups which provide support in their studies. Whilst it may look from the outside to be a series of student drinking escapades it is vitally important that the students support each other in their studies and the friendships they will form during their time at university will, in most cases, be friends for life that they will travel with on their journey outside the university. Students should be active in their chosen environment whether this means joining the rowing club, debating society or becoming an officer of the student union – all aspects of the growing and maturing process.

University tip

Hadlow College says:

We run a transition into higher education summer school which applicants are invited to attend. And at Freshers' Week students are introduced into the college and meet fellow students and staff, which allows students to settle in and meet people in an informal environment.

Student tip

'It's amazing how liberating it is, mixing with people from all over the world. You need to be really open to new friends; people with different backgrounds and interests can turn out to be the best mates.'

Some universities and colleges operate buddy programmes in which current students volunteer to make contact with new students and answer any questions about studying, about the university or about student life. If your university has such a scheme and you receive a letter, email or phone call from your buddy, do respond to it as it is well known to be a great way to find out more about what's about to happen.

The students' unions of many universities and colleges have a Facebook or other networking page which is yet another way you can compare notes and get to know friends before you arrive.

Meeting people when you're there

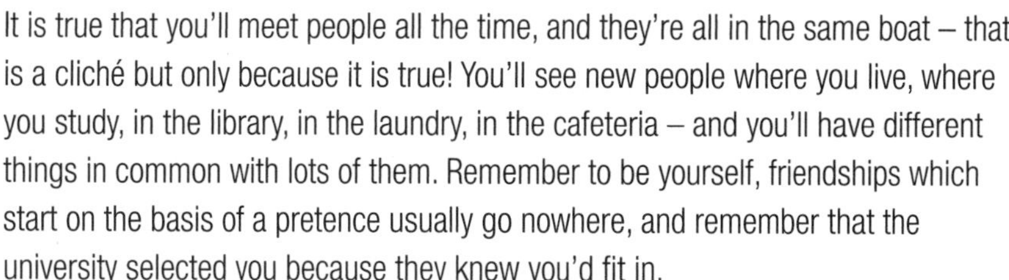

Student tip

'Your flatmates and the people on your course might not become your closest friends – don't worry about it. You'll work out the difference between people you can jog along with and the people you have more in common with. At uni you meet loads of new people all the time so the friendship landscape is always changing!'

It is true that you'll meet people all the time, and they're all in the same boat – that is a cliché but only because it is true! You'll see new people where you live, where you study, in the library, in the laundry, in the cafeteria – and you'll have different things in common with lots of them. Remember to be yourself, friendships which start on the basis of a pretence usually go nowhere, and remember that the university selected you because they knew you'd fit in.

Case study

Name: Yann Moysey
Course: Physiotherapy,
At: Nottingham University

Before starting my study, I felt the university was very helpful in preparing me to start the course. They sent through a "starter pack" including all the vital information about the course, tutorial groups, timetables etc. They also included helpful additional info like a bus timetable, as the course is based off campus. In addition, there was also a small section in the pack from the students about what to do in and around Nottingham. They also set up a Facebook group, allowing freshers to interact and ask questions before starting the course.

I attended two open days, the first being a general university open day, which I felt gave me a good idea about what the university, as a whole, was like. Then after being offered a place, post interview, I attended a departmental open day, which was much more specific and based upon the actual course I was doing. In retrospect I wish on the general open day I had got a better idea about the accommodation at Nottingham. I would advise going with a plan with what you want to do and see as you can quite easily get distracted as there is so much going on. I would also advise that during the department-specific open day ask all the questions you can, as it is at this stage where you may be choosing between different courses, and you want to make sure which one is right for you along with the university.

To find where I wanted to live in my first year I visited the university website which provided information on both catered and self-catered accommodation. As for deciding, I would advise speaking to friends at that university or past students, as they have been there and done it. Also consider where your course is based. For me it is a 5-minute walk to the bus stop, compared to someone else on the other side of the campus, taking 30 minutes, which you will appreciate in the morning, especially in your first year! Also, specifically for me at Nottingham, I think it is better to be on campus for your first year, as there are so many campus orientated events going on which you miss out on if you choose to live off campus. Also if you have less of a walk to lectures in the morning after a late night, you will appreciate the extra sleep I assure you.

I felt nervous on my first day, especially when walking into a room with 50 new course mates I had never met before. Initially you feel really awkward trying to start conversation. You are also bombarded with information from the staff and students about countless numbers of things to get involved with. All in all it is a bit daunting. However, the important thing to remember is that everyone is in the same position and before you know it you will be thinking, 'What was I worrying about?'

Freshers' week was brilliant at Nottingham, there was a specific night out organised every evening allowing you and our new block/course mates to socialise and just generally have an awesome time. A big part of freshers' week was the freshers' fair where information on all that the university had to offer was provided, ranging from all the different societies and sports clubs to taxi companies and free pizza. Literally anything going on at the university was there.

One major tip would be to get involved with as many extra-curricular things as possible, not only is it good fun but you also meet so many new people. At Nottingham I joined 'Karnival', the university's charity organisation and have ended up choosing to live next year with friends I made from that. It is beneficial to broaden your friendship circle especially for when choosing whom to live with in the second year as you have more options.

Starting university – leaving home

Student tip

'I can't wait! When I went on a tour of the campus and the accommodation it looked amazing. I'm so excited about going!'

You've got your place at university and are now thinking around the reality of starting your course, starting your new life. The nerves are no longer jangling at the thought of not getting into university – everything has changed and it is the thought of actually setting out that can seem overwhelming.

Student tip

'I'm dead nervous about this whole transition-into-adulthood thing, but it seems everyone else is really relaxed about it. Funny; I'm usually the one who's laid back when everyone else panics.'

The thing is to start planning as soon as you can, and to do things step-by-step.

UCAS would like to thank UNITE for their help and contribution to this chapter.

Accommodation

There are some key items you need to sort out if you are leaving home to go to university – and the first of those is accommodation. You may have already checked out the accommodation available at your firm and insurance choices, but now is the time to get serious. Contact your university to find out about the accommodation available. You can also search online to find out about other types of accommodation options available to you. Once your university offer arrives, it is often a good idea to arrange a viewing at your choice of accommodation and to visit the local area before signing your tenancy agreement. Some accommodation providers offer virtual or video tours, allowing you to see what their accommodation looks like if you're not able to visit. If, however, you need to go through Clearing, then there's no need to worry. There will most probably be plenty of options still available to you as you complete the process. Check descriptions carefully so that you know what you're getting in terms of what's included in the price, facilities, cleaning, sharing and so on. As a student you will typically have three accommodation options open to you: uni accommodation, also known as halls of residence, managed by the university; private houses or traditional student houses, managed by private landlords; and thirdly, privately managed, purpose-

Student tip:

'If I'd checked beforehand I'd have known to bring lots of cleaning products and cooking utensils.'

built student accommodation provided by private companies such as UNITE – the UK's largest student accommodation provider. Your uni accommodation office will have further information on many of the different types of accommodation available to you, including contact details for private landlords if you're looking for a private house, as well as details on university halls of residence and privately managed, purpose-built accommodation.

Price and quality for the different types of accommodation vary hugely, but there is something out there to suit everyone's taste and budget. Living in student accommodation while at uni is a great way to meet new people and make new friends easily. If, however, you have chosen not to live in student accommodation and are staying at home instead, you will still have plenty of opportunity to meet new people from your course through uni clubs and activities. The layout of the accommodation in university halls of residence and those run by private companies tends to be a large building divided into a number of flats or individual private rooms rented exclusively to students. In university halls of residence you can typically expect individual rooms with some communal living space, such as a common room and study area. You can also often choose between catered or self-catered halls, dependent on the level of cooking you are prepared to do! In shared flats, you can usually expect your own private bedroom with study area and a shared kitchen and lounge area.

The majority of managed, purpose-built accommodation providers typically offer a choice of living options, from single rooms to double self-contained studios, and is also likely to come complete with en-suite shower rooms. Their prices will often include utility bills, contents insurance and broadband. Students will have their own study space, a common room for socialising and would typically share a flat with between two and eight other students. Premium accommodation, which can include larger beds and mod cons such as wall-mounted flat screen TVs, may also be available.

Student tip:

'I wish I'd known that halls of residence would be so much fun!'

There is also the option of private housing or traditional student housing through a private landlord. This can be either a house or an apartment in a student area of the city, and of course gives you total control over who your flatmates are. This is particularly suitable to those returning to university after their first year, by which time they've made friends and decided whom they want to live with. (Remember though that the option to arrange a flatshare with friends is also available in the privately-managed sector.)

Whatever your choice, when you arrive you will probably have to show the letter or email confirming that you have already signed your contract, plus some photographic ID, before you can be given your key. There might be a compulsory health and safety talk by the hall or property managers.

Check whether there are rules concerning keeping items in your room such as candles, posters and electrical equipment such as kettles and sandwich toasters. Make sure you stick to these rules if you wish to get your deposit back, be covered by your contents insurance, etc.

When choosing which accommodation to apply for, you might ask yourself questions such as:

Self-catering or meals provided?

Catered sounds great, with meals provided and no washing up or cooking. But be aware that communal meals may have to be provided at set times so you will have to take breakfast when provided whether you are ready for it or not, and probably not in your dressing gown. Some mealtimes might clash with lectures around midday so you might end up doing some self-catering anyway. Think about what suits you best: catered may be great if cooking isn't your thing, self-catered will give you the experience of cooking for yourself and potentially the social aspect of cooking with your new flat mates. Self-catering can be better at matching special diets.

If you go for self-catering check where the nearest shops are and what equipment you're expected to supply yourself; and it might be a good idea to bring a few basics with you – some pasta, cheese, fruit, teabags or coffee and a pint of long-life milk, and a supply of your favourite snack.

Do I want my own bathroom?

Completely personal choice, but do question before you sign on the dotted line:

- whether the extra cost or saving is worth it
- how many people might be sharing the facilities
- what the cleaning arrangements are.

Student tip:

'Check how to get from the accommodation to uni and how long it takes (if I'd done that I wouldn't have been late on my first day!)'

Be aware that if you use shared shower facilities the flow of hot water might benefit from the demand being managed cooperatively. Some non-en-suite rooms have a hand-basin which can be useful, though again you might need to consider your budget. Fixed plumbing is convenient but can restrict the options for rearranging the layout of your room, for instance, and is occasionally noisy.

What location?

The location of your accommodation is important. Consider the balance of location against price carefully, as you might feel you're getting a bargain by opting for a cheaper area, but think about the added cost of travelling to and from uni or the city centre. Depending on the location of the accommodation you choose, getting around can be expensive. Weekly or monthly travel cards can shave pounds off your travel expenses and don't forget to see if there are student discounts – a Student Rail Card will save a third on rail fares.

Student tip:

'The city is exactly what my personality is like – small yet buzzing – and the campus is intimate and friendly. I recommend doing your research on everything about the university, and asking as many questions as you can.'

Is it secure?

You should also consider the security of the accommodation and the area and whether you'd feel safe living there. Some properties will come equipped with 24-hour security cover, secure door entry systems as well as security cameras, but this is not to be expected in all accommodation and you are frankly unlikely to find them in traditional student housing.

Mixed or single sex accommodation?

Again, personal preference will tell you what's right for you. If you're an outgoing person you will meet other people of both sexes anyway, and there is always a variety of clubs and societies for interest, relaxation and socialising. Your accommodation is where you are based, and for some people can be a bolt-hole while for others it is the central place for everything to happen. In the end it is as much about the individuals involved as their gender, and it is down to what you are used to and what you feel comfortable with.

Is there a deposit?

If you opt for a shared house or flat, you will be asked to pay a deposit, usually equivalent to one or three months' rent, and possibly one or two months' rent in advance. Privately managed accommodation providers will often ask for a fixed deposit amount, typically around £250, sometimes more in London. University halls may require a deposit too. Your deposit will be returned to you when you leave, provided that the place is in the same condition as it was when you moved in. The costs of repairs and cleaning can be deducted from the deposit returned to you, so read your tenancy agreement carefully to see what you might be liable for, and make careful notes of the condition of the rooms and their fixtures and fittings when you arrive.

Before moving into furnished accommodation, you might like to take photos of the general condition, scratches etc, and copy them onto a CD and hand it to the landlord. That way you should be less likely to have problems when checking out.

You should also agree an inventory, or list of items such as furniture, kitchen utensils etc, so that both you and the landlord know what should remain when you move out. Many accommodation providers will provide these but if not, your students' union or the Citizens Advice Bureau can give you advice and tips – see their websites.

Your rental deposit should be protected under a Tenancy Deposit Protection Scheme designed to stop landlords wrongly withholding all or part of the deposit and to help resolve any disputes – check before you hand over your deposit and sign the agreement.

What happens during the holidays?

Most tenancy agreements are for a fixed number of weeks so, depending on the length of your tenancy, holiday periods may be included. Tenancy lengths and start dates can vary, so before signing a tenancy agreement you should get clarification from your accommodation provider when the tenancy starts and its length in weeks.

Privately managed accommodation run by companies such as UNITE offer a mix of 43-week tenancies, starting in September and ending at the start of the following summer, and 51-week tenancies, though the options might vary. If you choose a 43-week tenancy, there may also be the option of extending your stay over the summer at a reduced rate. This can be useful if you're looking to stay in your university town or city to work, do additional study or use it as a base for the summer.

How do I manage my accommodation costs?

Accommodation prices vary by city with prices in London often higher than other parts of the country. When working out how much you can afford to pay, don't forget to make allowances for bills, contents insurance and a TV licence, which in some cases are not included in the rent. However, some accommodation providers include the price of utility bills, in-room internet access and contents insurance in the room price which makes it easier for you to manage your finances. When budgeting, remember to think about your financial needs over the holidays too.

It's vital that you read through a tenancy agreement before signing anything, as it's a legally binding document. The payment terms and options for different types of accommodation will vary considerably depending on the type of accommodation you choose. In some cases you may be required to pay the first term's rent in one sum at the beginning of your tenancy, while in others you may have the option to pay in smaller instalments.

What happens after my first year?

After you've completed your first year at uni, you will once again be faced with a choice of accommodation for your second and third years. If you have been living in halls of residence, you will probably need to look for alternative accommodation as university run halls are usually earmarked for first year and other priority students. Also, by now, you will have an idea if there's anyone you want to share with so could be looking for somewhere to accommodate you and your friends. Whether you are looking for a flat for two or a larger one for eight or nine of you, both managed, purpose-built accommodation and private houses may be able to cater for your choice. The accommodation office will be able to point you in the right direction or you can search online for providers or landlords.

Timings for finding your second year accommodation will vary by city. In some, students start booking before Christmas, whilst in others the majority of students will wait until their second term to start looking. Timings will often depend on the amount of good quality accommodation available. One of the key things to consider is who you want to live with and ensuring you find the right option for you. Don't forget, if you do want to live with a group of friends, private houses are not your only option. Private managed accommodation providers like UNITE also provide the option to book a flat with a group of friends and house students in all years of study.

Accommodation for international students

Students coming from abroad have access to the same accommodation choices as UK students and are often advised by their individual universities on the best places to live. It's a good idea for students from overseas to look at various accommodation options online for the full choice available to them.

If you're an overseas student, living in halls of residence or other purpose-built student accommodation is a great way to meet new people and mix with others from different backgrounds and on different courses; or the accommodation officer might be able to help you find a place with other students from your part of the world, if that is what you would prefer.

Being aware of the different accommodation options and knowing how to make the right decisions in choosing student accommodation will help you get off to the best start in your life at uni. Enjoy the experience!

General advice and news about student accommodation is also available at **www.nus.org.uk/en/advice.housing-advice**. You should also familiarise yourself with the Student Accommodation Code (see **www.thesac.org.uk**) which outlines and protects students' rights to safe, good quality accommodation. Check with your university whether they have signed up to the code.

www.ucas.com

If you have a disability...

Find out in advance, either by contacting the university or by visiting and seeing for yourself, whether buildings and facilities are accessible to you. Buildings you are likely to use include the students' union, bars, canteens, libraries, computer rooms, sports facilities, lecture theatres, teaching rooms and any departmental rooms. If you are deaf or hard of hearing, check if lecture theatres and teaching rooms have induction loops. You may also need to find out if there is parking for disabled people, good lighting and helpful signs around the university or college.

Often, disabled students are able to gain early access to their accommodation, to help them get settled in to their new life and surroundings, so check whether this is the case and whether someone from the disability office can be on hand when you arrive to make sure it all goes smoothly. The connections they can make for you can be of many kinds, for instance at Oxford, the Disability Advisory Service will liaise with the University Centre for Sport on behalf of disabled students who play a paralympic sport.

Do not be discouraged if some things are not right immediately. Talk to the disability coordinator about your needs and discuss what adaptations can be made to cater

Student tip:

'It's really important to know that the Disabled Students' Allowances (DSA) are there for people with less visible disabilities than wheelchairs etc – that if you are dyslexic you are eligible. You need to apply early.'

for your needs. Under the Equality Act (2010), all higher education institutions are obliged to make reasonable adjustments to the physical features of premises, where these are helpful to disabled students. If there is a physical barrier to access, universities must remove it, alter it or provide a reasonable means of avoiding the physical barrier to access. The Act also states that, most of the time, the costs of reasonable adjustments cannot be passed on to the disabled person.

It is nearly always a reasonable adjustment to provide information in an accessible or alternative format.

Freshers' week will normally include provision or special events for students with disabilities or support needs.

Examples of support

Support can be given to you to make your life easier and to remove barriers. The following is a list of examples of support (for further ideas, see **www.disabilityrightsuk.org/faqstudents.htm#Q8**). Whatever your needs, do discuss them with the disability support officer at the university or college.

- Access to occupational therapist
- Adapted accommodation
- Alternative methods of assessment
- Braille note-taker
- Careful timetabling, to minimise stress or maximise use of interpreter's availability
- Computer with specialist software or hardware
- Ergonomic chair
- Exercise facilities for guide dog
- Extensions in coursework deadlines
- Extra tutorials
- Flashing light doorbell
- Fridge for medication
- Materials in literal language
- Support worker, interpreter, medical assistant.

If things go wrong and you want to make a complaint

The student population of the UK is around two and a half million and for all but a handful their time at university or college goes pretty smoothly. However, from time to time, you or someone you know at university may become dissatisfied with one of the services provided by your institution. If you want advice on dealing with such a situation, you should remember that all universities and colleges have complaints procedures which are broadly similar and should be easily accessible (eg, in your student handbook). Complaints procedures normally contain the following stages.

- A requirement to try to resolve the matter informally with the person or service causing the problem.
- If a problem cannot be resolved informally, the formal procedure will usually start with filling in a complaints form. The students' union will be able to help with this if you wish and you will find information on your university website. You can search for 'Complaint' – the relevant section of the website will usually be under 'About us', 'Customer service' or 'If we don't come up to scratch' or something similar.

- The person dealing with complaints is usually the dean of school or faculty or the academic registrar, or in the case of a complaint from an international student, the International Office.
- If the complaint is not satisfactorily resolved, there's usually a review procedure that operates at vice-chancellor level.
- Only if you have exhausted the official internal complaints procedure of your university can you go beyond it to the Office of the Independent Adjudicator for Higher Education (OIAHE) at **www.oiahe.org.uk**. Anyone who is registered as a student at a participating higher education institution can make use of the OIAHE procedures. (Please note that the Browne Review of October 2010 recommended a change in the location of the independent complaints function to a new HE Council.)

It seems a bit negative to focus here on what might go wrong. For most people, the transition to higher education goes well, but if you are unfortunate enough to encounter problems, it is as well to have in advance a general idea of what might happen next. That will help you to keep things in proportion, share your experiences and seek help for yourself or give appropriate support to someone else in difficulties.

Remember that help with complaints, grievance issues or disciplinary matters can be given by the students' union, and you will normally be referred to an association or service which can support you through the process. Formal details of the processes involved will be in your student handbook and on the university website.

Money: making it go further

For students from England, Wales and Northern Ireland, student loans are paid in three instalments and so one of your top priorities has to be learning how to budget properly. For many of you this will be the first time you will have had charge of such a large sum of money. If you go out and spend it all at once, by week three of the term you will be struggling to make ends meet and will be fairly miserable too, besides possibly getting into debt.

Student tip:

'I wish I had known not to waste my student loan.'

When you get your funding it can seem like a lot of money, but it has to last you a whole term. (Exceptions to this rule are NHS bursaries and Scottish loans which are paid monthly.) Everyone's priorities vary but it's essential that you have enough money to pay your rent, food and utility bills. So pay your rent and any other essentials immediately and see what you have left for the rest of the term. You can work out a budget quite easily just by dividing this by the number of weeks until the next loan or grant payment. Life is very exciting at the start of your course and it is easy to put complicated things to one side and slip into bad habits.

Think carefully before you get any other loans or a credit card. Credit card debt is an easy trap to fall into but extremely hard to escape. Of course, if you manage the credit card well and pay off the balance every month, it can start to build up a positive credit rating which may benefit you if you later want loan funding for postgraduate study for example – but no record is much better than a poor record! Other forms of debt you should try to avoid include store cards, no matter how tempting the offer, they are one of the most expensive ways of borrowing money.

Sample student budget sheet

Income	£	Expenditure	£
Loan		Rent/hall fees	
Part-time wages		Food	
Grant		Household	
Other		Mobile telephone	
Bursary		Gas/electricity/water	
		TV licence	
		Books/stationery/photocopying	
		Socialising	
		Travel	
		Clothes	
		Other	
TOTAL		**TOTAL**	

Student tip:

'It can come as a surprise how much you have to spend on facilities like photocopying, books, etc.'

- Fill in a budget sheet for each term to learn more about managing your own finances.
- If your expenditure is more than your income, see if there are ways to increase your income – for example, getting a job. Maybe also contact the university for a 'wealth check' to make sure you are getting your full grant or loan entitlement.

- Once you have figured out how much you have left after paying your bills, set yourself a weekly amount for other costs and stick to it.
- Open your post! You should get in the habit of checking your bank statements as this will make it easier to keep track of your spending.
- Use cash rather than cards but remember that to budget properly you need to account for the money you spend, which can be difficult when the only evidence you have is an empty wallet or purse. Get used to keeping receipts and if using a card keep a sharp eye on your bank statements. Using cash makes spending very tangible but can also result in small change being wasted, and that also adds up over a term. Some people save their change in a jar which is great for times when funds are low.
- Go to the cash machine once or twice a week rather than every day. If you go and withdraw £10 every weekday in term time you will be withdrawing over £1500 a year!
- Make eating out a treat – not a daily event. This includes your lunch. Take a sandwich with you and save hundreds of pounds per year.
- Don't do your shopping in the convenience store next to your halls of residence – these are often far more expensive than a luxury delicatessen, let alone a regular supermarket. Use more economical shops, which often have a wider choice too. Get everyone in the flat to join in and help with the shopping.
- Buy supermarket own-brand toiletries and food.
- A student travel pass can save you a fortune each term, but do your sums. If you are not travelling the same route every day it may not be worth your while buying one.
- Look out for student discounts at the cinema, shops and restaurants – show your student card everywhere you go. Don't be embarrassed! If you live in a student town or city the shops and restaurants will nearly all offer discounts (but may not advertise them). We don't recommend you eat out but you will occasionally.

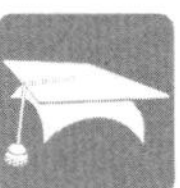

Student tip:

'I was so incredibly grateful that the university finance service was there when I had problems paying my fees.'

The majority of universities run free money management sessions either on a one-to-one basis or in groups. These are intended to be fun and interactive (not a lecture) and you will learn more about how to manage your money and get your spending habits under control.

Many advisers in universities are members of the National Association of Student Money Advisers (NASMA) and are supported to provide advice and information to students. The idea is to avoid financial problems and develop good money management skills. The sessions are intended to make your life easier by developing your skills and increasing your knowledge. Check out the student money advice pages on your university website to find out what help is on offer. Some useful information is also given at **www.savethestudent.org**.

Money Saving Expert (**www.moneysavingexpert.com/students**) offers advice on budgeting, banking and saving, as well as voucher schemes and shopping deals.

Working as a student

As a student in employment you will be liable for income tax and National Insurance just like anyone else. Students like any other employee can earn £8,105 before they have to pay income tax (2012-13 tax year). If your employer deducts tax from your wages you may be able to reclaim this from HM Revenue & Customs (HMRC) at the end of the tax year if your income is below this threshold.

At the time of writing HMRC is planning changes to the way students pay income tax. The website **www.studenttaxadvice.co.uk** and **www.gov.uk** (search on student tax) can give you more information about your tax liability.

Almost everyone has to pay National Insurance – students included. Make sure you give your employer your correct National Insurance number and check it on your payslips. Getting this wrong can have serious repercussions on your state pension later in life. Unlike income tax you cannot claim any overpayments back at the end of the year.

See Employment section on page 373 for further information about getting employment during your studies.

Council tax

Most full-time students do not have to pay council tax. When you enrol on your course you will be given an exemption certificate. It is your responsibility to give this to your landlord if you live in a privately rented house. It is a good idea to keep a copy of the certificate in case you receive a bill.

Students who live in purpose-built student accommodation (halls of residence) do not have to pay council tax.

Health care costs

You can have free NHS health care until your 19th birthday and even after this many students can get help with prescriptions, glasses or other health care costs, not because you are a student but because you have a low income. However, not many students know about this or make a claim.

You need to complete a form to be assessed. These are available from any large pharmacy, your university or can be downloaded from **www.nhsbsa.nhs.uk/792.aspx**.

Bank accounts

High street banks compete with each other for student business (they know that you should be a good earner over your lifetime and are likely to be too lazy ever to change banks) but don't be blinded by the free gifts on offer. Instead, look carefully at the level of support each bank offers and how they will treat you in various financial circumstances.

As a university student, you will normally qualify for an interest-free overdraft. This means that as long as you stay within the limit of your overdraft, you will not be charged for using it.

Most banks will require you to have all statutory funding, such as your maintenance loan and maintenance grant, paid directly into your bank account. Banks are entitled to and do close accounts and ask for any overdraft back, if you fail to pay your student funding into the account.

Domestic life

When you are living independently, the following points will be worth considering.

Safety and security

- Your landlord has a legal duty to have gas appliances checked for safety by a Gas Safe registered engineer and you should be given a copy of the safety check record. Faulty gas appliances which leak carbon monoxide can cause severe illness or even death. Carbon monoxide is odourless, so you cannot rely on recognising a smell of gas to protect you.
- Fires can be caused by electrical or other faults. Make sure that smoke detectors are installed and are working. Check the labels of all furniture and furnishings to see that they are made from fire-resistant material – if they are not, ask your landlord to replace them. Be careful about electrical wiring; plugging many items into one socket can overload the system besides leading to a tangle of wires over the floor. Make a mental note of the best means of escape in case of a fire.

- The first few weeks of the first term are often plagued by thefts as there are so many new faces around and nobody knows who is meant to be there and who is not. Think hard about leaving windows open, especially on the ground floor, and be careful about giving out entry codes to all and sundry. The NUS says that one in five students will be a victim of crime while at university – visit their website page The Lock (**www.nus.org.uk/campaigns/the-lock/**) for information and tips to help you protect yourself and your belongings.

Insurance

- You might be covered by your family's domestic contents policy which sometimes includes the possessions of students away from home, though watch out for any proviso which excludes instances of forced entry or items worth over a certain figure (say £1,000).
- Hall fees sometimes include insurance – check before buying separate cover.
- Don't leave anything valuable at university over the holidays.
- Old, well-used equipment (for instance, a laptop) is far less likely to attract unwelcome attention than a brand new top-of-the-range one.

Health

- Check whether there are conditions concerning health attached to your course – for instance if you're applying for courses to do with medicine or health care the UK health authorities recommend you should be immunised against Hepatitis B before you start training, and universities are likely to ask you for certificates to show that you are free of infection before confirming your place.
- Check your immunisation records. If there's an outbreak of something nasty it will help you to know where you stand. Some universities advise that all students should be vaccinated against meningitis C, which accounts for 40% of all meningitis cases in students. You may also explore the idea of getting a flu jab – a week or two in bed feeling dreadful can be a real interruption to your studies.
- Be aware that, as in boarding schools, concentrations of similar people in similar circumstances can lead to particular health issues. For instance there

have been recent outbreaks of mumps among students, the majority of whom today are among those who have not been vaccinated. Don't be alarmist but just log somewhere in your mind that the risks are slightly greater than back at home.

- Take a small first aid box, with a cold cure included for 'freshers' flu'. Unfamiliar kitchen knives can inflict a nasty gash, so include a few plasters and antiseptic cream. Check that you understand when you should call 999.
- Find out where the campus health service is situated before you need it, or register with a local surgery.
- Inform yourself about the risks associated with alcohol and drug abuse before you get tempted.
- Either you or some of those around you might be finding adjusting to student life particularly stressful. Try and look out for others and try and remember to look after yourself. Be active in looking for opportunities to make friends and for time to attend to your studies so that you don't fall behind. Remember that a chat to the student welfare office or your pastoral tutor can give you access to volumes of experience either in sorting out your own problems or how best to deal with having a neighbour in hall who is causing concern.

Laundry

- Dark clothes are easier to keep looking clean! As are dark bedding, towels and tea-towels.
- Washing tablets are easier than powder and don't spill into a wasteful mess, though they are more expensive.
- Take a big laundry bag with a starter supply of small change (not too small) for the laundrette. And don't forget coat-hangers so that creases have the chance to fall out!

Student tip:

'One of the most useful things I learnt was how to cook pasta for six people for £2.50!'

Cooking and eating

- If you don't cook, now might be a good opportunity to learn. Get a student cookbook such as *Four Ingredients*, or *The Ultimate Student Cookbook*, *Small Adventures in Cooking* or *Ultimate Student Vegetarian Cook Book*. Start small and then it is only you who has to eat the results of your early experiments.
- Collaborative cooking and eating is sociable and by sharing you can improve your cooking until you become a popular host yourself.
- Grilling is far healthier than frying!
- Find and note the whereabouts of a good cheap breakfast café so that you can start the day on the right foot even when the cupboard is bare.
- Check out the catering in the students' union.
- A list of basic equipment for self-catering might include: crockery for two, cutlery for two, a mug or two, two wooden spoons (to avoid your custard being tainted with the taste of onions), a pair of saucepans, a frying pan and maybe an oven tray, cheese grater, can opener, corkscrew, a couple of tea-towels, wooden chopping board and sharp knife, measuring jug. But remember there is also a case to be made for taking less rather than more – you don't know what is supplied (but can always ask) and most university towns will have cheap outlets for basics. If you're getting into cooking, a slow cooker can be great.

Domestic miscellany

- Big cushions can be useful to use as either chairs or spare beds.
- Don't take too much unless you know the size of your room – some are very compact indeed and can just about accommodate you and one spare sock. On the other hand, the further away from home you are, the harder it is to pop home to raid the family store.
- If you bring a television or a computer capable of relaying or replaying television programmes you must make sure you are covered by a valid TV licence.

- If you are eligible for Disabled Students' Allowances you may be able to receive support in the form of extra equipment, see pages 351-352.

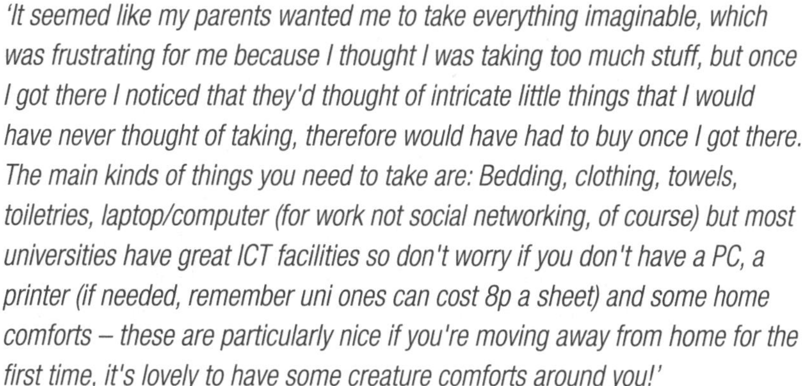

Student tip

'It seemed like my parents wanted me to take everything imaginable, which was frustrating for me because I thought I was taking too much stuff, but once I got there I noticed that they'd thought of intricate little things that I would have never thought of taking, therefore would have had to buy once I got there. The main kinds of things you need to take are: Bedding, clothing, towels, toiletries, laptop/computer (for work not social networking, of course) but most universities have great ICT facilities so don't worry if you don't have a PC, a printer (if needed, remember uni ones can cost 8p a sheet) and some home comforts – these are particularly nice if you're moving away from home for the first time, it's lovely to have some creature comforts around you!'

Practical matters

Important documents to bring with you

- Your AS12 Confirmation letter from UCAS confirming your place on your course
- Documents from Student Loans Company, SAAS or equivalent, bursary administrator, etc
- Letter from accommodation office with details of your university accommodation
- National Insurance number and tax details
- Passport, birth certificate, marriage certificate, immigration papers, national identity document or card etc (check with your university exactly what you need to bring)
- Driving licence, insurance and MOT
- Any other insurance certificates, or copy of your home insurance if it covers you at university – see page 362

- Medical card, details of repeat prescriptions, your home doctor's and dentist's details, any health insurance documents
- Travel discount card and travel tickets
- Bank details and bank, credit and debit cards, including recent statement from a UK bank, or a recent statement from a non-UK bank showing you have the funds to pay your fees.

You should check carefully that you are able to bring with you everything you need to enrol – check your university's website for full details. If you do not have all the necessary documents, you may not be able to enrol. This can mean withdrawal of your student entitlements, and if you are unable to supply documentation by a given deadline, you may even be excluded from the course.

Emergency contact

You will need to give the name and details of an emergency contact, so make sure you have up-to-date phone details and the email address of whomever it is you would want to be called in to help you in a crisis.

Getting around

- You'll probably need an ID card or pass to enter certain buildings or areas so find out how to get what you need. This may be included as part of your enrolment onto your course, and might involve production of your passport or driving licence or similar, or a photograph.
- Phoning up before a journey, even when you're travelling to the station, might get you a cheaper option than the ticket office.
- It is always worth checking the price of two singles as well as the price of a return on any public transport.
- Check parking availability before you go – how close is it to where you'll live, how secure, how expensive? Consider taking a bicycle instead of a car, especially if the university or college aspires to a green image. The only parking might be on side-streets which may be less safe, and can antagonise the local population.

We asked some universities what three things students should bring with them, and got a range of responses ...

A camera, a computer and a mobile phone that can do email!

Enthusiasm, commitment and sense of humour

- *Your own bed linen – to make you feel at home*
- *Identification – you may need this to open a student bank account, register for activities etc*
- *Pre-registration/welcome week information that will be sent to you before you arrive.*

1. Basic cookery skills are a good idea to be able to make a decent meal and help gain friends quickly
2. Enough money for those first few weeks (until the student support grants and loans clear)
3. Emergency phone contact details or an agreed way to contact friends and family.

- An alarm clock (don't rely on your mobile phone!)
- Food for first few days
- Laptop and USB

One university couldn't restrict itself to just three things ...

Desk lamp; laptop/desktop computer and memory stick; books and journals; A4 folders for written work; tool box and specialist course equipment; mug; mobile phone; digital camera ...

And we also asked a few first year students ...

If I were asked what three things a student should bring, I would say that it is good to have experience in what the student wants to study or have some knowledge of the course. Also, the student must be willing to be a team player and work as part of a team; and they must be willing to put hard work into their course and work.

- *Earplugs*
- *Chocolate*
- *Mousetrap*

- *Extension lead*
- *Kettle*
- *Sound system*

Induction and freshers' week

Robert Gordon University:

'Freshers' Week is aimed at bringing all new students together in order for them to settle in safely and make new friends. For a lot of people, starting university will mean leaving home and living away from parents for the first time. It is important for us to ensure all new students are acquainted with their new surroundings and opportunities in order to make sure they are safe and enjoy their student experience.

'There is a lot of information to digest when starting university and this is best dealt with as part of a group rather than 'going it alone'. As such, a big part of Freshers' Week is encouraging students to get involved in a number of activities, learn about their course and meet other students who are in the same position as them. Freshers' Week is great fun, like a big welcome party to university with events which cater to all tastes, but it is all built on the foundation of educating new students about the university and the city.'

Nottingham University:

'We run a welcome week designed to help students settle into university life as quickly as possible; this includes the academic side of university life as well as the social.

'Prior to Freshers' Week, the International Office also runs a welcome week for all new international students: a free week offering a fantastic introduction into life in the UK and at the university.'

Second year student:

'Freshers' Week: It was great, it's free – you only need to sort out your transportation, food and spending money. We had some ice-breakers, seminars about the uni etc, went bowling, clubbing and to the cinema.'

Induction days and Freshers' Weeks are designed to help you find your feet and settle in for the duration of your course. They are also very important for reminding you that extra-curricular activities such as sports are an important part of the higher education experience. Details are often on university websites. You might have to book in advance for very popular options. Beware of signing up for very esoteric clubs which might be very grateful for your joining fee but then fail to hold many or any meetings. Don't forget that if there is no club catering for your pet interest you can always start one yourself!

- Plan your Freshers' Week carefully with a variety of events around your course, your leisure interests and your location. Be aware that Freshers' Week will involve a mixture of campus-wide events and events devised to be of special interest to those in your department or faculty.
- Sometimes there are events that welcome parents and other family members.
- Most universities will have an orientation week for international students before the UK students move in, and sometimes airport pick-ups can be arranged. This will give you extra time to settle in and will help you find your way around the town and the campus, with special emphasis on the international clubs and societies and introductions to the international officers and, where possible, native speakers of newcomers' languages. Check the UKCISA website for information of general interest too; for instance every international student can benefit from reading the UKCISA information sheet on culture shock available at **www.ukcisa.org.uk/student/info_sheets/culture_shock.php**.

- Induction will involve an outline of your course or at least its early stages, introductions to key staff, notes on assessment and course work expected, and other important matters such as tours of key or specialist facilities, introduction to library usage, and will also have a section or two on more general matters such as student welfare and the students' union. You will often find out about student ambassadors during induction, who are usually second year students who remember just what it is like to be in your position. Make notes in case you are asked to be an ambassador next year!

- Study timetables might not be available until very near the start of the study year – check with your tutor or students' union who should be able to tell you where to look on the university or college website. Timetables are often a bit provisional at first, so check for updates even after you have found it.

Things to avoid

Some people see groups of new students as ripe for exploitation – so protect yourself by applying your common sense.

- Don't sign up for things you don't want or haven't had time to think about – store cards, credit cards, indeterminate commitments.
- Try not to deal with too many novelties or difficulties at once. There are many sources of help – make use of them. It might all be very different from what you expected; if this is the case, have a word with your pastoral tutor or find someone to talk to about it at the students' union or the welfare office, or you may find your new friends are feeling the same but hadn't liked to admit it.
- Be on the look-out for fraud – there are ever-increasing cases of email scams where a site looking just like a high street bank or the Student Loans Company, for instance, contacts you and asks you to confirm your personal details. No reputable institution would ever ask for such information to be verified in this way, so if you receive anything that arouses your suspicion, send it on to the real company. They will let you know if it is real and if so, how to deal with it. If it is a mistake or a scam they will be very grateful to you for helping them to stamp out such practices.

Employment

Nowadays two-thirds of students undertake paid work to help finance their studies. Roughly one in four freshers work during term time, about half of whom are in paid employment for 14 or more hours a week. Latest figures from the NUS suggest that about 40% of final year students rely on employment to secure adequate funding, attesting the extra costs of materials and final projects but also possibly a reflection of poor financial decision-making earlier on. Keeping the financial wolf at bay all adds to the stress of trying to succeed in your studies and social life. How to keep a healthy balance between building up debt and dedicating time to earning funds is delicate and different for every student. Again, the university authorities will have seen many solutions to this conundrum and will have advice to offer, for instance, they may recommend finding vacation work rather than working during term. One thing is certain, you can't begin to plan to work until your timetable and study commitments are clear.

Universities usually have recommended maximum employment hours for students, and there is a legal maximum of 20 hours a week for overseas students which makes a good rule of thumb. Talk to your tutor or welfare officer if you are tempted to work more than this to help cover your expenses. There might be employment possibilities within the university (for instance student ambassador roles for open days) or the students' union in the bars or shops for example, and these jobs might be easier to fit around your timetable as the employers will be sympathetic, and in any case try to get work nearby if you don't have transport otherwise the costs in time and travel will be out of proportion to your earnings.

It might be worth while giving a little attention to writing a CV before you go to university so that you can jump in quickly with your application while other people are still worrying about how to apply! If you get the outline done beforehand, with your school results, hobbies, interests and what you are studying, you can fill in any last minute details about availability once these become clear. Have a look at

- **www.e4s.co.uk**
- **www.justjobs4students.co.uk**
- **www.totaljobs.com**
- **www.studentjob.co.uk**
- **www.student-jobs.co.uk**

to get a flavour of the kinds of jobs that may be available.

It is a bonus, but one well worth giving some thought to, if you can find employment that could help your future career development. It is well known that employers are more likely to take on someone who has already spent time in their line of business, and even work placements elsewhere count, with four in ten employers as a mark in your favour. Progression within any sphere is worth mentioning on your CV; so make the most of any opportunity that comes your way. But try also to be aware that a highly competitive transient workforce is also ripe for exploitation, and check out anything that looks too attractive as the sting in the tail can be difficult to escape – remember to check whether you can work more flexibly when you are taking exams, for instance, and whether you are committed to working the same hours or shifts in holiday and term time, or if you are offered a premium for unsocial hours, do check what these actually are and what the transport implications are. You need to stay safe, too, and walking home alone in an unfamiliar area in the small hours may not be the best way to do that.

Parents, grandparents, guardians, pets and other family members

Saying goodbye to you is probably something new for them as well as for you. They'll regard you as more adult when you come home for the Christmas holidays than they do now. For them it might seem like only last week that they cheered you on at your nursery school sports day (they're sometimes silly like that) and now you're suddenly very grown up and they're having to do a lot of adjusting in a very short time. If you're living at home while you study you'll have more chance to explain but they might be less aware of the changes going on around you than if you were physically far away. So the potential problems are different if you are living at home while studying: your family might not recognise how much things are changing for you and might not realise the new ways in which you need both freedom and support. You'll still be a part of the student community and fully involved in evening events and weekend outings, which will be different from your life before university. Your dog won't forget you but its loyalties are heavily influenced by pragmatism. If you have children they might take time to adjust to the new you!

Student tip:

'I'm really excited though nervous cos this will be the first time I'm so far from home!'

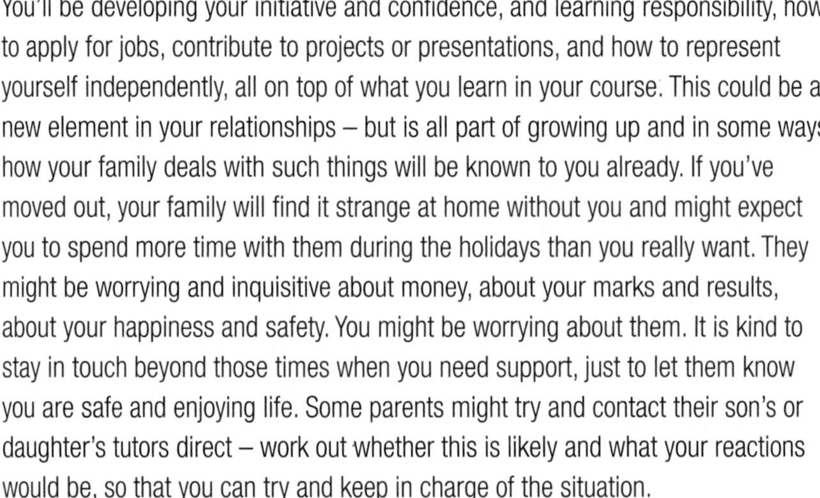

You'll be developing your initiative and confidence, and learning responsibility, how to apply for jobs, contribute to projects or presentations, and how to represent yourself independently, all on top of what you learn in your course. This could be a new element in your relationships – but is all part of growing up and in some ways how your family deals with such things will be known to you already. If you've moved out, your family will find it strange at home without you and might expect you to spend more time with them during the holidays than you really want. They might be worrying and inquisitive about money, about your marks and results, about your happiness and safety. You might be worrying about them. It is kind to stay in touch beyond those times when you need support, just to let them know you are safe and enjoying life. Some parents might try and contact their son's or daughter's tutors direct – work out whether this is likely and what your reactions would be, so that you can try and keep in charge of the situation.

Strange things can happen. You might miss them more than you think, and they might miss you for unexpected reasons – are you the one who always removes spiders from the bathroom? Try to see the funny side if you can.

Did you know?

Unis have loads of societies you can join

Each uni has a long list of groups you can join, from political and religious societies to social societies – one uni has a cheese and chocolate club... Joining a society is a great way to meet people with the same interests. Check the unis' websites or speak to the students' union.

Myth buster

You're not on your own

Although you might be nervous about starting uni on your own, you're not alone. Everyone is going through the same experience, and if you have any concerns when you're at uni, there's always someone available to help. Most unis have their own welfare, advice or guidance centres.

Whatever your problem, big or small, they'll be able to advise you or point you in the right direction for help. To find out what your uni offers, go to their website and look up student support, or go into the students' union and ask staff there.

Chapter checklist

These are the things you should be doing and thinking about in Step 6 of your applicant journey:

- [ ] Check the correspondence you receive from your university or college and take the relevant action on:
  - accommodation options
  - reading lists
  - preparation advice for your course
  - assembling your important papers and documentation
  - liaising with the disability officer
  - booking your place on Freshers' Week events.
- [ ] Check out your accommodation options if you want to be independent of the uni.
- [ ] Finalise your finance arrangements.
- [ ] Meet people through social networking sites.
- [ ] Think about part-time work options.
- [ ] Pack bags and make travel arrangements, if moving away from home.

www.ucas.com

Resources

This section of the book will help you understand some of the jargon you may hear when making your UCAS application, including information about the UCAS Tariff. We've also included links to other organisations you may find useful during your journey into higher education and a map of the UK to help you locate your institutions.

www.ucas.com

UCAS Tariff

Finding out what qualifications are needed for different higher education courses can be very confusing.

The UCAS Tariff is the system for allocating points to qualifications used for entry to higher education. Universities and colleges can use the UCAS Tariff to make comparisons between applicants with different qualifications. Tariff points are often used in entry requirements, although other factors are often taken into account. Information on Course Finder at **www.ucas.com** provides a fuller picture of what admissions tutors are seeking.

The tables on the following pages show the qualifications covered by the UCAS Tariff. There may have been changes to these tables since this book was printed. You should visit **www.ucas.com** to view the most up-to-date tables.

Further information?

Although Tariff points can be accumulated in a variety of ways, not all of these will necessarily be acceptable for entry to a particular higher education course. The achievement of a points score therefore does not give an automatic entitlement to entry, and many other factors are taken into account in the admissions process.

The Course Finder facility at **www.ucas.com** is the best source of reference to find out what qualifications are acceptable for entry to specific courses. Updates to the Tariff, including details on how new qualifications are added, can be found at **www.ucas.com/students/ucas_tariff/**.

How does the Tariff work?

- Students can collect Tariff points from a range of different qualifications, eg GCE A level with BTEC Nationals.
- There is no ceiling to the number of points that can be accumulated.
- There is no double counting. Certain qualifications within the Tariff build on qualifications in the same subject. In these cases only the qualification with the higher Tariff score will be counted. This principle applies to:
  - GCE Advanced Subsidiary level and GCE Advanced level
  - Scottish Highers and Advanced Highers
  - Speech, drama and music awards at grades 6, 7 and 8.
- Tariff points for the Advanced Diploma come from the Progression Diploma score plus the relevant Additional and Specialist Learning (ASL) Tariff points. Please see the appropriate qualification in the Tariff tables to calculate the ASL score.
- The Extended Project Tariff points are included within the Tariff points for Progression and Advanced Diplomas. Extended Project points represented in the Tariff only count when the qualification is taken outside of these Diplomas.
- Where the Tariff tables refer to specific awarding organisations, only qualifications from these awarding organisations attract Tariff points. Qualifications with a similar title, but from a different qualification awarding organisation do not attract Tariff points.

How do universities and colleges use the Tariff?

The Tariff provides a facility to help universities and colleges when expressing entrance requirements and when making conditional offers. Entry requirements and conditional offers expressed as Tariff points will often require a minimum level of achievement in a specified subject (for example, '300 points to include grade A at A level chemistry', or '260 points including SQA Higher grade B in mathematics').

Use of the Tariff may also vary from department to department at any one institution, and may in some cases be dependent on the programme being offered.

In July 2010, UCAS announced plans to review the qualifications information provided to universities and colleges. You can read more about the review at **www.ucas.com/qireview**.

What qualifications are included in the Tariff?

The following qualifications are included in the UCAS Tariff. See the number on the qualification title to find the relevant section of the Tariff table.

1	AAT NVQ Level 3 in Accounting
2	AAT Level 3 Diploma in Accounting (QCF)
3	Advanced Diploma
4	Advanced Extension Awards
5	Advanced Placement Programme (US and Canada)
6	Arts Award (Gold)
7	ASDAN Community Volunteering qualification
8	Asset Languages Advanced Stage
9	British Horse Society (Stage 3 Horse Knowledge & Care, Stage 3 Riding and Preliminary Teacher's Certificate)
10	BTEC Awards (NQF)
11	BTEC Certificates and Extended Certificates (NQF)

12	BTEC Diplomas (NQF)
13	BTEC National in Early Years (NQF)
14	BTEC Nationals (NQF)
15	BTEC QCF Qualifications (Suite known as Nationals)
16	BTEC Specialist Qualifications (QCF)
17	CACHE Award, Certificate and Diploma in Child Care and Education
18	CACHE Level 3 Extended Diploma for the Children and Young People's Workforce (QCF)
19	Cambridge ESOL Examinations
20	Cambridge Pre-U
21	Certificate of Personal Effectiveness (COPE)
22	CISI Introduction to Securities and Investment
23	City & Guilds Land Based Services Level 3 Qualifications
24	Graded Dance and Vocational Graded Dance
25	Diploma in Fashion Retail
26	Diploma in Foundation Studies (Art & Design; Art, Design & Media)
27	EDI Level 3 Certificate in Accounting, Certificate in Accounting (IAS)
28	Essential Skills (Northern Ireland)
29	Essential Skills Wales
30	Extended Project (stand alone)
31	Free-standing Mathematics
32	Functional skills
33	GCE (AS, AS Double Award, A level, A level Double Award and A level (with additional AS))

34	Hong Kong Diploma of Secondary Education (from 2012 entry onwards)
35	ifs School of Finance (Certificate and Diploma in Financial Studies)
36	iMedia (OCR level Certificate/Diploma for iMedia Professionals)
37	International Baccalaureate (IB) Diploma
38	International Baccalaureate (IB) Certificate
39	Irish Leaving Certificate (Higher and Ordinary levels)
40	IT Professionals (iPRO) (Certificate and Diploma)
41	Key Skills (Levels 2, 3 and 4)
42	Music examinations (grades 6, 7 and 8)
43	OCR Level 3 Certificate in Mathematics for Engineering
44	OCR Level 3 Certificate for Young Enterprise
45	OCR Nationals (National Certificate, National Diploma and National Extended Diploma)
46	Principal Learning Wales
47	Progression Diploma
48	Rockschool Music Practitioners Qualifications
49	Scottish Qualifications
50	Speech and Drama examinations (grades 6, 7 and 8 and Performance Studies)
51	Sports Leaders UK
52	Welsh Baccalaureate Advanced Diploma (Core)

Updates on the Tariff, including details on the incorporation of any new qualifications, are posted on **www.ucas.com**.

UCAS TARIFF TABLES

1

AAT NVQ LEVEL 3 IN ACCOUNTING	
GRADE	TARIFF POINTS
PASS	160

2

AAT LEVEL 3 DIPLOMA IN ACCOUNTING	
GRADE	TARIFF POINTS
PASS	160

3

ADVANCED DIPLOMA

Advanced Diploma = Progression Diploma plus Additional & Specialist Learning (ASL). Please see the appropriate qualification to calculate the ASL score. Please see the Progression Diploma (Table 47) for Tariff scores

4

ADVANCED EXTENSION AWARDS	
GRADE	TARIFF POINTS
DISTINCTION	40
MERIT	20

Points for Advanced Extension Awards are over and above those gained from the A level grade

5

*ADVANCED PLACEMENT PROGRAMME (US & CANADA)	
GRADE	TARIFF POINTS
Group A	
5	120
4	90
3	60
Group B	
5	50
4	35
3	20

6

ARTS AWARD (GOLD)	
GRADE	TARIFF POINTS
PASS	35

7

ASDAN COMMUNITY VOLUNTEERING QUALIFICATION	
GRADE	TARIFF POINTS
CERTIFICATE	50
AWARD	30

8

ASSET LANGUAGES ADVANCED STAGE			
GRADE	TARIFF POINTS	GRADE	TARIFF POINTS
Speaking		Listening	
GRADE 12	28	GRADE 12	25
GRADE 11	20	GRADE 11	18
GRADE 10	12	GRADE 10	11
Reading		Writing	
GRADE 12	25	GRADE 12	25
GRADE 11	18	GRADE 11	18
GRADE 10	11	GRADE 10	11

9

BRITISH HORSE SOCIETY	
GRADE	TARIFF POINTS
Stage 3 Horse Knowledge & Care	
PASS	35
Stage 3 Riding	
PASS	35
Preliminary Teacher's Certificate	
PASS	35

Awarded by Equestrian Qualifications (GB) Ltd (EQL)

*Details of the subjects covered by each group can be found at www.ucas.com/students/ucas_tariff/tarifftables

UCAS TARIFF TABLES

10

*BTEC AWARDS (NQF) (EXCLUDING BTEC NATIONAL QUALIFICATIONS)			
GRADE	TARIFF POINTS		
	Group A	Group B	Group C
DISTINCTION	20	30	40
MERIT	13	20	26
PASS	7	10	13

11

*BTEC CERTIFICATES AND EXTENDED CERTIFICATES (NQF) (EXCLUDING BTEC NATIONAL QUALIFICATIONS)					
GRADE	TARIFF POINTS				
	Group A	Group B	Group C	Group D	Extended Certificates
DISTINCTION	40	60	80	100	60
MERIT	26	40	52	65	40
PASS	13	20	26	35	20

12

*BTEC DIPLOMAS (NQF) (EXCLUDING BTEC NATIONAL QUALIFICATIONS)			
GRADE	TARIFF POINTS		
	Group A	Group B	Group C
DISTINCTION	80	100	120
MERIT	52	65	80
PASS	26	35	40

13

BTEC NATIONAL IN EARLY YEARS (NQF)					
GRADE	TARIFF POINTS	GRADE	TARIFF POINTS	GRADE	TARIFF POINTS
Theory				Practical	
Diploma		Certificate			
DDD	320	DD	200	D	120
DDM	280	DM	160	M	80
DMM	240	MM	120	P	40
MMM	220	MP	80		
MMP	160	PP	40		
MPP	120				
PPP	80				

Points apply to the following qualifications only: BTEC National Diploma in Early Years (100/1279/5); BTEC National Certificate in Early Years (100/1280/1).

*Details of the subjects covered by each group can be found at **www.ucas.com/students/ucas_tariff/tarifftables**

UCAS TARIFF TABLES

14

BTEC NATIONALS (NQF)					
GRADE	TARIFF POINTS	GRADE	TARIFF POINTS	GRADE	TARIFF POINTS
Diploma		Certificate		Award	
DDD	360	DD	240	D	120
DDM	320	DM	200	M	80
DMM	280	MM	160	P	40
MMM	240	MP	120		
MMP	200	PP	80		
MPP	160				
PPP	120				

15

BTEC QUALIFICATIONS (QCF) (SUITE OF QUALIFICATIONS KNOWN AS NATIONALS)					
EXTENDED DIPLOMA	DIPLOMA	90 CREDIT DIPLOMA	SUBSIDIARY DIPLOMA	CERTIFICATE	TARIFF POINTS
D*D*D*					420
D*D*D					400
D*DD					380
DDD					360
DDM					320
DMM	D*D*				280
	D*D				260
MMM	DD				240
		D*D*			210
MMP	DM	D*D			200
		DD			180
MPP	MM	DM			160
			D*		140
PPP	MP	MM	D		120
		MP			100
	PP		M		80
				D*	70
		PP		D	60
			P	M	40
				P	20

UCAS TARIFF TABLES

16

BTEC SPECIALIST (QCF)			
GRADE	TARIFF POINTS		
	Diploma	Certificate	Award
DISTINCTION	120	60	20
MERIT	80	40	13
PASS	40	20	7

17

CACHE LEVEL 3 AWARD, CERTIFICATE AND DIPLOMA IN CHILD CARE & EDUCATION					
AWARD		CERTIFICATE		DIPLOMA	
GRADE	TARIFF POINTS	GRADE	TARIFF POINTS	GRADE	TARIFF POINTS
A	30	A	110	A	360
B	25	B	90	B	300
C	20	C	70	C	240
D	15	D	55	D	180
E	10	E	35	E	120

18

CACHE LEVEL 3 EXTENDED DIPLOMA FOR THE CHILDREN AND YOUNG PEOPLE'S WORKFORCE (QCF)	
GRADE	TARIFF POINTS
A*	420
A	340
B	290
C	240
D	140
E	80

19

CAMBRIDGE ESOL EXAMINATIONS	
GRADE	TARIFF POINTS
Certificate of Proficiency in English	
A	140
B	110
C	70
Certificate in Advanced English	
A	70

20

CAMBRIDGE PRE-U					
GRADE	TARIFF POINTS	GRADE	TARIFF POINTS	GRADE	TARIFF POINTS
Principal Subject		Global Perspectives and Research		Short Course	
D1	TBC	D1	TBC	D1	TBC
D2	145	D2	140	D2	TBC
D3	130	D3	126	D3	60
M1	115	M1	112	M1	53
M2	101	M2	98	M2	46
M3	87	M3	84	M3	39
P1	73	P1	70	P1	32
P2	59	P2	56	P2	26
P3	46	P3	42	P3	20

UCAS TARIFF TABLES

21

CERTIFICATE OF PERSONAL EFFECTIVENESS (COPE)	
GRADE	TARIFF POINTS
PASS	70

Points are awarded for the Certificate of Personal Effectiveness (CoPE) awarded by ASDAN and CCEA

22

CISI INTRODUCTION TO SECURITIES AND INVESTMENT	
GRADE	TARIFF POINTS
PASS WITH DISTINCTION	60
PASS WITH MERIT	40
PASS	20

23

CITY AND GUILDS LAND BASED SERVICES LEVEL 3 QUALIFICATIONS				
GRADE	TARIFF POINTS			
	EXTENDED DIPLOMA	DIPLOMA	SUBSIDIARY DIPLOMA	CERTIFICATE
DISTINCTION*	420	280	140	70
DISTINCTION	360	240	120	60
MERIT	240	160	80	40
PASS	120	80	40	20

24

GRADED DANCE AND VOCATIONAL GRADED DANCE					
GRADE	TARIFF POINTS	GRADE	TARIFF POINTS	GRADE	TARIFF POINTS
Graded Dance					
Grade 8		Grade 7		Grade 6	
DISTINCTION	65	DISTINCTION	55	DISTINCTION	40
MERIT	55	MERIT	45	MERIT	35
PASS	45	PASS	35	PASS	30
Vocational Graded Dance					
Advanced Foundation		Intermediate			
DISTINCTION	70	DISTINCTION	65		
MERIT	55	MERIT	50		
PASS	45	PASS	40		

25

DIPLOMA IN FASHION RETAIL	
GRADE	TARIFF POINTS
DISTINCTION	160
MERIT	120
PASS	80

Applies to the NQF and QCF versions of the qualifications awarded by ABC Awards

UCAS TARIFF TABLES

26

DIPLOMA IN FOUNDATION STUDIES (ART & DESIGN AND ART, DESIGN & MEDIA)	
GRADE	TARIFF POINTS
DISTINCTION	285
MERIT	225
PASS	165

Awarded by ABC, Edexcel, UAL and WJEC

27

EDI LEVEL 3 CERTIFICATE IN ACCOUNTING, CERTIFICATE IN ACCOUNTING (IAS)	
GRADE	TARIFF POINTS
DISTINCTION	120
MERIT	90
PASS	70

28

ESSENTIAL SKILLS (NORTHERN IRELAND)	
GRADE	TARIFF POINTS
LEVEL 2	10

Only allocated at level 2 if studied as part of a wider composite qualification such as 14-19 Diploma or Welsh Baccalaureate

29

ESSENTIAL SKILLS WALES	
GRADE	TARIFF POINTS
LEVEL 4	30
LEVEL 3	20
LEVEL 2	10

Only allocated at level 2 if studied as part of a wider composite qualification such as 14-19 Diploma or Welsh Baccalaureate

30

EXTENDED PROJECT (STAND ALONE)	
GRADE	TARIFF POINTS
A*	70
A	60
B	50
C	40
D	30
E	20

Points for the Extended Project cannot be counted if taken as part of Progression/ Advanced Diploma

31

FREE-STANDING MATHEMATICS	
GRADE	TARIFF POINTS
A	20
B	17
C	13
D	10
E	7

Covers free-standing Mathematics - Additional Maths, Using and Applying Statistics, Working with Algebraic and Graphical Techniques, Modelling with Calculus

32

FUNCTIONAL SKILLS	
GRADE	TARIFF POINTS
LEVEL 2	10

Only allocated if studied as part of a wider composite qualification such as 14-19 Diploma or Welsh Baccalaureate

UCAS TARIFF TABLES

33

GCE AND VCE									
GRADE	TARIFF POINTS	GRADE	TARIFF POINTS	GRADE	TARIFF POINTS	GRADE	TARIFF POINTS	GRADE	TARIFF POINTS
GCE & AVCE Double Award		GCE A level with additional AS (9 units)		GCE A level & AVCE		GCE AS Double Award		GCE AS & AS VCE	
A*A*	280	A*A	200	A*	140	AA	120	A	60
A*A	260	AA	180	A	120	AB	110	B	50
AA	240	AB	170	B	100	BB	100	C	40
AB	220	BB	150	C	80	BC	90	D	30
BB	200	BC	140	D	60	CC	80	E	20
BC	180	CC	120	E	40	CD	70		
CC	160	CD	110			DD	60		
CD	140	DD	90			DE	50		
DD	120	DE	80			EE	40		
DE	100	EE	60						
EE	80								

34

HONG KONG DIPLOMA OF SECONDARY EDUCATION					
GRADE	TARIFF POINTS	GRADE	TARIFF POINTS	GRADE	TARIFF POINTS
All subjects except mathematics		Mathematics compulsory component		Mathematics optional components	
5**	No value	5**	No value	5**	No value
5*	130	5*	60	5*	70
5	120	5	45	5	60
4	80	4	35	4	50
3	40	3	25	3	40

No value for 5** pending receipt of candidate evidence (post-2012)

UCAS TARIFF TABLES

35

IFS SCHOOL OF FINANCE (NQF & QCF)			
GRADE	TARIFF POINTS	GRADE	TARIFF POINTS
Certificate in Financial Studies (CeFS)		Diploma in Financial Studies (DipFS)	
A	60	A	120
B	50	B	100
C	40	C	80
D	30	D	60
E	20	E	40

Applicants with the ifs Diploma cannot also count points allocated to the ifs Certificate. Completion of both qualifications will result in a maximum of 120 UCAS Tariff points

36

LEVEL 3 CERTIFICATE / DIPLOMA FOR iMEDIA USERS (iMEDIA)	
GRADE	TARIFF POINTS
DIPLOMA	66
CERTIFICATE	40

Awarded by OCR

37

INTERNATIONAL BACCALAUREATE (IB) DIPLOMA			
GRADE	TARIFF POINTS	GRADE	TARIFF POINTS
45	720	34	479
44	698	33	457
43	676	32	435
42	654	31	413
41	632	30	392
40	611	29	370
39	589	28	348
38	567	27	326
37	545	26	304
36	523	25	282
35	501	24	260

38

INTERNATIONAL BACCALAUREATE (IB) CERTIFICATE					
GRADE	TARIFF POINTS	GRADE	TARIFF POINTS	GRADE	TARIFF POINTS
Higher Level		Standard Level		Core	
7	130	7	70	3	120
6	110	6	59	2	80
5	80	5	43	1	40
4	50	4	27	0	10
3	20	3	11		

UCAS TARIFF TABLES

39

IRISH LEAVING CERTIFICATE			
GRADE	TARIFF POINTS	GRADE	TARIFF POINTS
Higher		Ordinary	
A1	90	A1	39
A2	77	A2	26
B1	71	B1	20
B2	64	B2	14
B3	58	B3	7
C1	52		
C2	45		
C3	39		
D1	33		
D2	26		
D3	20		

40

IT PROFESSIONALS (iPRO)	
GRADE	TARIFF POINTS
DIPLOMA	100
CERTIFICATE	80

Awarded by OCR

41

KEY SKILLS	
GRADE	TARIFF POINTS
LEVEL 4	30
LEVEL 3	20
LEVEL 2	10

Only allocated at level 2 if studied as part of a wider composite qualification such as 14-19 Diploma or Welsh Baccalaureate

42

MUSIC EXAMINATIONS					
GRADE	TARIFF POINTS	GRADE	TARIFF POINTS	GRADE	TARIFF POINTS
Practical					
Grade 8		Grade 7		Grade 6	
DISTINCTION	75	DISTINCTION	60	DISTINCTION	45
MERIT	70	MERIT	55	MERIT	40
PASS	55	PASS	40	PASS	25
Theory					
Grade 8		Grade 7		Grade 6	
DISTINCTION	30	DISTINCTION	20	DISTINCTION	15
MERIT	25	MERIT	15	MERIT	10
PASS	20	PASS	10	PASS	5

Points shown are for the ABRSM, LCMM/University of West London, Rockschool and Trinity Guildhall/Trinity College London Advanced Level music examinations

43

OCR LEVEL 3 CERTIFICATE IN MATHEMATICS FOR ENGINEERING	
GRADE	TARIFF POINTS
A*	TBC
A	90
B	75
C	60
D	45
E	30

UCAS TARIFF TABLES

44

OCR LEVEL 3 CERTIFICATE FOR YOUNG ENTERPRISE	
GRADE	TARIFF POINTS
DISTINCTION	40
MERIT	30
PASS	20

45

OCR NATIONALS					
GRADE	TARIFF POINTS	GRADE	TARIFF POINTS	GRADE	TARIFF POINTS
National Extended Diploma		National Diploma		National Certificate	
D1	360	D	240	D	120
D2/M1	320	M1	200	M	80
M2	280	M2/P1	160	P	40
M3	240	P2	120		
P1	200	P3	80		
P2	160				
P3	120				

46

PRINCIPAL LEARNING WALES	
GRADE	TARIFF POINTS
A*	210
A	180
B	150
C	120
D	90
E	60

47

PROGRESSION DIPLOMA	
GRADE	TARIFF POINTS
A*	350
A	300
B	250
C	200
D	150
E	100

Advanced Diploma = Progression Diploma plus Additional & Specialist Learning (ASL). Please see the appropriate qualification to calculate the ASL score.

48

ROCKSCHOOL MUSIC PRACTITIONERS QUALIFICATIONS					
GRADE	TARIFF POINTS				
	Extended Diploma	Diploma	Subsidiary Diploma	Extended Certificate	Certificate
DISTINCTION	240	180	120	60	30
MERIT	160	120	80	40	20
PASS	80	60	40	20	10

UCAS TARIFF TABLES

49

SCOTTISH QUALIFICATIONS

GRADE	TARIFF POINTS
Advanced Higher	
A	130
B	110
C	90
D	72
Ungraded Higher	
PASS	45

GRADE	TARIFF POINTS
Higher	
A	80
B	65
C	50
D	36
NPA PC Passport	
PASS	45
Core Skills	
HIGHER	20

GRADE	TARIFF POINTS
Scottish Interdisciplinary Project	
A	65
B	55
C	45

GROUP	TARIFF POINTS
Scottish National Certificates	
C	125
B	100
A	75

Details of the subjects covered by each Scottish National Certificate can be found at www.ucas.com/students/ucas_tariff/tarifftables

50

SPEECH AND DRAMA EXAMINATIONS

GRADE	TARIFF POINTS
PCertLAM	
DISTINCTION	90
MERIT	80
PASS	60

GRADE	TARIFF POINTS
Grade 8	
DISTINCTION	65
MERIT	60
PASS	45

GRADE	TARIFF POINTS
Grade 7	
DISTINCTION	55
MERIT	50
PASS	35

GRADE	TARIFF POINTS
Grade 6	
DISTINCTION	40
MERIT	35
PASS	20

Details of the Speech and Drama Qualifications covered by the Tariff can be found at www.ucas.com/students/ucas_tariff/tarifftables

51

SPORTS LEADERS UK

GRADE	TARIFF POINTS
PASS	30

These points are awarded to Higher Sports Leader Award and Level 3 Certificate in Higher Sports Leadership (QCF)

52

WELSH BACCALAUREATE ADVANCED DIPLOMA (CORE)

GRADE	TARIFF POINTS
PASS	120

These points are awarded only when a candidate achieves the Welsh Baccalaureate Advanced Diploma

Jargon buster

When applying through UCAS, you may hear or read the commonly used words and phrases shown below. To help you, we've provided this list, with a summary of their meanings.

APEL: Accreditation of Prior Experiential Learning.

APL: Accreditation of Prior Learning.

Apply: the UCAS online application system for applying for higher education courses.

Adjustment: applicants who have met and exceeded the conditions of their firm choice are given an opportunity to look for an alternative place while holding their original confirmed place.

Clearing: a system used towards the end of the academic cycle. If you have not secured a place, it enables you to apply for course vacancies.

Conditional offer: an offer made by a university, whereby you must fulfil certain criteria before you can be accepted on the course.

Confirmation: when conditional offers that you have accepted become unconditional or are declined. Confirmation is usually dependent on your qualification or exam results.

Deferral: holding an offer of a place until the following year.

Exam board: an organisation that sets exam questions and is responsible for marking them and distributing results. Also known as examination board, awarding organisation, or awarding body.

Extra: the opportunity to apply for another course if you have used all five choices and not secured a place. Extra runs from the end of February until the end of June.

FE: further education.

Firm offer: the offer that you have accepted as your first choice.

Fresher: a first year undergraduate student.

HE: higher education.

Institution: a university or college offering higher education courses.

Insurance offer: the offer that you have accepted as your second choice, in case you do not meet the requirements for your firm offer.

Invitation: an invitation from a university to attend for interview, audition, or provide a portfolio, essay or other piece of work.

NSS: National Student Survey.

Personal ID: a 10-digit individual number assigned to you when you register to use Apply. It is printed on every letter we send you. You will be asked to provide this number if you contact our Customer Contact Centre.

Point of entry: your year of entry to the course, for example, 2 refers to the second year of the course.

Scheme Code: used in conjunction with your Personal ID to uniquely identify your application.

Track: a system where you can track the progress of your application at **www.ucas.com**, reply to any offers received, and make certain amendments, for example, change of address or email.

UCAS Card: this scheme is the start of the UCAS journey. Registered students have access to a host of information about courses, life in higher education, the application process and a free discount card that can be used in the high street.

UCAStv: our video guides to help you apply to university and find out what other students think about higher education. You can learn how to use our systems and make the most of the resources available at **www.ucas.tv**.

Unconditional offer: an offer given to you by a university if you have satisfied the criteria and can attend the course.

Unsuccessful: you have not been accepted by the university concerned.

Withdrawal: either you or a university cancels a choice before a decision has been made – a reason will be included if the withdrawal was issued by an institution.

Useful contacts

In this section we've provided contact details for other sources of information and advice you may find helpful.

UCAS Connect: connect with UCAS online at **www.ucasconnect.com** – it shows the latest advice we've posted on Twitter (**twitter.com/ucas_online**) and Facebook (**www.facebook.com/ucasonline**), and useful hints, tips, and reminders about important dates. There's student blogs from current applicants writing about their experiences of applying through UCAS, and 'how-to' video guides, like writing a personal statement, attending a higher education event, or going to an open day. You can watch and share more video guides at **www.ucas.tv**. You'll also find a link to the **UCAS Advisers' blog** (**http://ucasonline.blogspot.co.uk/**) which allows us to push out key messages to applicants, and publish Q&A sessions with guests, such as university admissions departments and student finance organisations.

Higher education – general advice

Your school or college: if you are currently studying at a school or college, you can contact your tutor for help. You may also have a school careers adviser who can look at your skills and interests and help you identify suitable courses.

Careers centres: contact your local careers advisory service and careers library for more advice and guidance.

Depending on where you live, visit the websites listed below for advice:

- **England – National Careers Service:** impartial careers advice and practical help for 13 – 19 year olds, with a focus on careers and learning. Advisers are available between 08:00 – 22:00 seven days a week – **www.gov.uk/careers-helpline-for-teenagers**
- **Northern Ireland – Careers Service Northern Ireland:** provides an impartial, all-age careers information, advice and guidance service. Professionally qualified careers advisers are based in careers resource centres and offices, jobs and benefits offices and job centres – **www.nidirect.gov.uk/careers**
- **Scotland – Skills Development Scotland:** can help you make well-informed decisions about learning and your career. Visit your local Skills Development Scotland centre or **www.myworldofwork.co.uk**
- **Wales - Careers Wales:** provides people of all ages with free, bilingual, impartial, careers information, advice and guidance at **www.careerswales.com**

The Complete University Guide: includes university league and subject tables – **www.thecompleteuniversityguide.co.uk**

Department for Education: the Department for Education is responsible for education and children's services – **www.education.gov.uk**

Quality Assurance Agency for Higher Education (QAA): safeguards quality and standards in UK higher education, checking how well universities and colleges meet their responsibilities – **www.qaa.ac.uk**

National Union of Students (NUS): is the national voice of students, helping them to campaign, get cheap student discounts and provide advice on living student life to the full – **www.nus.org.uk**

Students with disabilities and special needs

Disability Rights UK
Skill is a UK independent charity that provides advice to disabled students who are studying in England. They also support students who are studying in Wales and Scotland – **www.disabilityrightsuk.org/disabledstudents.htm**

Royal National Institute of Blind People: **www.rnib.org.uk**

Royal National Institute for the Deaf: **www.rnid.org.uk**

British Dyslexia Association: **www.bdadyslexia.org.uk**

Disabled Students' Allowances (DSAs): more information can be found at **www.gov.uk/disabled-students-allowances-dsas**

Student finance and money matters

Depending on where you live, contact the relevant organisation below for advice:

Student Finance England – **www.gov.uk/student-finance**

Student Finance Northern Ireland – **www.studentfinanceni.co.uk**

Student Awards Agency for Scotland – **www.saas.gov.uk**

Student Finance Wales – **www.studentfinancewales.co.uk**

EU students (living outside the UK) who want to study in England, Northern Ireland or Wales should visit **www.gov.uk/student-finance** for further information. EU students who want to study in Scotland should visit **www.saas.gov.uk**

NASMA: The National Association of Student Money Advisers strives to relieve the poverty of students through the provision of advice, information and training – **www.nasma.org.uk**

Student Calculator powered by Brightside: an online budgeting tool provided by the education charity Brightside to help students manage their money – **www.studentcalculator.org.uk**

Student Bank Accounts: compare and choose the best student bank account for you – **www.studentbankaccounts.co.uk**

Money Saving Expert: advice on budgeting, banking and saving, as well as voucher schemes and shopping deals – **www.moneysavingexpert.com/students**

Lifestyle and accommodation

UNITE is the UK's leading developer and manager of purpose-built student accommodation – **www.unite-students.com**

Studentpad.co.uk was set up in December 1999 as an independent adviser and provider of a database of private and university accommodation.

Push.co.uk is the 'ruthlessly independent guide' to UK universities, student life, gap years, open days and student finance.

Cheap and healthy recipe ideas for students and anyone else on a budget can be found at **www.beyondbakedbeans.org**

Bright Knowledge: a guide to careers, education and student life – **www.brightknowledge.org**

Studential: aims to help all students aged 16 and older with their academic journey, by offering information and advice on all stages of education – **www.studential.com**

Universitiesnet: a student guide offering advice on studying at universities in the UK. From debating whether the cost of going to university is worth it, to knowing what to look out for when renting a student house, to finding a recipe, or deciding whether to start a graduate career or take a gap year – **www.universitiesnet.com**

The Student Accommodation Code: the Code protects students' rights to safe, good quality accommodation, wherever they are studying, and makes sure they get the best out of their time living in university or college residences – **www.thesac.org.uk**

Student Beans: providing students with discounts, entertainment and advice on all things student, Student Beans speaks directly to over 500,000 UK students every month – **www.studentbeans.com**

Studentstories.co.uk features students talking about their experiences of university, gap years, finding a job and getting career experience.

The Student Pocket Guide: provides UK students with discounts, entertainment and tips to help save money and get the most out of student life – **www.thestudentpocketguide.com**

16-25 Railcard: saving 16-25 year olds or over 26s in full-time education 1/3 off rail fares across Britain – **www.16-25railcard.co.uk**

StudentParents.org: tips and information about student finance and university life as a parent – **www.studentparents.org**

Getting support when you're at university or college

Students' unions: your students' union will probably be the hub of your university or college. The union is responsible for social events, sports events, discounts, music and, most importantly, for representing students. Details of students' unions within UK universities and colleges are available on the UCAS website at **www.ucas.com/students/startinguni/studentsunions**. (Also see NUS details on page 403.)

Nightline: Nightline is a confidential and anonymous listening, support and information service, run by students for students. Nightline operates in many universities and usually offers a phone service through the night. Email services and drop-in centres are also available in many universities – **www.nightline.ac.uk**

Lifetracks: Lifetracks offers help and advice for students at university or college. It contains useful articles, videos, features and a free question and answer service, all aimed at helping you while you're studying, and when making choices about your future – **www.lifetracks.com**

International students

Visa requirements

The UK Border Agency website contains all the information you need when applying for a student visa under Tier 4 of the points based system for immigration. For up-to-date details of the requirements for the student visa category and the relevant application process, visit **www.ukba.homeoffice.gov.uk/visas-immigration/studying/**

There's also a lot of useful immigration information for international students on the UKCISA (UK Council for International Students) website at **www.ukcisa.org.uk/student/immigration.php**

English language courses

Most universities and colleges provide English language courses and other forms of support to help you with your studies. The British Council also provides information about English language support at **www.britishcouncil.org/new**

You may want to take English classes when you arrive in the UK. English UK is the world's leading language teaching association with more than 400 members – all accredited by the British Council – including private language schools, educational trusts and charities and language centres in further education colleges and universities. More information can be found at **www.englishuk.com**

If you are also interested in improving your academic listening skills, ease (essential academic skills in English) may be able to help: **www2.warwick.ac.uk/fac/soc/al/leap/listeningandspeaking/**

Other links you may find useful:

Prepare for success: an interactive web learning tool for international students who are getting ready to come to the UK for study in further or higher education – **www.prepareforsuccess.org.uk**

Education UK: a website brought to you by the British Council to inspire and guide you throughout your study abroad journey in the UK – **www.educationuk.org**

UK NARIC: the national agency responsible for providing information, advice and expert opinion on vocational, academic and professional skills and qualifications from over 180 countries worldwide – **www.naric.org.uk**

Mature students

Access to HE courses

Access to HE courses are designed for people who want to take a university level course, but who didn't gain the necessary qualifications while at school. More information and a course search for QAA-recognised Access courses in England, Wales and Northern Ireland can be found at **www.accesstohe.ac.uk**

Information about Access courses in Scotland is available on the Scottish Wider Access Programme (SWAP) website at **www.scottishwideraccess.org**

Advice from further and adult education

If you are currently studying in further or adult education, it is worth asking your tutor for help, as well as your careers advisory service and careers library.

Advice from higher education

School and college liaison units within universities and colleges will also help mature applicants. Some institutions have city centre advice shops.

Careers companies

Some local careers companies offer an all-age information and advisory service. This is sometimes free, but a charge may be made. Look in your local telephone directory under Careers Service.

C2 – The Graduate Careers Shop

Operated by the University of London Careers Service, but open to any graduates at any point in their careers, C2 offers impartial, independent advice on any matter related to jobs and careers. Several services are available, on a sliding scale of charges: **www.c2careers.co.uk**

Educational Grants Advisory Service (EGAS)

Provides advice on funding available for post-16 education and training within the UK. Primarily concerned with helping disadvantaged students: **www.family-action.org.uk**

Gov.uk

Gov.uk is the website of the UK Government providing information and online services. Information about options for older people looking to get into higher education, and ways to combine study with work and family life can be found at **www.gov.uk/mature-student-university-funding**

Information, advice and guidance (IAG)

Local IAG services for adults are delivered by a variety of organisations, including Skills Development Scotland, educational institutions, and voluntary and community bodies. They offer free information and advice to individuals. You can find contact details for your nearest IAG service at your local library.

Learndirect

Guidance about training and employment opportunities in England. Working to rigorous standards monitored by the Department for Education: **www.learndirect.co.uk**

National Careers Service

A free, impartial and confidential service provided over the phone and on the web for adults seeking information and advice on courses and careers: **https://nationalcareersservice.direct.gov.uk**

National Extension College

With over 150 home-study courses and 200 resource titles, the NEC offers a range of nationally recognised qualifications in a wide variety of subjects: **www.nec.ac.uk**

National Open College Network (NOCN)

The National Open College Network (NOCN) is the leading credit-based awarding organisation in the UK, offering high quality, flexible, credit-based qualifications: **www.nocn.org.uk**

The Open University (OU)

The OU is the UK's only university dedicated to distance learning: **www.open.ac.uk**

Workers' Educational Association (WEA)

The UK's largest voluntary provider of adult education: **www.wea.org.uk**

Gap years

Year Out Group: to help you find a suitable and worthwhile project. Year Out Group provides references and resources to help you make the most of a year out – **www.yearoutgroup.org**

Foreign & Commonwealth Office travel & living abroad: provides travel advice by country, guidance to travellers before embarking on their trip, tips on staying safe and healthy, and travel news – **www.fco.gov.uk/en/travel-and-living-abroad**

vinspired: connects 16-25 year olds with volunteering opportunities in England – **http://vinspired.com**

Gapwork is an independent information provider specialising in gap years, gap jobs, gap year vacancies, activities and voluntary work either in the UK or abroad – **www.gapwork.com**

CSV is a volunteering and training charity, founded in 1962 – **www.csv.org.uk**

www.ucas.com

UK map of major cities and airports

Acknowledgements

UCAS is tremendously grateful to the many individuals and organisations for their invaluable contributions to our guide. Without their help we would not have been able to make the book come alive with their experiences and knowledge.

Individuals: Dr Nina Reeve, GP and Caroline Queen, veterinary surgeon.

Case studies: Catherine Alexander, Emma Alexander, Sara Dalton, Lucy Fenwick, Melissa Gloria Larsson, Alina Ludviga, Danielle de Massimi, Kevin Minors, Yann Moysey, Jane Pratt at The Grammar School at Leeds, Fred Suter, Jenny Vowles, Rochelle Weir and Nicky West.

Universities and colleges: James Seymour at Aston University, Victoria Bel Gil at Bournemouth University, Michelle Millar at Bradford College, Dr Roseanna Cross and Christine Moroney at the University of Bristol, Sarah Hannaford at the University of Cambridge, Richard Emborg at Durham University, Alix Delany and Dr Harriet Jones at the University of East Anglia, Rebecca Gaukroger at Edinburgh University, Neil Lakeland at Hadlow College, Mel Peter at Imperial College London,

Paul Stafford at Kingston University, Carolyn Williams at Liverpool John Moores University, Sean Threlfall at The University of Manchester, Stuart Davidson at Myerscough College, Nathalie Mortimer at the University of Nottingham, Jeni Aldridge at the Open University, Christopher Boulle and Helen Charlesworth at the University of Oxford, Sue Davey at Peninsula Schools of Medicine & Dentistry at Plymouth University, Rachel Creegan at Robert Gordon University, Lynsey Hopkins at the University of Warwick and Antonia Beringer at the University of West of England.

Organisations: José Ángel García for British Council Mexico, Emma Warboys for Cambridge Assessment, Jennifer Koller for College & University Consultants of Geneva, Dr Bernard Kingston for The Complete University Guide, Tony Stevens for Disability Rights UK, Paul Ireland for the Higher Education Liaison Officers Association (HELOA), Simon Kemp for Higher Education Statistics Agency (HESA), Elisabeth Marksteiner for International School of Zug and Luzern, Switzerland, Joyce Hong for HPAT Ulster, Jo Gibson for NASMA, Jeannette Law for Sage Advising, Milan, Italy, Andy Blaikie of Compass Group on behalf of STA Travel, Tim Devlin for Sutton Trust, Rachel Greatrix at UKCAT, Elizabet Sanchez for UNITE and David Allen for Univisits Ltd.

Special thanks to all the students who gave us their UCAS experiences on the UCAS Connect blogs and yougo forums.

Finally, thanks must also go to our UCAS colleagues, not only for their contributions, but also their enthusiasm and encouragement toward the production of the guide.

What do you think?

We welcome your feedback – good and bad – about our second edition of *The UCAS Guide to getting into University and College*, so that we can improve our next edition for future readers.

What did you think of this book?

____

____

____

What did you like best about it?

____

____

____

Was there anything you disliked about it? What was it?

____

____

____

Was there anything missing? Let us know what it was.

____

____

____

Would you recommend it to a friend?

____

Are you: (Tick ✓)

- ☐ planning to apply to university or college?
- ☐ a parent?
- ☐ an adviser in a school or college?
- ☐ or none of these – please say. ____________________

We do hope that you'll be able to spend a few minutes to give us your feedback about this book. You can either email us at ucas.editors@ucas.ac.uk or send a copy of this comment slip to UCAS, Rosehill, New Barn Lane, Cheltenham, Glos GL52 3LZ.

www.ucas.com